BRIDGING THE MUL

BRIDGING THE MULTIMODAL GAP

From Theory to Practice

EDITED BY
SANTOSH KHADKA
J. C. LEE

UTAH STATE UNIVERSITY PRESS
Logan

© 2019 by University Press of Colorado

Published by Utah State University Press
An imprint of University Press of Colorado
245 Century Circle, Suite 202
Louisville, Colorado 08827

All rights reserved
Manufactured in the United States of America

 The University Press of Colorado is a proud member of
the Association of University Presses.

The University Press of Colorado is a cooperative publishing enterprise supported,
in part, by Adams State University, Colorado State University, Fort Lewis College,
Metropolitan State University of Denver, University of Colorado, University of Northern
Colorado, Utah State University, and Western State Colorado University.

∞ This paper meets the requirements of the ANSI/NISO Z39.48–1992
(Permanence of Paper)

ISBN: 978-1-60732-796-7 (paperback)
ISBN: 978-1-60732-797-4 (ebook)
DOI: https://doi.org/10.7330/9781607327974

Library of Congress Cataloging-in-Publication Data

Names: Khadka, Santosh, 1977– editor. | Lee, J. C., 1979– editor.
Title: Bridging the multimodal gap : from theory to practice / edited by Santosh Khadka
    and J. C. Lee.
Description: Logan : Utah State University Press, [2018] | Includes bibliographical refer-
    ences and index.
Identifiers: LCCN 2019001999| ISBN 9781607327967 (pbk.) | ISBN 9781607327974
    (ebook)
Subjects: LCSH: English language—Rhetoric—Study and teaching (Higher) | Modality
    (Linguistics) | Interdisciplinary approach in education.
Classification: LCC PE1404 .B7355 2018 | DDC 415/.6—dc23
LC record available at https://lccn.loc.gov/2019001999

Cover illustration © clivewa/Shutterstock

CONTENTS

BRIDGING THE MULTIMODAL GAP

Introduction

EXTENDING THE CONVERSATION
Theories, Pedagogies, and Practices of Multimodality

Santosh Khadka and J. C. Lee

SITUATING THE COLLECTION

In the last two decades following the publication of the New London Group's (1996) "A Pedagogy of Multiliteracies: Designing Social Futures," the notion of literacy has significantly changed. The group called for an expansion of the definition of literacy beyond the alphabetic-only to account for meaning-making practices in visual, auditory, behavioral, and spatial modes. Many rhetoric and composition scholars have theorized similar multimodal approaches to engage the notion of literacy, specifically writing, in the composition classroom. The list includes, among others, scholars like Cynthia Selfe, Kathleen Blake Yancey, Stuart Selber, Anne Wysocki, Geoffrey Sirc, and Jody Shipka, who contend that since writing includes signifying practices in multiple mediums—print, visual, aural, graphics, animation, and such—writing instruction should consider this plurality of composing mediums and attempt to scaffold students' composing abilities in all possible modalities of expression, hence engaging multimodal theories and pedagogies in writing classrooms.

A quick review of scholarship in the field reveals that the theoretical conversations around multimodal composing are already quite sophisticated in some respects, but the pedagogical translation of those conversations has not reached the same level, particularly among instructors new to multimodal practices, who often struggle with the question of *how* to adopt multimodal instruction in their classrooms. This situation has created an uneasy gap between theory and practice and between students' preferred literacy practices and actual instruction in writing classrooms. Multiple studies into students' literacy practices have found our students are writing more than ever with a great variety of composing technologies and forums widely available to them (Lenhart 2012; Lenhart et al. 2008; Madden et al. 2013; Purcell, Buchanan, and

DOI: 10.7330/9781607327974.c000

Friedrich 2013; Yancey 2009), but the primary focus and medium of our instruction has mostly remained traditional print.

Cognizant of this discrepancy between students' regular literacy practices and composition instruction, Jessie L. Moore, Paula Rosinski, Tim Peeples, Stacey Pigg, Martine Courant Rife, Beth Brunk-Chavez, Dundee Lackey, Suzanne Kessler Rumsey, Robin Tasaka, Paul Curran, and Jeffrey T. Grabill (2016) express the fear that our "students are moving beyond the scope of many writing pedagogies" (9). In fact, Moore et al. raise a serious question about pedagogical approaches being adopted in first-year writing courses across institutions of higher education in this country: "Many universities have required first-year writing courses, presumably with the goal of preparing students for future writing in and beyond the academy, but are they meeting this goal if they are not accounting for these 21st century differences?" (9). Similar questions and concerns are also raised by other scholars in the field. For instance, Geoffrey Sirc (2012) notes that rhetoric and composition has yet to fully embrace composing technologies other than traditional print. If this continues, he adds, it's very likely our writing instruction will become increasingly irrelevant to the literate lives of our students. Along similar lines, Collin Brooke (2009) openly warns, "Our disciplinary insistence upon the printed page, if it persists unchecked, will slowly bring us out of step with our students, our institutions, and the broader culture of which we are a part" (23).

Even though some scholars in the field have persuasively argued for the value of multimodal composing practices and the learning that occurs in the process, implementation of multimodal instruction has remained nominal in many writing programs. Attempts at implementing multimodal approaches are sporadic at best. Even those attempts are mostly individual instructors' initiatives in a handful of institutions. Multimodality—so highly hailed in scholarship as the means of preparing the writers and communicators of the future—is largely ignored in most of writing classrooms. Frankly speaking, multimodality is still far from being a norm in the majority of writing classes, and it is miles away from being adopted by a large section of writing instructors and programs. Even the scholarship is not adequate; it must further expand its horizon by being more aggressive in exploring the pedagogical potentials of a new and evolving set of composing technologies. New composing technologies keep coming, and the current ones keep changing; therefore, we must keep abreast of them first and then regularly theorize them in our disciplinary frames, with particular focus on their pedagogical value for writing classrooms.

This anthology moves in that direction by helping both veteran instructors and newer entrants into multimodality map its scope and its pedagogical potentials. The fourteen chapters in this collection explore new horizons of the scholarly conversation on multimodality while presenting an array of theories, pedagogies, and strategies for engaging multimodality in classrooms. By presenting research on the implementation of multimodality in diverse contexts, this collection attends to the ever-increasing chasm between those scholars and instructors who are already confident and competent with multimodal theories and pedagogies and those who are not but are interested to move in that direction.

A BRIEF REVIEW OF SOME RECENT MULTIMODAL THEORIES AND PRACTICES

As indicated above, the theoretical conversations surrounding multimodality have been quite sophisticated. Randall McClure (2011), for instance, introduces the idea of web 3.0 and discusses "how the Semantic Web might alter the research process and, more importantly, the research-writing relationship" (316). William I. Wolff (2013) similarly investigates what counts as writing in a web 2.0 environment and finds that web 2.0 spaces such as blogs, wikis, Twitter, and so on are spaces for writing like traditional print medium and "have their own grammars, styles, and linguistics" (212). He argues that "effective and successful compositional engagement with Web 2.0 applications—Yancey's 'new composition'—requires an evolving interactive set of practices" (212). He further claims that our learning about these practices has the potential to transform how we conceptualize writing and how we teach this art within and outside a Web 2.0 ecosystem. The point Wolff is trying to make is that we must productively engage these various writing spaces and modes in our composition classrooms.

Moore et al. (2016) actually present a little snapshot of the composing technologies our students use on a daily basis: "Notebook paper and pencil, word-processing programs, cell phones, and Facebook: these are just a few of the composing technologies today's students use to write in their everyday, academic, and professional lives" (2). Rebecca Tarsa (2015), a digital writing and rhetoric scholar, calls new forums of writing available to students "digital participation sites," which "offer a wide range of opportunities for deploying both digital and alphabetic literacy skills, and have proven incredibly successful in creating the literacy engagement that frequently proves elusive in composition instruction" (12). She maintains that since most of our students "are active in digital participation spaces at some point in their lives (Jenkins et al.), this makes them a rich site of inquiry for theorizing literacy engagement, especially in relation to students' existing everyday literacy activity and practices" (12). All these scholars are pointing to an exigence that calls for a more robust engagement with multimodality in writing classrooms.

The notion of multimodality itself is deeply explored and fleshed out in published scholarship. Yancey (2004), in "Looking for Sources of Coherence in a Fragmented World: Notes toward a New Assessment Design," writes that "print and digital overlap, intersect, become intertextual" (89), implying that multimodality is closely connected with digitality. In fact, the field of digital rhetorics in general has framed multimodal writing as composing with digital technologies and has explored ways to develop assignments that facilitate students' work with a great variety of semiotic resources. But Jody Shipka (2009) is cautious about not conflating multimodal with digital. For Shipka, multimodal is more inclusive than digital alone. She quotes Russel Wiebe and Robert S. Dornsife Jr. to illustrate her point:

> Instead of seeing the computer as the only technology with which composition ought to be concerned, we wish to show that only when other contemporary media—television, video, photography, music, and so forth—are considered, and the notion of a "text" broadened to include everything from conventional essays, to paintings, photographs, videos, and hybrids that we have yet to imagine, can "computer composition" really become a living discipline in an academy that responds seriously to the lives its students live. (Shipka W349)

Shipka theorizes multimodal composing as what she calls "a composition made whole" that invites students to purposefully utilize a wide variety of texts, tools, and practices while composing a text of their choosing (W363).

This is a small sample of recent scholarship published in the field, which shows it is trying to keep up with innovations happening in the field of information and communication technologies, but it is not yet comprehensive enough and requires further expansion with the study of different unexplored dimensions of multimodality. This collection takes a small step in that direction.

While stating there has not been much multimodal instruction in the majority of composition classrooms across the nation, we do not mean to imply there have not been any attempts to engage multimodality in writing classrooms. In fact, there are some excellent examples of instructors implementing multimodal curriculum successfully in their classrooms. Diana George (2002), for example, takes up the New London Group's literacy-as-design paradigm, saying it is relevant for composition in a visual age: "For students who have grown up in a technology-saturated and an image-rich culture, questions of communication and composition absolutely will include the visual, not as attendant to the verbal but as complex communication intricately related to the world around them" (32). By practicing design as a teaching trope, George attempts to undo the privileging of print over other semiotic modes.

Similarly, John Pedro Schwartz (2008) discusses a course he taught at American University in Beirut using a "Museum-based Pedagogy" with "the museum as a means for teaching the five literacies that are already or rapidly becoming central to our curriculum: verbal, visual, technological, social, and critical" (29). He sees museums as feasible and potential sites for "teaching students to understand multimodal ways of meaning-making in their social, technological, and institutional contexts" (29). He further adds that "the discovery and employment of the museum's means of persuasion develop competence at analyzing and using forms of communication that are common to other spaces and texts" (29).

Furthermore, Dale Jacobs (2007) implements composition as a design trope by making comics the major resources and assignments in his composition classroom. He posits that media convergence—convergence of image and text—is evident in comics, and comics can be the sponsors of multimodal literacy. According to him, students' engagement with comics both as classroom resource and the medium of composition could be a productive way to introduce students to the notion of multimodality in action. Yet another instance of innovative pedagogical response is Rebecca Wilson Lundin's (2008) "networked" pedagogy, which she believes "gives us an opportunity to make visible, and subsequently reevaluate, the received wisdom of our field concerning the definition of writing, models of authorship, classroom authority, and more" (433). She discusses and embraces wikis as productive sites for practicing networked pedagogy, as students interact with each other in the network in "a completely user-editable environment" (434) blurring the roles of author and reader, thus calling into question the traditional authority of writers and readers. Steven Fraiberg's (2010) multilingual-multimodal framework of writing, which engages "students in activities involving juxtaposition, filtering, selection, and recombining" (118), adds another innovation in pedagogy.

Along similar lines, J. Elizabeth Clark (2010) adopts ePortfolios, blogging, and digital storytelling as assignments in order to prepare students for the future of writing which, in her view, will be "based on a global, collaborative text, where all writing has the potential to become public"

(28). She calls it "an intentional pedagogy of digital rhetoric" (28) aimed to foster interactivity, collaboration, and sense of ownership and authority among students.

WHAT THIS COLLECTION DOES AND HOW IT DOES IT

Our collection builds on and extends existing theoretical and pedagogical conversations pertaining to multimodality in writing classrooms. It speaks to a diverse set of audiences from different academic levels and institutional contexts. One of our anonymous reviewers summarizes what this collection is all about in this succinct statement:

> I was particularly struck by the range (or diverse sampling) of contexts, issues, and concerns represented in this collection—face-to-face and online instruction, instruction at both the graduate and undergraduate levels, L2 instruction, discussions about UDL, assessment, process, transfer, risk-taking/experimentation and dealing with resistance and frustration. I was equally impressed by the range of media types covered in the collection: audio assignments, blogs, comics, videos, digital stories, photo essays, and screen casts, just to name a few. The range and diversity exhibited in this collection helps to underscore the great variety of ways in which, audiences with which, and contexts in which one might engage as well as research multimodal texts and practices. . . . I expect this collection will have something (or, in fact, many things) for anyone interested in multimodal practice. Importantly, while celebrating many of the benefits and outcomes associated with multimodal approaches, the collection does not shy away from shedding light on (and offering suggestions for coping with) the frustration, fear or doubt that often accompanies multimodal practice. Put simply, the chapters of this collection do a fine job of articulating, exploring, and situating (theoretically and in terms of other scholarship in the field) key questions and issues of concern to those who are practicing multimodal approaches to composing, often times by underscoring how multimodal approaches and techniques relate to, build upon, and remediate more familiar/traditional practices, methods, and concerns.

More important, this collection attempts to bridge the existing gap between many theories and practices of multimodality, hence the title *Bridging the Multimodal Gap: From Theory to Practice.* A majority of chapters in the collection bring scholarly frameworks and practices of multimodality together and offer theoretically grounded strategies, suggestions, and best practices for teachers and scholars interested in further exploring and engaging the emerging theories and practices of multimodal composition.

Fourteen excellent chapters are organized into four thematic sections and an afterword, namely, discourses in multimodality; multimodal process work; composing across media: affordances, learnings, and challenges; multimodal assessment; and afterword. These categories are arbitrary, of course, created for the convenience of readers, but many of the chapters across these sections intersect and nicely complement one another in both theoretical and pedagogical terms. The thematic grouping is done only on the basis of the primary focus or orientation of the chapters. No question, many of the chapters would fit into more than one section, but doing so would confuse readers. So, we have chosen a safer option and placed a set of thematically aligned chapters under four different sections.

CHAPTER SUMMARIES

In the first chapter, "On Multimodality: A Manifesto," Rick Wysocki, Jon Udelson, Caitlin E. Ray, Jessica S. B. Newman, Laura Sceniak Matravers, Ashanka Kumari, Layne M. P. Gordon, Khirsten L. Scott, Michelle Day, Michael Baumann, Sara P. Alvarez, and Dànielle Nicole DeVoss present a wonderful and passionate manifesto that provides a foundation of principles that can underlie the conceptualization and application of multimodality. The tenets in this chapter emphasize the need for critically considered and self-reflexive multimodal composition, providing a foundation that echoes throughout the other chapters of this collection.

In the second chapter, "Re-imagining Multimodality through UDL: Inclusivity and Accessibility," Elizabeth Kleinfeld places multimodality into conversation with architectural principles of universal design in order to advocate for a universal design for learning (UDL); such a design ensures reflexive, multimodal practices that accommodate all student needs even before students declare those needs. By preemptively addressing the heterogeneity of our classrooms, UDL-informed multimodal composition challenges assumptions about communication while allowing instructors to emphasize traditional, rhetorical appeals to logos, pathos, and ethos. Rather than single out students by accommodating needs individually, UDL-informed composition allows instructors to frame accessibility rhetorically.

In chapter 3, "Dissipating Hesitation: Why Online Instructors Fear Multimodal Assignments," Jessie Borgman shares experiences that will help online writing instructors new to multimodality take their first steps toward multimodal assignments. Acknowledging such impediments as the lack of face-to-face time in online writing classes and instructors' hesitancy when new to multimodal assignments, Borgman applies a cost-value assessment of multimodal composing in online (only) instructional settings, ultimately offering concrete suggestions for incorporating multimodal assignments in the online writing course.

Mark Pedretti and Adam Perzynski explore the value of recordings in their composition classrooms in the fourth chapter, "Reversing the Process: Video Composition and the Ends of Writing." Students in Pedretti and Perzynski's study composed separately in both video- and text-based formats, which allowed for a comparative analysis of students' experiences, and the findings indicated increased awareness of process and varied perceptions of product. These findings challenge prevailing theories of process-oriented composition instruction that dominate our classrooms, as students reported video production required more advanced planning and allowed for less postcomposing revision.

In the fifth chapter, "Thinking beyond Multimodal Projects: Incorporating Multimodal Literacy into Composing and Reflection Processes," Tiffany Bourelle, Angela Clark-Oates, Andrew Bourelle, Matthew Irwin, and Breanne Potter help instructors enter the world of multimodal reflections and process work. While most discussions of multimodal practices focus on multimodal composition as the telos of an assignment (a trend reflected within this very collection), these authors share their practice of using multimodality during the early-composing and final-reflection stages. They note that broadening the use of multimodality can help instructors and scholars develop their pedagogies and practices.

Steven Alvarez's work for chapter 6, "Archiving Digital Journaling in First-Year Writing," centers on blogs, and it takes a more practice-oriented approach by discussing the use of blogs to bridge students' formal and informal language use as they transition into academic English. Through comparative evaluation of the transition from informal, online journaling into formal and revised, multimodal portfolios, his participants developed a more rhetorically nuanced and process-oriented understanding of writing and academic English.

In chapter 7, "Blogging Multimodally: A Multiyear Study of Graduate Student Composing Practices," Kathleen Blake Yancey reviews students' self-expression through multimodal composition. The setting of the graduate classroom sets her work apart from many of the chapters that precede it. In the absence of directions for word count, students responded to the multimodal syllabus and early assignments that integrated images, taking up the invitation to become (increasingly) multimodal. Yancey analyzes eleven student blogs that formed essential classroom discussion, noting changes that occurred over a ten-year span, by the end of which students inclined toward fully multimodal blog entries that used as many words as those sparsely multimodal entries of preceding years.

Jennifer Buckner reminds readers not to limit multimodality to common expectations for (often visually dominated) digitality in chapter 8, "When Multimodality Gets Messy: Perception, Materiality, and Learning in Written-Aural Remediation." She reports findings from an empirical study of six first-year composition students' remediation from written to audio modalities, anchoring it to her conception of semiotic synesthesia. Ultimately, she finds that remediation can lead students into generative moments of dissonance that produce resonance, as students strengthen their understanding of composition through overcoming the challenges of remediation.

Rebecca Thorndike-Breeze, Aaron Block, and Kara Mae Brown approach multimodal practice from the genre of comics in chapter 9, "Entering the Multiverse: Using Comics to Experiment with Multimodality, Multigenres, and Multiliteracies." The authors introduce instructors to the practice of using serial art in the classroom as subject matter with which to develop critical thinking skills, to increase students' awareness of multiliteracy and genre, and to provide inspiration and modeling for students' remediation of their compositions.

Like Buckner's work and that of Thorndike-Breeze, Block, and Brown, Joel Bloch discusses remediation in chapter 10, "Digital Storytelling in the L2 Graduate Writing Classroom: Expanding the Possibilities of Personal Expression and Textual Borrowing." Bloch shares a detailed account of his practices with graduate students, wherein students remediate a text essay on their discipline and enter it into a digital story. In this interdisciplinary, graduate writing classroom, students furthered their understanding of writing in their respective disciplines through multimodal compositions in which students defined their fields of study and their individual relationships thereto.

In chapter 11, "Multimodality, Transfer, and Rhetorical Awareness: Analyzing the Choices of Undergraduate Writers," Stephen Ferruci and Susan DeRosa address the challenges and benefits of bringing multimodal projects into diverse classrooms of predominately first-generation college students, many of whom enter college having had little access to the technologies that allow for multimodal composition. The authors discuss their use of creative discourse-community ethnographies (DCEs), which led students to compose public-service announcements. They analyze students' textual and multimodal compositions, along with metanarratives students tracked throughout the process of remediation, concluding that students' engagement with multimodal compositions increased their understanding of the rhetorical situation while facilitating their ability to critically discuss their rhetorical choices.

Chapter 12 switches gears and moves the discussion towards addressing the questions of assessing multimodal projects. In "Distributed Assessment from the Runway to the Classroom: A Model for Multimodal Writing Assessment," Areti Sakellaris makes a passionate argument for establishing a material connection to multimodality as demonstrated by the fashion industry. Like many of our authors, Sakellaris marks the conflation of multimodality with digitality and argues that evaluating tangible multimodality through Rei Kawakubo's fashion designs expands understandings of composing and the ways in which the composition classroom relates to knowledge across the curriculum.

In chapter 13, "Multimodal Pedagogy and Multimodal Assessment: Toward a Reconceptualization of Traditional Frameworks," Shane Wood further explores assessment in the multimodal classroom. While retaining the notion of grading multimodal projects, Wood advocates for the use of alternative assessment methods, namely the grading contract, to account for students' process throughout multimodal composition rather than exclusively grading the final product. Through contracts, he contends, instructors can emphasize the value of process work to the students.

Finally, in the afterword, titled "(In Lieu of an) Afterword: Rewriting the Difference of Multimodality: Composing Modality and Language as Practice," Bruce Horner observes that, by definition, notions of difference, such as those used to understand language and multimodality in relation to one another, derive from and reinforce prevailing hierarchies, hegemonies, and norms. He then advocates that composition's scholarship and practice resituate difference as a natural and neverending product of composition. Situating his discussion within translingual and transmodal theory, Horner argues for the subversion of dominant conceptions of multimodality and language (their segregation and definition through difference), which will increase students' agency over their composing processes and rhetorical choices.

REFERENCES

Brooke, Collin Gifford. 2009. *Lingua Fracta: Towards a Rhetoric of New Media.* Cresskill, NJ: Hampton.

Clark, J. Elizabeth. 2010. "The Digital Imperative: Making the Case for a 21st-century Pedagogy." *Computers and Composition* 27 (1): 27–35.

Fraiberg, Steven. 2010. "Composition 2.0: Toward a Multilingual and Multimodal Framework." *College Composition and Communication* 62 (1): 100–126.

George, Diana. 2002. "From Analysis to Design: Visual Communication in the Teaching of Writing." *College Composition and Communication* 54 (1): 11–39.

Jacobs, Dale. 2007. "Marveling at 'The Man Called Nova': Comics as Sponsors of Multimodal Literacy." *College Composition and Communication* 59 (2): 180–205.

Lenhart, Amanda. 2012. *Teens, Smartphones, and Texting*. Pew Research Center, Internet and Technology. http://www.pewinternet.org/Reports/2012/Teens-and-smartphones.aspx?src=prc-headline.

Lenhart, Amanda, Sousan Arafeh, Aaron Smith, and Alexandra Macgill. 2008. *Writing, Technology and Teens*. Pew Research Center, Internet and Technology. http://pewinternet.org/Reports/2008/Writing-Technology-and-Teens.aspx.

Lundin, Rebecca Wilson. 2008. "Teaching with Wikis: Toward a Networked Pedagogy." *Computers and Composition* 25 (4): 432–48.

Madden, Mary, Amanda Lenhart, Maeve Duggan, Sandra Cortesi, and Urs Gasser. 2013. *Teens & Technology 2013*. Pew Research Center, Internet and Technology. http://www.pewinternet.org/2013/03/13/teens-and-technology-2013/.

McClure, Randall. 2011. "WritingResearchWriting: The Semantic Web and the Future of the Research Project." *Computers and Composition* 28 (4): 315–326.

Moore, Jessie L., Paula Rosinski, Tim Peeples, Stacey Pigg, Martine Courant Rife, Beth Brunk-Chavez, Dundee Lackey, Suzanne Kessler Rumsey, Robin Tasaka, Paul Curran, and Jeffrey T. Grabill. 2016. "Revisualizing Composition: How First-Year Writers Use Composing Technologies." *Computer and Composition* 39: 1–13.

New London Group. 1996. "A Pedagogy of Multiliteracies: Designing Social Futures." *Harvard Educational Review* 66 (1): 60–93.

Purcell, Kristen, Judy Buchanan, and Linda Friedrich. 2013. *The Impact of Digital Tools on Student Writing and How Writing Is Taught in Schools*. Pew Research Center, Internet and Technology. http://www.pewinternet.org/2013/07/16/the-impact.

Schwartz, John Pedro. 2008. "Object Lessons: Teaching Multiliteracies through the Museum." *College English* 71 (1): 27–47.

Sirc, Geoffrey. 2012. "Resisting Entropy." *College Composition and Communication* 63 (3): 507–19.

Shipka, Jody. 2009. "Negotiating Rhetorical, Material, Methodological, and Technological Difference: Evaluating Multimodal Designs." *College Composition and Communication* 61 (1): W343–W366.

Tarsa, Rebecca. 2015. "Upvoting the Exordium: Literacy Practices of the Digital Interface." *College English* 78 (1): 12–33.

Wolff, William I. 2013. "Interactivity and the Invisible: What Counts as Writing in the Age of Web 2.0." *Computers and Composition* 30 (3): 211–225.

Yancey, Kathleen Blake. 2004. "Looking for Sources of Coherence in a Fragmented World: Notes Toward a New Assessment Design." *Computers and Composition* 21 (1): 89–102.

Yancey, Kathleen Blake. 2009. "A Call to Support 21st Century Writing." In *Writing in the 21st Century: A Report from the National Council of Teachers of English*. Urbana, IL: NCTE. http://www.ncte.org/library/NCTEFiles/Press/Yancey_final.pdf.

SECTION I

1

ON MULTIMODALITY
A Manifesto

Rick Wysocki, Jon Udelson, Caitlin E. Ray, Jessica S. B. Newman,
Laura Sceniak Matravers, Ashanka Kumari, Layne M. P. Gordon,
Khirsten L. Scott, Michelle Day, Michael Baumann,
Sara P. Alvarez, and Dànielle Nicole DeVoss

INTRODUCTION

We offer this chapter as a manifesto; specifically, it acts as a set of
tenets about multimodality and its place in our pedagogy and research.
Additionally, this manifesto articulates and frames activities of thinking,
being, and making from our perspectives as rhetoric and composition
scholar–teachers occupying a particular cultural, historical, and technological moment. We draw our manifesto approach from design studies
and employ the genre in a way that ties it to scholarship in and histories
of design thinking, but our work is anchored in writing studies.

The *First Things First Manifesto* was originally published in 1964 and
primarily drafted in England; it responded to a particular cultural
moment of advertising, capitalism, and speed—that is, to the Modern
values dominant in the culture at the time (e.g., the individual Self,
Science, Technology, Progress, and other capital-letter values that
trumped notions of complex subjectivity; more cautious, critical engagement, and multivocality; truths rather than Truth). In it, the twenty-one
authors called for a more humanistic approach to design—a reversal of
priorities away from gimmickry and slick sales and toward the importance of street signs, books, catalogues, and other design objects that
influence our everyday lives.

In 1999, "First Things First Revisited" was published by Rick Poynor
in *Emigre Magazine*. In this text, Poynor offers a rich historical and
cultural discussion of the importance of context to the original 1964
piece. Poynor argues further that although historically anchored, the
claims of the original piece are as meaningful in 1999 as they were in
the 1960s, and that, indeed, "we live and breathe design. . . . Designers

DOI: 10.7330/9781607327974.c001

are engaged in nothing less than the manufacture of contemporary reality." That same year, a "First Things First Manifesto 2000," authored and signed by thirty-three designers, was published simultaneously in *Emigre, AIGA Journal of Graphic Design, Eye Magazine,* and *Blueprint.* In it, the authors point back to the 1964 document and toward the future of design, arguing that design has a significant role to play in public discourse.

In 2014, the website firstthingsfirst2014 was launched, and it attracted more than one thousand six hundred signatures and continued the distribution of the 1964 tenets along with new tenets. By drawing attention back to the effects of design on the lived experiences of human 'beings, "First Things First" marked a particularly significant moment for design studies that has rippled throughout these later texts. While we are not necessarily claiming writing studies is in a historical, institutional, or cultural position similar to the one design studies was in the 1960s (indeed, we argue we are not), we do want to leverage the rhetorical velocity (Ridolfo and DeVoss 2009) of the manifesto genre in similar ways and for similar purposes to those of "First Things First."

Our manifesto is multivocal. It emerges from the combination and pluralism of our voices and positionalities as we articulate our shared—and, at times, conflicting—perspectives on multimodal composing. We also draw in voices from scholars in our field to situate and amplify our claims. We lean on stories and experiences. As Malea Powell (2012) has importantly reminded us, "Stories take place. Stories practice place into space. Stories produce habitable spaces" (391). Although the bullet points below in some ways obscure the rich tapestry of stories underneath them, this piece is informed by story—by the research shared by scholars, by our experiences in classrooms and discussions in our hallways, and by the narratives we weave as we present our work at conferences. In this piece, then, we combine our voices with others in order to further situate rhetoric and composition as a habitable space for multimodality.

Manifestos, moreover, can live and breathe. They can circulate. Their tenets are organic, flexible, and malleable. Ideally, they have rhetorical velocity and are repurposed, taken up, adopted, altered, and live beyond their original contexts and places of publication. Taking up these affordances, what we hope to offer in the chapter is a replicable stance—a series of processes, approaches, and practices readers can adapt and put to use in their scholarship, at their institutions, and in their classrooms.

THE TENETS

On Thinking Rhetorically

Rhetorically informed scholarship shapes our thinking on multimodality and technology. Stuart Selber (2004), for instance, calls attention to the ways functional, critical, and rhetorical literacies must be balanced in fostering digital literacy, and we extend that perspective to multimodality writ large. Such a perspective, specifically, can help composers employ appropriate modalities and technologies, and approaching composing processes *rhetorically* can also emphasize an orientation toward social efficacy and action. We also agree with Cynthia L. Selfe (2009) and Bump Halbritter (2013) that an attention to less-privileged semiotic modes can reveal alternative forms of rhetorical activity: "With the yoke of language . . . lifted, writing may not only be and do new work, it may live and breathe in scenes of symbolic action that we may not have been recognizing as scenes of writing" (Selfe 2009, 8).

Here we offer tenets for thinking about multimodality and composing generally as markedly rhetorical activities:

- Technology is not an end but rather a pedagogical means; we should never teach technology for technology's sake, nor multimodal composing for multimodality's sake, but rather as a way of supporting particular individuals and groups trying to achieve defined aims within socially contextualized spheres of action, for whom multimodality may be an effective method of rhetorical communication (Adsanatham 2012; Borton and Huot 2007).

- Writing and technology are not monolithic, determined, or static entities but exist at a nexus of complex and nonlinear historical developments, social and economic situation(s), and political and institutional apparatuses. They are dynamic and multilocal, and thus we must resist totalizing narratives that position technology as necessarily tied to Western development and instead interrogate the heterogeneity of technologies through and with which humans act to make meaning in the world (Fraiberg 2010; Haas 2007; Zielinski 2006).

- Students need to engage in not only the technical (how-to) aspects of work with digital communication and composition media and technologies but also in critical analysis of that media. At the same time, scholars, teachers, and students alike should recognize that distinctions between theory and practice are not necessarily tenable, and we should keep in mind the recursive, co-constitutive, and to some degree inseparable natures of thinking, acting, making, and doing.

- Students—along with their teachers—should explore different computer and communication technologies so they may choose the best medium to facilitate their writing and respond to the rhetorical situation. We cannot split practices of making from those of critiquing and making knowledge. Practices of multimodality, like digital literacy, are best comprised by a balance among functional, critical, and rhetorical orientations (Selber 2004).

On Making

Practices of designing and making have become increasingly important to our field and to pedagogy-driven initiatives in general (see, for instance, EDUCAUSE posts and initiatives: Labb and Neely 2014; Pirani 2014). One strand of designing-as/and-composing has been with us since the New London Group, who argued in 1996 for a pedagogy of multiliteracies that "focuses on modes of representation much broader than language alone" and that attends to the resources of meaning as "constantly being remade by their users as they work to achieve their various cultural purposes" (64). While the NLG highlighted the semiotics of composing, more recent scholarship has attended to making as a material practice of composing, and Richard Marback (2009) articulates design thinking as a paradigm for composition, arguing that design "is the making of a meaningful thing, an artifact that means in the world independently of the meaning created for it by the designer" (402). Jim Purdy (2014) also explores a design thinking approach for composition, arguing that design thinking produces composition processes that are generative and focused on creating rather than analysis. Angela Haas (2007) has called us to think about how making-as-semiosis is not as a novel practice but one that has been culturally and rhetorically employed in American Indian communities for some time.

In the larger world of education, we are currently witnessing a developing interest in sites of making. The *New Media Consortium Horizon Report* (Johnson et al. 2016), for example, has given makerspaces an estimated time to adoption of two to three years within university structures (42). Given that both practices and spaces of making tend to be unevenly associated with STEM fields, scholars of rhetoric and composition must contend with and respect new forms of composing that integrate and hybridize computational, digital, and material processes. We offer the following tenets of how making can and should inflect our work:

- To truly address multimodal meaning making, we must work across a bandwidth of critical analysis and constructive production: making. Material artifacts are not only objects to be analyzed, as has generally been the tendency in our field, but products and containers of the semiotic activities invested in them. They are, in this respect, compositions.

- Furthermore, practices of making and critical activity must be rendered mutually supportive. Such a perspective does not privilege one or another paradigm but sees them as two sides of the same coin: analysis informs production; production informs analysis (Halbritter 2013; Murray 2010; Shipka 2011).

- Similarly, we must negotiate and continuously reorient ourselves across a spectrum of theoretical framing and practical doing. Multimodal composing requires that we interrogate and negotiate different tools, technologies, languages, and interfaces and that we also use them, experiment with them, make with them, and reimagine them. Making meaning requires taking chances, and taking chances requires the risk of failure. Failure itself can be generative and productive and is often a necessary iterative component to making. We see all of these, perhaps most especially failure, as necessary to developing robust, multimodal pedagogies that integrate practices of making.

- Just as we ask students to integrate maker identities into their composing ethos and activity, we must also demand the same of ourselves. If we ask students to ideate, compose, and produce in particular genres and/or with particular modes, we ourselves should create with them so we too experience the challenges and pleasures of "composition in a new key" (Yancey 2004).

On Teaching and Curriculum Building

Multimodal composing cannot exist outside a larger ecology of teaching and curriculum building. Scholars ask us to consider ourselves as students (always learning) in our process of building multimodal pedagogies, as well as to include students in our curriculum development (Ball 2004; Sealy-Ruiz 2016; Selfe 2004; 2009; Shipka 2011; Yancey 2004). As Selfe (2004) persuasively asserts, "If our profession continues to focus solely on teaching alphabetic composition—either online or in print—we run the risk of making composition studies increasingly irrelevant to students engaging in contemporary practices of communicating" (72). Teaching and curriculum building are fundamentally important to the undergraduate students we teach, to ourselves as graduate students and emerging scholars, to the pedagogical practices we take up, and to the ways in which we develop practices that span both classrooms and programs. Thus:

- Teaching multimodally and teaching multimodality are *not* the same as simply adding a "digital assignment." A multimodal pedagogy is not just additive; rather, it is a stance, an orientation, and a privileging of the many ways of making and receiving meaning. This work challenges the perceived primacy of "traditional" modes of meaning making, as well as the outcomes of "traditional" composition practices.

- We must remember we continue to learn and grow with our students. We should develop low-stakes assignments for our students to engage with first as they encounter new technologies (Sheridan and Rowsell 2010). Allowing students to explore before delving into more complex applications of a tool helps build both our students' and our own comfort level with the possible applications of technology.

- We must include student voices and, when possible, the ideas of other stakeholders in our curriculum-building processes. Our pedagogy should attend to student needs. Asking students what benefits they seek in our multimodal pedagogies allows us to attend to the knowledge they bring to the classroom so we can help them move beyond the classroom. By asking alumni and community partners what they look for from multimodal composers, we attend to the professional practices, processes, and places beyond our classrooms.

- We must work to create, foster, and sustain cultures of multimodal composing in our departments and the institutions in which they are situated. This project demands conscientious attention to theories of multimodal composing, as well as to its practices, processes, and products as manifested across all the stakeholders in our professional worlds: undergraduate and graduate students, staff, faculty, administrators, advisors, and others.

- The multimodal work we do will not always be understood, supported, or valued by institutions or our students. We must anticipate this resistance and be prepared to articulate clearly why multimodality matters in the context of our classrooms, our curricula, and our programs.

- We must be attentive to the larger curricular, departmental, institutional, and professional contexts in which we work. Our courses do not exist in a vacuum, nor does multimodal composing. We should look toward committees, caucuses, community organizations, corporations, and others to help inform the ways in which we understand multimodal composing and how, where, when, and so on it enters the world.

On Approaching Evaluation and Assessment

As our field has said of print texts for some time, evaluation and assessment should be directly informed by and clearly linked to the rhetorical purposes of any activity or assignment. This context is, arguably, even more true of multimodal composing. We must always attend to the rhetorical dimensions of such composition, asking questions like: What modes and media are engaged by a piece? How do these choices fit audience needs and expectations? How does the composer's engagement with the modes and media speak to or work against the exigency being responded to? These questions draw us to a rhetorical understanding of multimodal evaluation and assessment, a perspective described by Sonya Borton and Brian Huot (2007) and by Heidi McKee and DeVoss (2013), among others.

We assert, then, the following:

- We should evaluate multimodal compositions with a frame and lens of remediation; composers do not necessarily abandon "old" literacies or "traditional" practices when composing multimodally. Rather, we are working across a span of meaning-making practices that include these processes and others, and our assessment practices should account for this fact. More specifically, we must create evaluation structures that do not ask students to abandon our best rhetorical processes and practices in the face of new tools, spaces and places for composing, or "different" types of compositions.

- When possible, we should build rubrics for multimodal assignments *with* students and use evaluation approaches as a heuristic for thinking about composing multimodal products. We should seek out examples with students and approach these examples to cultivate an understanding of best practices that influence composing and evaluating (Adsanatham 2012; Stedman 2012).

- Practices and processes of multimodal composing are best supported by approaches both formative and summative, with each type of response anchored to the particular composing moment. They are also best supported by assessment practices that encourage play and exploration (Sheridan and Rowsell 2010) and design thinking (Purdy 2014).

On Considering Embodiment and Performance

Unlike many "traditional" texts, multimodal compositions afford composers the ability to engage all the senses, and thus embodiment is a necessary consideration when engaging in multimodal composing. Not only do our bodies react to the spaces and interfaces—digital and physical—in which we compose, but we have the opportunity to engage readers/viewers aesthetically and materially with our compositions.

The embodied aspects and often digital delivery of multimodal composing also implicate performance. Compositional practice is necessarily a performance, and we might situate embodiment as part of the enactment of our identities within the writing artifacts we produce (Frith 1998; Ratcliffe 2005). Further, as Marita Sturken and Lisa Cartwright (2001) contend, the act of composition constructs readers when rhetors and interlocutors together perform multimodal compositions.

This attention to performance and embodiment leads us to make the following statements:

- Multimodal composing is always and necessarily embodied. While our fingers might be seen as the primary digits in "digital writing" (Haas 2007), they are not the only parts of our bodies engaged in multimodal composing. We ought not to separate our computational writing processes and practices from the bodies through which these occur (McCorkle 2012; Wysocki 2003; 2012).

- With embodiment comes material influences. We are influenced by the sounds of the coffee shops where we work, the interruptions of students and colleagues in our offices, the quiet reprieve of a library cubby. We feel ground beneath our feet—the rough carpet or the spring of the floorboards. We feel the soft cushion of the chairs as we sit, the ache of our legs as we decide to stand and stretch, the widening of our chest cavity as we take a deep breath, our arms extending and sinews expanding as we stretch them above our heads. The false Cartesian divide between our minds and bodies is challenged by multimodal composition.

- We should compose multimodally by attending to the senses that inform the work we produce: our perceptions of sound, sight, and touch influence how we compose and what we intend our readers/ viewers to experience. Our use of still images with moving images, with voice, with music, and more engage not only the mind of the reader/ viewer but also the *sensory experience* the reader/viewer has as well. Attending to the balance of this sensory experience is essential; we must consider how all these elements work together to create meaning.

- We must attend to issues of accessibility and usability, recognizing that not all individuals experience multimodal compositions in the same ways. A reader/viewer with motor issues, for instance, might have to slow their mouse movements and clicks. A reader/viewer with limited hearing might rely upon textual transcripts to experience a multimodal text. Thus, we must, as much and as robustly as possible, open our multimodal texts to all readers/viewers (Yergeau et al. 2013).

On Working Infrastructurally

As James Porter, Patricia Sullivan, Stuart Blythe, Jeff Grabill, and Libby Miles (2000) argue, institutions are powerful but are by no means monolithic: "Institutions, as unchangeable as they may seem (and, indeed, often are), do contain spaces for reflection, resistance, revision, and productive action" (613). Extending this claim, we understand that while the localized pedagogical practices of individual teachers can be effective in creating space for multimodality, it is also imperative to contend with the larger institutional and cultural environments within which these practices are, to some degree, circumscribed and to find tactics to work within such environments productively. Moreover, as Erin Karper (2013) makes clear, not all institutions are created equal when it comes to providing resources for multimodality, and we must, therefore, attend to these differences and develop theories and practices that work across institutions and contexts and, at the same time, inform localized activity within them. To this end,

- We must attend to the larger curricular, departmental, and institutional environments in which we work. Our multimodal work is framed and, in many ways, influenced by a large range of everyday contexts related to issues of computer-lab access, networks and storage capabilities, and so forth (DeVoss, Cushman, and Grabill 2005).

- We must attend to the policies and laws that surround multimodal work. Institutional policies may regulate network bandwidth and use, for instance, or may suggest approaches to using copyright-protected work. Laws may provide us with the tools and affordances of fair use and the ability to use circulating work for purposes of our research, cultural critique, parody, and so forth (DeVoss and Porter 2006; DeVoss and Webb 2008; Herrington 2010; Westbrook 2006; 2009).

- We should pay attention to issues of space. Robust, accessible, sustainable spaces designed to best support multimodal composing take time to imagine, iterate, test, launch, and refine. Further, space is *always already* a living entity that requires near-constant attention to upkeep, maintenance, and user needs. Therefore, we must be cognizant and critical of the spaces in which multimodality is practiced; work both within and against these spaces; and, when necessary, hack spaces to suit purposes aligned with sound rhetorical and pedagogical practices (Walls, Schopieray, and DeVoss 2009).

- We should reconsider what work is valued in the field for hiring, annual review, and tenure and promotion processes, specifically with multimodal compositions in mind. The valuation of work should extend beyond traditional print publications and conference presentations to include digitally rich, multimodal-anchored service-learning work; computational and digital humanities-anchored projects; and born-digital scholarship (Eyman and Ball 2015; Glaser and Micciche 2015).

- We must understand that the university is not the sole province of the practices described in this manifesto. Therefore, scholars should examine not only multimodality and making-as-composing within the university but also look to, study, and support alternative communities of meaning-making practice. This perspective requires, we suggest, not just a commitment to expanding what "counts" as composing but a commitment to human-centered research and ethical scholarship.

On Advocating

Here, we anchor advocacy as braided with community engagement and the drive to look outside our own academic contexts and into the ways our knowledge and resources might enable us to establish reciprocal relationships with communities and other institutions. Multimodal work positions us to be advocates because it asks us to acknowledge the fact that our departments, institutions, and field at large are changing in response to the increasingly networked systems of composing and consuming in global economies. Advocacy is intimately tied to activism;

while the two are not synonymous, they are closely related and require complementary approaches and dedications.

We see advocacy as a way to use our particular positions as multimodal thinkers, composers, and makers in higher education to do the work of knowledge activism, which Eli Goldblatt (2005) describes as bringing our own personal resources, our institutional resources, and our composing skills and experiences to our relationships with community partners. Although multimodal scholarship and pedagogy are not intrinsic to community-engagement work, these intellectual commitments overlap in their advocacy for habitable futures that expand the purview of universities and cast a wider net for what "counts" as scholarly work.

Ellen Cushman (1996) argues that "activism means accepting a civic duty to empower people with our positions" (14). In adopting this disposition toward advocacy and activism in multimodal scholarship and pedagogy, we should thus advocate for structures that empower others to both critique and create multimodal work. Here, we adopt Cushman's multiple definitions of "empower" as "(a) to enable someone to achieve a goal by providing resources for them; (b) to facilitate actions—particularly those associated with language and literacy; (c) to lend our power or status to forward people's achievement" (14). Reciprocity is a key element of responsible advocacy work.

Keeping these definitions and concerns in mind, we put forward the following tenets about advocacy and multimodality:

- We should consider that institutional and departmental environments can have a significant impact on multimodal teaching and research practices, we should have a robust infrastructural understanding of the spaces in which we work, teach, and play (Karper 2013; Sheppard 2009; Walls, Schopieray, and DeVoss 2009). We should use these understandings of infrastructures to advocate for inclusive spaces and environments that enable multimodal teaching, scholarship, and play.

- We must listen. To best advocate, we must be informed about the ways in which various individuals, communities, organizations, and so forth make meaning multimodally. We must pay close attention to how various stakeholders engage multimodal practices—to act, to live, to learn, to make change, and more—in the context of their particular cultural spaces (Fraiberg 2010; Lauer 2009; New London Group 1996).

- By listening to the ways people engage multimodal practices, we should craft contexts and cultures of support and access so all learners have the opportunity to work with and across media. Access may relate to network/bandwidth access, to particular tools or devices, to time to develop experience with various tools, and so on. This concern for access should also reach beyond our departmental contexts into other disciplines and departments and into communities and institutions outside academia.

- In taking our broad view of multimodal advocacy, we must consider issues of sustainability as part of our advocacy work—sustainability in terms of both environmental advocacy and championing sustainability in terms of the long-term life of both the practices and technologies for which we advocate. Sustainability will be important as we go into a changing future in which understandings of and contexts for writing are shifting. A commitment to multimodality therefore enables us to be agents of change in our institutions and communities.

CONCLUSION

Manifestos are beginnings, not ends. We offer these tenets and hope that readers find them to be flexible, nimble, adoptable, and malleable considerations to guide the ways in which they approach multimodal composing. Each tenet embodies the contribution of multiple voices that were informed by plural perspectives and encourages the very flexibility that constituted its development. That is to say, the flexibility we used to compose this manifesto is the very flexibility necessary for putting these tenets to good use. This flexibility allows the tenets to be adoptable and malleable for a range of institutional and/or community contexts and introduces the possibility of conversations that will contribute to our further understanding and practice of multimodality. These conversations themselves should take place across media, practices, and modes with hopes of increasing the pluralism of voices, compositions, and stories.

REFERENCES

Adsanatham, Chanon. 2012. "Integrating Assessment and Instruction: Using Student-generated Grading Criteria to Evaluate Multimodal Digital Projects." *Computers and Composition* 29(2): 152–74.

Ball, Cheryl E. 2004. "Show, Not Tell: The Value of New Media Scholarship." *Computers and Composition* 21(4): 403–25.

Borton, Sonya, and Brian Huot. 2007. "Responding and Assessing." In *Multimodal Composition: Resources for Teachers*, edited by Cynthia L. Selfe, 99–111. Cresskill, NJ: Hampton.

Cushman, Ellen. 1996. "The Rhetorician as an Agent of Social Change." *College Composition and Communication* 47(1): 7–28.

DeVoss, Dànielle Nicole, Ellen Cushman, and Jeffrey T. Grabill. 2005. "Infrastructure and Composing: The When of New-Media Writing." *College Composition and Communication* 57(1): 14–44.

DeVoss, Danielle Nicole, and Jim Porter. 2006. "Why Napster Matters to Writing: Filesharing as a New Ethic of Digital Delivery." *Computers and Composition* 23(2): 178–210.

DeVoss, Dànielle Nicole, and Suzanne Webb. 2008. "Media Convergence; Grand Theft Audio: Negotiating Copyright as Composers." *Computers and Composition* 25(1): 79–103.

Eyman, Douglas, and Cheryl Ball. 2015. "Digital Humanities Scholarship and Electronic Publication." In *Rhetoric and the Digital Humanities*, edited by Bill Hart-Davidson and Jim Ridolfo, 65–79. Chicago, IL: University of Chicago Press.

"First Things First Manifesto." 1964. Design is History. http://www.designishistory.com /1960/first-things-first/.

"First Things First Manifesto 2000." 1999. *Emigre Magazine.* http://emigre.com/Editorial .php?sect=1&id=14 (also appeared in *AIGA Journal of Graphic Design, Eye Magazine,* and *Blueprint*).

Fraiberg, Steven. 2010. "Composition 2.0: Toward a Multilingual and Multimodal Framework." *College Composition and Communication 62*(1): 100–25.

Frith, Simon. 1998. *Performing Rites: On the Value of Popular Music.* Cambridge, MA: Harvard University Press.

Glaser, Jennifer, and Laura Micciche. 2015. "Digitizing English." In *Rhetoric and the Digital Humanities*, edited by Bill Hart-Davidson and Jim Ridolfo, 199–209. Chicago, IL: University of Chicago Press.

Goldblatt, Eli. 2005. "Alinsky's Reveille: A Community-Organizing Model for Neighborhood-Based Literacy Projects." *College English 67*(3): 274–95.

Haas, Angela M. 2007. "Wampum as Hypertext: An American Indian Intellectual Tradition of Multimedia Theory and Practice." *Studies in American Indian Literatures 19*(4): 77–100.

Halbritter, Bump. 2013. *Mics, Cameras, Symbolic Action: Audio-Visual Rhetoric for Writing Teachers.* Anderson, SC: Parlor.

Herrington, TyAnna. 2010. *Intellectual Property on Campus: Students' Rights and Responsibilities.* Carbondale: Southern Illinois University Press.

Johnson, Larry, Samantha Adams Becker, Michele Cummins, Victoria Estrada, Alex Freeman, and Courtney Hall. 2016. *NMC Horizon Report: 2016 Higher Education Edition.* Austin, TX: New Media Consortium. http://cdn.nmc.org/media/2016-nmc-horizon -report-he-EN.pdf.

Karper, Erin. 2013. "Make It Do or Do Without: Transitioning from a Tech-Heavy to a Tech-Light Institution: A Cautionary Tale." *Computers and Composition 30*(1): 16–23.

Labb, Alan, and Elizabeth Neely. 2014. "Making Way for Maker Culture." *EDUCAUSE Review.* http://er.educause.edu/articles/2014/3/making-way-for-maker-culture.

Lauer, Claire. 2009. "Contending with Terms: 'Multimodal' and 'Multimedia' in the Academic and Public Spheres." *Computers and Composition 26*(4): 225–39.

Marback, Richard. 2009. "Embracing Wicked Problems: The Turn to Design in Composition Studies." *College Composition and Communication 61*(2): 397–417.

McCorkle, Ben. 2012. "Whose Body? Looking Critically at New Interface Designs." In *Composing Media Composing Embodiment*, edited by Kristin R. Arola and Anne Wysocki, 174–87. Logan: Utah State University Press.

McKee, Heidi A., and Dànielle Nicole DeVoss., eds. 2013. *Digital Writing Assessment and Evaluation.* Logan, UT: Utah State University Press / Computers and Composition Digital Press.

Murray, Joddy. 2010. *Non-discursive Rhetoric: Image and Affect in Multimodal Composition.* Albany: SUNY Press.

New London Group. 1996. "A Pedagogy of Multiliteracies: Designing Social Futures." *Harvard Educational Review 66*(1): 60–93.

Pirani, Judith A. 2014. "Student as Designer: Making Edtech that Increases Student Success." EDUCAUSE Blog. https://er.educause.edu/blogs/2014/11/student-as-designer -making-edtech-that-increases-student-success

Porter, James E., Patricia Sullivan, Stuart Blythe, Jeffrey T. Grabill, and Libby Miles. 2000. "Institutional Critique: A Rhetorical Methodology for Change." *College Composition and Communication 51*(4): 610–42.

Powell, Malea. 2012. "2012 CCCC Chair's Address: Stories Take Place—A Performance in One Act." *College Composition and Communication 64*(2): 383–406.

Poynor, Rick. 1999. "First Things First Revisited." *Emigre Magazine.* https://www.emigre.com/Magazine/51.

Purdy, James P. 2014. "What Can Design Thinking Offer Writing Studies?" *College Composition and Communication 65*(4): 612–41.

Ratcliffe, Krista. 2005. *Rhetorical Listening: Identification, Gender, Whiteness.* Carbondale: Southern Illinois University Press.

Ridolfo, Jim, and Dànielle Nicole DeVoss. 2009. "Composing for Recomposition: Rhetorical Velocity and Delivery." *Kairos: A Journal of Rhetoric, Technology, and Pedagogy 13*(2). http://kairos.technorhetoric.net/13.2/topoi/ridolfo_devoss/velocity.html

Sealy-Ruiz, Yolanda. 2016. "Why Black Girls' Literacies Matter: New Literacies for a New Era." *English Education, 48*(4), 290–298.

Selber, Stuart. 2004. *Multiliteracies for a Digital Age.* Carbondale: Southern Illinois University Press.

Selfe, Cynthia L. 2004. "Taking Up the Challenges of Visual Literacy." In *Writing New Media: Theory and Applications for Expanding the Teaching of Composition,* edited by Anne Frances Wysocki, Johndan Johnson-Eilola, Cynthia L. Selfe, and Geoffrey Sirc, 67–110. Logan: Utah State University Press.

Selfe, Cynthia. 2009. "The Movement of Air, the Breath of Meaning: Aurality and Multimodal Composing." *College Composition and Communication 60*(4): 616–63.

Sheppard, Jennifer. 2009. "The Rhetorical Work of Multimedia Production Practices: It's More Than Just Technical Skill." *Computers and Composition 26*(2): 122–31.

Sheridan, Mary P., and Jennifer Rowsell. 2010. *Design Literacies: Learning and Innovation in the Digital Age.* New York: Routledge.

Shipka, Jody. 2011. *Toward a Composition Made Whole.* Pittsburgh, PA: University of Pittsburgh Press.

Stedman, Kyle D. 2012. "Remix Literacy and Fan Compositions." *Computers and Composition 29*(2): 107–23.

Sturken, Marita, and Lisa Cartwright. 2001. *Practices of Looking: An Introduction to Visual Culture.* New York: Oxford University Press.

Walls, Douglas, Scott Schopieray, and Dànielle Nicole DeVoss. 2009. "Hacking Spaces: Place as Interface." *Computers and Composition 26*(4): 268–87.

Westbrook, Steve. 2006. "Visual Rhetoric in a Culture of Fear: Impediments to Multimedia Production." *College English 68*(5): 457–80.

Westbrook, Steve, ed. 2009. *Composition and Copyright: Perspectives on Teaching, Text-making, and Fair Use.* New York: SUNY Press.

Wysocki, Anne Frances. 2003. "With Eyes That Think, and Compose, and Think: On Visual Rhetoric." In *Teaching Writing with Computers,* edited by Pam Takayoshi and Brian Huot, 182–201. Boston, MA: Houghton Mifflin.

Wysocki, Anne Frances. 2012. Introduction to *Composing Media Composing Embodiment,* edited by Kristin R. Arola and Anne Wysocki, 1–24. Logan: Utah State University Press.

Yancey, Kathleen Blake. 2004. "Made Not Only in Words: Composition in a New Key." *College Composition and Communication 56*(2): 297–328.

Yergeau, Melanie, Elizabeth Brewer, Stephanie Kerschbaum, Sushil Oswal, Margaret Price, Cynthia L. Selfe, Michael J. Salvo, and Franny Howes. 2013. "Multimodality in Motion: Disability in Kairotic Spaces." *Kairos: A Journal of Rhetoric, Technology, and Pedagogy 18*(1). http://kairos.technorhetoric.net/18.1/coverweb/yergeau-et-al/index.html.

Zielinski, Siegfried. 2006. *Deep Time of the Media.* Cambridge: MIT Press.

2

REIMAGINING MULTIMODALITY THROUGH UDL
Inclusivity and Accessibility

Elizabeth Kleinfeld

INTRODUCTION

Last week, a student and I were looking for information online together on a website I use regularly. I told her I love the website because it has so much useful information but that I was constantly frustrated by the fact that it doesn't have a search box, so I often had trouble finding the information I knew was there. "It does have a search box," she replied, and pointed to it on my screen. Sure enough, there *is* a search box, a rather large one, in fact. I had simply missed it every time I'd gone to the website because, while it is large, it is light gray against a white background, and I have low contrast sensitivity, a visual impairment that makes it difficult for me to see things that do not have highly contrasting colors. This is a typical example of the ways in which webtexts can fail to include all users.

This impairment is not limited to webtexts, of course. I regularly miss signs for buildings, streets, restrooms, and classrooms because those signs are designed for people who do not depend, as I do, upon high contrast. If the signs on my campus were designed according to the principles of universal design, a concept that originated in architecture, they would likely be larger and use higher contrast but would be no less attractive. Applying universal design to the signs would not make them any less usable for people who already use them easily, but it would simply increase the number of people for whom the signs are helpful. Sheryl Burgstahler (2015), founder and director of the Disabilities, Opportunities, Internetworking, and Technology (DO-IT) Center and Access Technology Center at the University of Washington in Seattle, describes universal design as "proactively designing a space to meet the needs of potential visitors with a wide range of physical capabilities. The design feature itself sends a message to anyone who requires its

DOI: 10.7330/9781607327974.c002

use, 'We expected that you would come to our home. You are welcome here'" (xi). In contrast, the signs on my campus communicate the message every day that I was not expected, just as the invisibility (to me) of the search box on the website indicated that my use of the website was not expected by its creators.

Rhetoricians, perhaps, understand better than most how important it is to welcome our audience into our texts, but we can lose sight of that when we forget that our audiences are not homogeneous and that our classes themselves are texts. Taken together, the ideas that our texts should welcome heterogeneous audiences and that our classes should welcome students, regardless of physical ability, race, linguistic variety, gender, sexual orientation, and age form an argument for using the principles of universal design for learning (UDL) to help us reimagine aspects of multimodal composition and pedagogy. UDL is a framework for educational practice that encourages flexibility in how material is presented, how students engage with material, and how they demonstrate knowledge and skills. UDL reduces barriers in instruction while maintaining high achievement expectations for all students, especially supporting those who may learn differently (King-Sears 2014). Significantly, UDL—like universal design in architecture—enhances experiences for people with disabilities *and for everyone else.*

Considering multimodality through the lens of UDL is particularly appropriate for a collection aimed at a global audience, as notions of accessibility can be broadened to include geographical and cultural diversity. I argue, in fact, that they *should* be broadened to include geographical and cultural diversity and that such notions are particularly important when we think about multimodal compositions because the usually online aspect of those compositions invite culturally diverse audiences.

UNIVERSAL DESIGN FOR LEARNING

The guiding principle of UDL is to reduce obstacles to students' accessing and engaging with instructional material. Research indicates that UDL also helps instructors maintain high achievement expectations for all students (King-Sears 2014). Just as increasing the contrast on a website or a sign allows people with some forms of low vision to access the website or sign without impacting the ability of people who do not have low vision to access the website or sign, UDL allows students to access educational opportunities in whatever ways work best for them without limiting the ways in which other students access educational opportunities.

The term *universal design learning* originated with David Rose and Anne Meyer in 1990, based on the ideas of universal design in architecture, which were created by Ron Mace (Rose et al. 1990). The idea behind universal design is to make buildings accessible to everyone, "considering the needs of . . . buildings' potential users at the outset," and by doing such, architects could design buildings that would not later need to be retrofitted to accommodate visitors in wheelchairs or with other types of disabilities. David H. Rose, Anne Meyer, Nicole Strangman, and Gabrielle Rapport use the example of the Louvre's well-known entrance, with a staircase spiraling around an elevator shaft. By integrating both a staircase and an elevator into the design, the architects were able to ensure all visitors, regardless of mobility, could ascend and descend as needed, and because they designed the multiple modes of moving between floors into the building from the beginning, rather than retrofitting, they were able to achieve a thoughtful and distinctive aesthetic effect. Although universal design in architecture is now associated with clever, forward-thinking design, universal design in learning (UDL), which aims to apply the basic concepts of UD to the classroom, continues to be often associated with disability.

The more traditional way of dealing with student disability in higher education has been accommodation, which means changing an assignment or classroom activity for one individual with a disability to allow that person to complete the assignment or participate in the activity. This is the equivalent of retrofitting an existing building with a ramp to allow alternative ways to access the building. An example of accommodation in the classroom is giving a hearing-impaired student a transcript of an audio file the rest of the class listens to. The accommodation helps that one student in that one instance. In contrast, a UDL approach builds options into the course design that give everyone, not only students with disabilities, different ways to complete assignments or participate in activities. This approach eliminates the stigma associated with disability and the concept that an accommodation is a form of preferential treatment or lowering of standards.

There are other significant differences between the accommodation model and UDL. The accommodation model hinges on disclosure of difference, while UDL acknowledges that difference exists and plans for it in advance. In fact, accommodation relies on a notion of disability as abnormal, strange, or special in a negative way. In contrast, UDL relies on a notion of difference *as normal*, welcoming difference, communicating to every student an echo of Burgstahler's message of hospitality: "I expected you to be in my classroom. You are welcome here" (2015, xi.). A UDL approach means building options for engagement and demonstration into a course, just as the Louvre's elevator with a staircase builds options for moving between floors into the museum without compromising anyone's ability to go up or down a flight. Visitors in wheelchairs might be the obvious beneficiaries of the elevators, but they are not the only ones: parents pushing strollers and visitors who went a little overboard buying coffee-table books at the gift shop also use the elevators, and so do people who are simply feeling a little too tired to navigate the stairs.

Significantly, UDL—like universal design in architecture—enhances experiences for people with disabilities *and for everyone else.* In a classroom designed around principles of UDL, three principles are activated: students are provided with multiple avenues into course content, multiple avenues to engage with course content, and multiple avenues to express their understanding of course content. This principle typically manifests itself as course content being presented in different ways, such as through lecture, visuals, demonstrations, and field trips; students being presented with different ways to engage with content in class, such as discussion, freewriting, hands-on activities, and role-playing; and students being given open-ended assignments, such as the option to demonstrate their understanding through writing a paper, having a conversation with the professor, doing a performance, or creating a work of visual art.

A growing body of research connects UDL to enhanced learning for all students (Benton-Borghi 2013; Lopes-Murphy 2012; McGuire-Schwartz and Arndt 2007; Spooner et al. 2007; Strobel et al. 2007). Just as universal design in architecture enhances experiences for people with disabilities and for everyone else, UDL enhances experiences for all students. An excellent example of this is simply turning on the captions when showing a video in class. While instructors might think turning on the captions is only necessary when hearing-impaired students are in the class, Robert Collins (2013) found that turning the captions on helped Native American students who were not hearing impaired with comprehension. This practice is a perfect example of UDL in action—turning on the captions does not hinder anyone's ability to engage with the video, and it certainly enables a hearing-impaired student to engage. Additionally, students who may not be hearing impaired, such as the Native American students Collins studied, may find the captions enhance their experience.

While Collins (2013) focused on Native American students, he found that when he turned video captions on, "*all* students seemed to perform better" (77; italics mine), being more active in class discussions following the videos and demonstrating higher levels of critical thinking (81). Being able to read the words on the screen in addition to hearing them may have enabled students who are visual learners to engage more deeply or on more levels with the material presented in the videos. As our student populations continue to diversify, it becomes more important for us to acknowledge and plan for differences in how students learn, how they identify, and how they interact with the world. One important group of students to consider is what Gail E. Hawisher, Cynthia L. Selfe, Gorjana Kisa, and Shafinaz Ahmed (2010) call "transnational"—that is, "the growing group of students who are at home in more than one culture and whose identities [span geographical and political borders]. These students typically speak multiple languages, often including varieties of English from outside the United States, and maintain networks of friends, family members, and other contacts around the globe" (56). In fact, Gunther Kress (2009) attributes the "explosive interest in the issue of multimodality over the last decade or so" to globalization (5). As I said earlier, I think notions of diversity should include geographical and cultural diversity. As our student populations become more geographically and culturally diverse, our assignments, assessments, and classroom activities must acknowledge that our classrooms are not the homogenous spaces we may have imagined them to be in the past. In a twenty-first-century classroom that may include students who range in age over several generations, come from different cultures, speak different varieties of English, and have varying degrees of abilities and disabilities, we must plan for difference.

Assigning multimodal compositions to students can, in itself, be a UDL move. A multimodal approach asks students to compose using some combination of alphabetic text and electronic, audio, and/or visual components. When students compose in multiple modes and are allowed to make choices about which modes they will use, they must make nuanced decisions about how they can best convey their message to their audience. Students can choose which modes to use and how heavily to rely on different modes to make their points and take advantage of their own skills and technological prowess. Assigning multimodal compositions also provides an excellent opportunity to encourage student composers to take the concepts central to UDL, universal access and acknowledgement of diversity, into account as they create their pieces. In the classroom, universal design means enacting a pedagogy that welcomes learners regardless of age, race, ability, location, and other factors and saying, "Welcome to my classroom. I was expecting you." As a composer of multimodal pieces, universal design means enacting an ethos that welcomes readers, viewers, and users regardless of age, race, ability, location, and other factors and saying, "Welcome to my text. I was expecting you." Assigning students multimodal texts gives them the opportunity to compose in ways that work for them; in turn, students can give readers and users the opportunity to engage with their texts in ways that work for the readers and users. A multimodal pedagogy informed by the principles of UDL emphasizes the heterogeneity of that audience—in terms of linguistic, racial, ethnic, religious, socioeconomic, cultural, and physical diversity—destabilizing assumptions about what constitutes clear, accessible communication while shining a spotlight on traditional rhetorical concerns such as appealing to ethos, logos, and pathos.

Considering multimodal approaches to composition and pedagogy in light of the principles of UDL presents the opportunity to situate accessibility as a rhetorical issue more than as an "accommodation." For example, how and why to make a webtext accessible to someone using adaptive software becomes contextualized when the audience for the website is understood as diverse. Especially when students' multimodal projects will be available on the Internet, it makes sense for us to help them think about the broad and heterogeneous nature of their audiences. Because digital projects are so easy to share, they are much more likely to be seen by diverse audiences than are hard copies, which can be seen as an affordance. A compelling multimodal project could potentially go viral, or a homebound reader who might have been isolated in the past can now log on to the Internet, and voila!, access your student's multimodal project that advocates for something that homebound reader is invested in—and a partnership is born. There is great opportunity in helping students think more expansively about the audiences for their multimodal projects, especially when the broad audiences are real, authentic audiences the Internet makes possible.

CASE STUDIES

I want to share a few brief examples of how UDL and multimodality function together in my classes to illustrate what planning for difference can look like. I will begin with a discussion of an assignment in my first-year writing course and then discuss one in an upper-division course for English majors and minors. My purpose in sharing examples from these two classes in particular is to show that UDL and multimodality can be integrated into a class at any level, whether it is an introductory, general studies course or a more specialized course focused on advanced study.

In my first-year writing course, students read four articles and then compose responses that are posted to our course-management system. The assignment lists comprehension and application questions for each article and then instructs students, "For each of the four scholarly articles assigned, compose a response in written, audio, visual, or video format that answers the questions." For example, after reading Joseph Bizup's "BEAM: A Rhetorical Vocabulary for Teaching Research-Based Writing," students are asked to describe in their own words each of the four ways of using sources Bizup describes and then locate examples of each in a scholarly article of their choice. Of the twenty-four students in the course last semester, two opted to create a static visual, three recorded audio responses, one made a video, and the remaining eighteen wrote their answers. The video was a particularly strong response, with the student zooming in on the pages of a scholarly article to show examples of the source-use strategies Bizup describes while the student explained in a voiceover what each example was doing. Interestingly, this student had earned an F on the previous week's article response, which he wrote. The option to choose the mode of his response allowed him to show me he understood the concepts in Bizup's article. Because the video was posted to the course-management system for other students to view, it also served as an instructional material for classmates who did not fully grasp the ideas in the Bizup article, perhaps because reading about the ideas was not the optimal way for those students to comprehend the content. The student who made the video opted not to caption it, and when he posted the video to the course-management system, he included a note apologizing for the lack of captions and any inconvenience it might cause to his classmates.

Each of the four reading responses in this class are worth 25 out of 1,000 points; because of the low point values, students feel free to experiment and try modes that might be somewhat outside their comfort zones. The stakes were higher for students in my 3000-level theory-of-authorship course. In that class, 25 percent of the grade comes from a collaborative project in which students analyze authorship scenarios that challenge conventional notions of authorship. The assignment gives students latitude to determine the mode(s) they want to use, with the stipulation that the finished project must be available to the public to view or read. The students decided to work together as an entire class to create a wiki that studied the plagiarism charges against Martin Luther King Jr. Each student took a different topic to write up for the wiki, such as how plagiarism was defined at the time King wrote his dissertation, what the authors of the allegedly plagiarized work said about the charges, conventions of source use in sermon writing, and more recent studies on the prevalence of plagiarism in master's theses. Students also included links to pieces they composed related to contested source use in general, such as a slide show about the sampling practices of slam poets and a choose-your-own-adventure-type website about how students in creative-writing workshops appropriate ideas from each other.

In both classes, work is accessible to a wider audience, and the student composer's sense of audience is expanded simply because of the digital and easily shared nature of the projects. That sense of an expansive audience is something we deal with at length in class as students think through and compose their projects. While it isn't possible with the time constraints of a typical college semester to teach students how to make fully accessible texts,[1] it is possible to engage students in discussions and deliberation of accessibility issues. As the apologetic note from the student who opted not to include captions demonstrates, students can begin to think through how their composing choices might be excluding some potential audience members and thus limiting their composition's potential for advocacy.

Composing multimodal texts engages students more powerfully as authors than composing traditional academic essays does. In his discussion of his experience with assigning multimodal compositions to students, Peter Kittle (2009) notes the powerful way students' sense of identity was affected.

> Students adopted an identity as composer (or director, or writer, as these terms were used rather synonymously by students). In past classes, students in the midst of writing more traditional essays often found themselves somewhat lost, feeling neither sure where their compositions were leading, nor how to find (and reach) their destinations. The genre of the multimodal document, coupled with the technology used to produce it, seemed to support students' ability to vest themselves in what Gee (2003) calls a "projective identity" . . . This is the simultaneous creation of a new identity related to a particular project . . . and the projection of oneself into that identity, a process reinforced when the project's efforts are marked by some degree of success. (55, 178).

When students identify as composers in this way, they are more likely to have a keen sense of responsibility to their audience. We can help shape that sense of responsibility to include making texts accessible to diverse audiences.

MULTIMODALITY, INCLUSIVITY, AND FEMINISM

Traditional approaches to composition emphasize teacher-student com-munication, with the student composing a piece only the teacher will see, even if the assignment imagines a wider audience. This approach is echoed in traditional class discussions. Multimodal composition can disrupt these dynamics by providing students with real, authentic audi-ences on the Internet, and a pedagogy informed by UDL and concepts of inclusivity can take this approach one step further by engaging stu-dents to think about the audiences for their multimodal pieces in terms of accessibility and inclusivity. The difference between the dynamics of a traditional writing class and a twenty-first-century writing class mirrors the difference between a traditional classroom and a feminist classroom. In a traditional writing class, students compose academic essays, while in a twenty-first-century writing class, students compose multimodal texts. In a traditional classroom, students sit in neat rows and even during "class discussion" make comments directed at the teacher rather than at the classroom community, whereas in a feminist classroom, students sit in a circle, making eye contact with and speaking to the entire class-room community. In the traditional writing class and the traditional classroom, communication is bi-directional, between the student and teacher. In the twenty-first-century writing class and the feminist class-room, communication is dispersed and democratic.

In fact, I suggest that assigning multimodal compositions can be a feminist pedagogical project, destabilizing the notion of instructor-as-audience and actively engaging issues of ownership and authority as they relate to textual production and reception. In a class informed by prin-ciples of UDL, students can conduct usability testing for each other's texts, engaging with the content and form of compositions in ways far more meaningful and authentic than the traditional peer-review work-shop an academic essay allows. Multimodal composing invites usability testing, as students are often already aware of ways different web brows-ers render text and images.

In these ways, a class informed by UDL principles in which students produce multimodal texts can be seen as enacting a feminist pedagogy, as Kay Siebler (2008) describes it here:

> Feminist pedagogy is a keen awareness of classroom dynamics, continually striving to confront issues of owner and authority as they play out between students and teachers; it is an attempt to move students to critical con-sciousness, especially in regards to racism, classism, sexism, homophobia and other ideological forces that create hierarchies; it is a commitment to creating connections between the external world and the classroom,

creating a learning environment that is high energy, using the kinetics of a classroom as a critique of traditional models of education. (3)

By asking students to produce texts that will be read and heard and used by real audiences beyond the teacher, and by asking students to consider the diversity of those real audiences, teachers are challenging the traditional academic order and empowering students to consider the real-world consequences of their composing choices.

Asking students (and ourselves) to consider the diversity of real audiences challenges our notions of normalcy. In their essay arguing for closer alignments between rhetoric and disability studies, Jay Dolmage and Cynthia Lewiecki-Wilson (2010) remind us that "normate thinking is deeply entrenched within the academy and deviations from the norm make people uncomfortable and become justifications for exclusion" (25). When we and our students consider that our audiences may not be white and male and able bodied and design multimodal projects with diverse users in mind, we push back against the idea that people who are not white and not male and not able bodied are somehow less than those who are. We acknowledge that the white, male, able-bodied audience is not, in fact, "normal" but rather is privileged, and we take responsibility and hold ourselves accountable for not perpetuating exclusionary composing practices.

As I said earlier, the constraints of the typical academic semester make it difficult to prepare assignments that require students to produce fully accessible texts, but the consideration of how texts exclude or privilege some audiences is useful. Questions I find very powerful in my classes are, who would feel invited into this text? and who would be excluded from this text? Making students (and ourselves) aware of who is being invited and who is being excluded by the design of a text helps them understand their composing choices as having ramifications beyond the classroom. For example, I often give assignments that allow students to choose the genre or mode for their response; students then compose a rationale for their genre or modal choice. When students choose academic essay, their rationales are often apologetic in tone, as they acknowledge that the academic essay excludes many of the people they hope would be exposed to the message of their composition. Putting myself through a similar exercise motivated me to include fewer technology-reliant activities in my classes, as I realized the commonplace that everyone has Wi-Fi access all the time is not necessarily true for the students at my modified open-enrollment institution. One of the more effective multimodal activities I've used recently involves students in producing zines.² Most significantly, when instructors and students consider whom their texts include and exclude, attention is called to issues of accessibility and inclusivity in broader society. We ask such questions as, why is it considered acceptable to design a class or a text around the assumption that everyone has perfect vision when one out of twenty people is visually impaired? Playing with the framing of that question can be useful, too—phrasing it as, why is it considered acceptable to exclude one out of twenty students from the class we design or one out of twenty people from the text we design? can help put the focus on the real consequences of our composing choices.

Calling our students' attention to who is included and excluded by their (and our) compositions invokes both feminist and disability studies critiques, but it is also just good rhetorical practice. In analyzing any rhetorical situation, the rhetor should consider who their audience is and the impact of their own composing choices on their ability to reach that audience.

CONCLUSION

Ironically, though it's common for college classes today to include a companion website or make extensive use of e-mail and even social media for class-related communications, assignments themselves still tend to privilege print. Perhaps as a result, Hawisher et al. (2010) note that "some of our students . . . raised on visual media find school increasingly irrelevant" (57). Incorporating multimodal assignments into our classes is a way to help students see school as relevant. Doing so with UDL principles in mind can help expand their classroom experiences to mirror the diversity and multiple perspectives their lives are telling them matter. Designing our classes to be inclusive and asking our students to compose for diverse audiences—or interrogating our reasons for making choices that exclude students or audiences—is a productive response to questions about the relevance of our classes and assignments.

Multimodal work can give students the means to acknowledge multiple subject positions in ways traditional academic essays, with their reliance on a unified, consistent voice, actually erase. Hawisher et al. (2010) note that the transnational students they have studied see themselves as "citizens dwelling on the blurred borders of nation-states" (66). I suggest we are all, to some degree, citizens dwelling on blurred borders. The distinctions between ethnicities, genders and sexualities, abilities and disabilities, and other markers are becoming more blurred every day, which makes any assumption of a homogeneous audience suspect. We need a pedagogy that not only acknowledges this diversity but actually embraces it as an affordance of composing in the twenty-first century. Our classrooms should say to all students who enter, "Welcome. I expected you," and we should help our students compose texts that say to all users, "Welcome. I expected you."

NOTES

1. The two-day grant-funded Building an Accessible Future for the Humanities Project workshops are an excellent way for faculty to learn about how to make digital texts accessible; however, the very fact that it takes a two-day workshop to help faculty learn about accessibility indicates how difficult it would be to fully immerse students in the experience. More information on the workshops can be found here: http://www.accessiblefuture.org/.
2. This assignment was inspired by Hillery Glasby's presentation, "Writing as Making: Making as Writing: DIY Multimodality in the Composition Classroom," at the Feminisms and Rhetorics Conference 2015.

REFERENCES

Benton-Borghi, Beatrice Hope. 2013. "A Universally Designed for Learning (UDL) Infused Technological Pedagogical Content Knowledge (TPACK) Practitioners' Model Essential for Teacher Preparation in the 21st Century." *Journal of Educational Computing Research* 48 (2): 245–65.

Bizup, Joseph. 2008. "BEAM: A Rhetorical Vocabulary for Teaching Research-Based Writing." *Rhetoric Review* 27 (1): 72–86.

Burgstahler, Sheryl E. 2015. Preface to *Universal Design in Higher Education: From Principles to Practice*, edited by Sheryl E. Burgstahler. Cambridge, MA: Harvard Education Press.

Collins, Robert Keith. 2013. "Using Captions to Reduce Barriers to Native American Student Success." *American Indian Culture and Research Journal* 37 (3): 75–86.

Dolmage, Jay, and Cynthia Lewicki-Wilson. 2010. "Refiguring Rhetorica: Linking Feminist Rhetoric and Disability Studies." In *Rhetorica in Motion: Feminist Rhetorical Methods and Methodologies*, edited by Eileen E. Schell and K. J. Rawson. Pittsburgh, PA: U of Pittsburgh Press.

Glasby, Hillery. 2015. "Writing as Making: Making as Writing: DIY Multimodality in the Composition Classroom." Paper presented at the Feminisms and Rhetorics Conference. Tempe, AZ. October 28–31, 2015.

Hawisher, Gail E., Cynthia L. Selfe, Gorjana Kisa, and Shafinaz Ahmed. 2010. "Globalism and Multimodality in a Digitized World: Computers and Composition Studies." *Pedagogy* 10 (1): 55–68.

King-Sears, Peggy. 2014. "Introduction to *Learning Disability Quarterly* Special Series on Universal Design for Learning: Part One of Two." *Learning Disability Quarterly* 37 (2): 68–70.

Kittle, Peter. 2009. "Student Engagement and Multimodality: Collaboration, Schema, Identity." In *Teaching the New Writing: Technology, Change, and Assessment in the 21st-Century Classroom*, edited by Anne Herrington, Kevin Hodgson, and Charles Moran. New York: Teachers College Press.

Kress, Gunther. 2009. *Multimodality: A Social Semiotic Approach to Contemporary Communication*. New York: Routledge.

Lopes-Murphy, Solange. 2012. "Universal Design for Learning: Preparing Secondary Education Teachers in Training to Increase Academic Accessibility of High School English

Learners." *The Clearing House: A Journal of Educational Strategies, Issues and Ideas* 85 (6): 226–30.

McGuire-Schwartz, Mary Ellen, and Janet S. Arndt. (2007). "Transforming Universal Design for Learning in Early Childhood Teacher Education from College Classroom to Early Childhood Classroom." *Journal of Early Childhood Teacher Education* 28 (2): 127–139.

Rose, David H., Anne Meyer, Nicole Strangman, and Gabrielle Rappolt. *Teaching Every Student in the Digital Age.* http://www.ascd.org/publications/books/101042/chapters/What-Is-Universal-Design-for-Learning%C2%A2.aspx.

Siebler, Kay. 2008. *Composing Feminisms: How Feminists Have Shaped Composition Theories and Practices.* Cresskill, NJ: Hampton.

Spooner, Fred, Joshua N. Baker, Amber A. Harris, Lynn Ahlgrim-Delzell, and Diane M. Browder. 2007. "Effects of Training in Universal Design for Learning on Lesson Plan Development." *Remedial and Special Education* 28 (2): 108–16.

Strobel, Wendy, Sajay Arthanat, Stephen Bauer, and Jennifer Flagg. 2007. "Universal Design for Learning: Critical Need Areas for People with Learning Disabilities." *Assistive Technology Outcomes and Benefits* 4 (1): 81–98.

3

DISSIPATING HESITATION
Why Online Instructors Fear Multimodal Assignments and How to Overcome the Fear

Jessie C. Borgman

INTRODUCTION

In their book *Multimodal Composition: Resources for Teachers*, Pamela Takayoshi and Cynthia Selfe (2007) indicate that "many composition teachers—raised and educated in the age and the landscape of print—feel hesitant about the task of designing, implementing and evaluating assignments that call for multimodal texts—texts that incorporate words, images, video, and sound" (3). James Purdy and Joyce Walker (2010) further complicate the assessment of multimodal texts when they write that "discussions have tended to focus primarily on establishing digital work as equivalent to print publications . . . instead of considering how digital scholarship might transform knowledge-making practices" (178). Yet, technology has forced the field to rethink what writing courses should look like, what they should teach, and how they should be evaluated. Technology has made learning through online writing courses (OWCs) possible, which has shifted the landscape even further for what face-to-face (f2f) writing courses should look like. Reassessment of the first-year writing class has become common, as has discussion of what should be taught in these classes. Definitions of "writing instruction" have become blurred due to these huge shifts in technology and a new-found dependence on composing with computers.

This chapter examines why online instructors often hesitate to use multimodal assignments in the OWC and why online instructors debate whether the use of multimodal assignments is worth the extra challenges brought on by online settings. It outlines the additional uncertainties of using multimodal assignments in the online writing classroom and the benefits the technology of online courses yields to multimodal assignments. While there is not a lot of scholarship on multimodality in online writing classrooms, the scholarship that does exist focuses mostly

DOI: 10.7330/9781607327974.c003

on the logistics (Blair 2016; Minter 2016). This chapter takes a different approach, addressing the fear instructors have about using multimodal assignments. The chapter also discusses the value of using multimodal assignments in an online setting, and it assess the cost value of using multimodal assignments in a virtual setting, focusing on the challenges versus rewards. Last, the chapter offers suggestions for how online writing instructors (OWIs) can squelch their fears and begin incorporating at least one multimodal assignment per semester with success.

In looking at the NCTE's position statement on multimodal literacies, a clear argument can be made for how multimodal texts enhance the ability to make meaning. For example, the first declaration suggests that "integration of multiple modes of communication and expression can enhance or transform the meaning of the work beyond illustration or decoration" (National Council of Teachers of English 2005). Yet with this argument to use multimodal assignments comes hesitation. This hesitation is also underscored in two other declarations in the statement: "There are increased cognitive demands on the audience to interpret the intertextuality of communication events that include combinations of print, speech, images, sounds, movement, music and animation. Products may blur traditional lines of genre, author/ audience and linear sequence"; "With the development of multimodal literacy tools, writers are increasingly expected to be responsible for many aspects of the writing, design, and distribution process that were formerly appointed to other experts." While these statements provide great goals for utilizing multimodal assignments in writing courses, they also create hesitation on the part of instructors due to the vague descriptions for application in classrooms. Hesitation comes in many forms, and one of the reasons for hesitation is the discomfort with teaching composition through more than just words and sentences, which is a very traditional approach English teachers are all quite comfortable with (Dunn 2001, 50), but hesitation can manifest in other ways as well and becomes exacerbated when considering the use of multimodal assignments, especially in an online setting. Using multimodal assignments is scary and exciting; however, it is beneficial to students to use such assignments in order to expand their understanding of composing. While it is often assumed that multimodal means digital, this is not the case, as is pointed out by Jody Shipka (2011) in *Toward a Composition Made Whole.* Many other scholars have made this distinction as well (Wysocki 2004; Ball 2014), and yet, the tendency to group multimodal texts as digital remains, as does the fear: "Anxiety about works that blur the boundaries dividing alphabetic text from these 'new' nonlinear, born-digital texts remains a force in our field" (Benson 2014, 166). In other words, fear of the new and digital paralyzes instructors and creates an unnecessary division between old and new texts. This anxiety permeates instructors who teach in f2f settings but is somehow exacerbated when instructors move their writing courses online.

In "Teaching Multimodal Assignments in OWI Contexts," Kris Blair (2015) argues, "Moving beyond a functional view of multimodal literacy not only aligns technology with rhetoric to foster a critical citizenry that communicate in a range of media, but in the case of OWI, also allows students to deploy multimodal genres to critically and rhetorically explore identity and the role that various tools play in shaping and representing that identity through a broadened definition of writing" (488). Furthermore, while using multimodal assignments expands student definitions of writing, many online instructors are hesitant to assign any type of multimodal work due to the logistics of working with students in a digital environment with no f2f time. Yet, as this chapter suggests, many continue to hesitate and refrain from including multimodal assignments in online courses due to fear, three different kinds of fear to be exact: fear of the logistics, fear of the big and bold, fear that students will not understand the meaning of multimodal texts.

DEFINITIONS

In order to get a full context of multimodality and the OWC, it is important to have a definition of multimodality. In the course of my research, it became clear that while many definitions exist, they share a common understanding that multimodality involves the use of multiple modes of delivery in order to create one cohesive meaning. This commonality stems from the New London Group's (NLG) (Cope et.al 2003) definition of multiliteracy, which encompasses five modes of making meaning (linguistic, aural, visual, gestural and spatial). Multiliteracy research examines texts as composed through multiple modes (not only written/text based) because it argues that the very act of writing requires the use of multiple modes (linguistic, aural, visual, gestural, and spatial). A more specific definition of multimodality was formulated by Gunther Kress and Theo Van Leeuwen (2001) in *Multimodal Discourse: The Modes and Media of Contemporary Communication*, in which they state that multimodality can be defined "as the use of several semiotic modes in the design of a semiotic product or event, together with the particular way in which these modes are combined" (20). Cheryl Ball and Colin Charlton (2015) define it further in their piece "All Writing Is Multimodal," suggesting that multimodal simply put means "multiple + mode," and these authors use the NLG's five modes of making meaning (linguistic, aural, visual, gestural and spatial) to argue that, essentially, all writing is multimodal because "every piece of communication a human composes—uses more than one mode" (42).

Although there are several definitions of the term multimodality, it seems that short and simple definitions offer the most flexibility in use and understanding of the general premise of multimodality. For example, in the first chapter of their textbook *Writer/Designer: A Guide to Making Multimodal Projects*, Kristin Arola, Ball, and Jennifer Sheppard (2014) simplify the definition for students, stating, "Multimodal describes how we combine multiple different ways of communicating in everyday life" (1). With this definition, the authors also illustrate the functionality of multimodal texts with visual examples and discussions thereof. In the introduction to her book *Multimodal Composition: A Critical Sourcebook*, Claire Lutkewitte (2013) offers this: "In a broad sense, multimodal composition can be defined as communication using multiple modes that work purposely to create meaning . . . multimodal composition is situated and thus shaped by context, history, audience, place, time, and other factors" (2–3). Combining these definitions and reflecting on their differences allow readers to understand the complexity of multimodality and to have one set, working definition. Looking at multimodality in the most basic sense, "multiple + mode," allows a general working definition for instructors and students alike.

RECALLING HISTORY: HAVE WE ALWAYS BEEN MULTIMODAL?

The multimodal-literacies discussion began most fervently with *Multiliteracies: Literacy Learning and the Design of Social Futures*, in which Bill Cope and Mary Kalantzis (2000) explore issues of language and cultural diversity and raise questions regarding the future of literacy pedagogy in response to the ever-changing technological advances infiltrating workplaces, public spaces, and community lives—"lifeworlds" (4), to use their term. They identify four components of pedagogy ("situated practice, overt instruction, critical framing and transformed practice") and six design elements of the meaning-making process ("linguistic, visual, audio, gestural, spatial and the patterns that relate to these five modes") that they use to test these ideas in their curriculum and explore the "what" and "how" of literacy pedagogy as a changing entity (7). Cope and Kalantzis (2000) ask readers to consider broader definitions of literacy teaching and learning, including two key components they identify as:

1. "Extend[ing] the idea and scope of literacy pedagogy to account for the context of our culturally and linguistically diverse and increasingly globalized societies" (9).

2. "Argu[ing] that literacy pedagogy now must account for the burgeoning variety of text forms associated with information and multimedia technologies" (9).

In *Remixing Composition: A History of Multimodal Writing Pedagogy*, Jason Palmeri (2012) expands on Cope and Kalantzis's (2000) idea of literacy's involvement with social and cultural change. Palmeri (2012) challenges theories that treat composition's history as focused solely on the study of words and alphabetic texts. He reveals, instead, that compositionists have been using multimodal approaches to composition since the 1970s and that many of the approaches anticipated the future of composition studies in the digital age. Palmeri argues that composition has a rich history of interacting in multiple modes, and he suggests that using this history can help us reexamine our current pedagogical practices (149). Palmeri suggests that we embrace our multimodal history and explore multimodality with our students to enact social change.

Countering Palmeri's (2012) argument that we have always been multimodal, Takayoshi and Selfe (2007) point out that while we as a field (and the work we produce) may have always been multimodal, the assignments in the composition classes we teach remain largely unchanged: "The texts that students have produced in response to composition assignments have remained essentially the same for the past 150 years. . . . The information within these is conveyed primarily by two modalities—words and visual elements (e.g., layout, font, font size, white space)—and is often distributed in the medium of print . . . students are producing essays that look much the same as those produced by their parents and grandparents" (1–2). So, while the field may have been participating in multimodality, the composing tasks we have given our students and our focus on the essay have remained largely static. We still privilege alphabetic text over multimodality; we still assign largely text-focused writing assignments and teach students how to be better communicators through words (Dunn 2001, 47). Ball (2014) also notes that composition scholarship often argues for the value of multimodality but the rarely does so through multimodal texts. In looking at the history of multimodal composition and the above viewpoints on our field's use of multimodality, it becomes clear that ambiguity is high and definitions are at best gray, resulting in fear and hesitation, which complicates some arguments that there could be a standard definition of multimodality, as mentioned earlier.

ONLINE WRITING INSTRUCTION (OWI)
EMERGES AND FURTHER COMPLICATES

And yet, with the explosion of online writing instruction (OWI) in the late 2000s, the composition field has encountered a new struggle: how to deal with multimodal writing in nontraditional school environments. Blair (2015) reminds us of the tension between OWI and multimodal composition, and she suggests that the field must rethink its goal in order to transform the field's understanding of writing as multimodal because multimodal composing better prepares students to communicate in contexts outside academics (474–75). Blair further notes, "The distinction between 'writing' versus 'composing' frequently is positioned as an either/or argument—that in privileging one over the other, we do a disservice to students either in not sufficiently introducing them to more traditional print-based discourse crucial to their academic success, or in not bridging the gap between how students use technologies to compose outside the classroom and how we use (or do not use) those same technologies" (474–75). Among the questions OWIs must ask when thinking about adding multimodal assignments, three stand out: Are these beneficial to the students' understanding of composing texts in the real world? Is the use of multimodal assignments expanding students' definitions of writing? Is it allowing them options of writing and or composing as textual and/or multimodal? In thinking about the use of multimodal assignments in the composition classroom, Takayoshi and Selfe (2007) remind us that "before teachers can begin to explore the possibilities of multimodal composition classes, they must reflect on their pedagogical assumptions about writing instruction generally" (6). And yet, as Blair (2015) reminds us, the conversation must be larger than just an individual assessment of one's teaching philosophy. The field, as a whole, must reflect on its "pedagogical assumptions about writing instruction generally," and we must stop thinking "either/or" and start "bridging the gap between how students use technologies to compose outside the classroom and how we use (or do not use) those same technologies" (475). This perspective of teaching students to compose beyond the classroom applies most certainly to the OWC. Just because a course is online does not absolve instructors or writing programs from trying to "bridge the gap" and teach students how to use their daily composing skills/strategies in their school and work lives. The OWC is a perfect venue to help students combine their multiple literacies (New London Group 1994) and utilize these already-developed skills in other venues.

THE FEARS THAT BIND US

As an OWI, I fear multimodal composition assignments. I do, and I stand in admiration of those who actually have the guts to use them in their OWCs. I have taught composition f2f and online for over a decade, and I still do not want to use multimodal assignments in my online courses; this reluctance is based solely on fear . . . period. I know I am not alone. I have talked with my peers at conferences; I have read the very few pieces of research that exist on multimodal assignments in the OWC, and it remains clear that there is an ever-present fear of bringing multimodal assignments into the OWC. One of the reasons fear might pervade is that, in the field, misconceptions still exist regarding multimodal assignments, and instructors sometimes allow misunderstanding to guide their fears. Ball and Charlton (2015) identify these two misconceptions as (1) some assume all multimodal texts are digital and (2) some assume that the opposite of multimodal is monomodal (42). However, the hesitation to incorporate multimodal assignments into the OWC is a bit more complex than just misconceptions and a lack of a definition. There are several reasons OWIs like myself indulge the fear and refrain from using multimodal assignments in their OWCs. The hesitation is still largely fear based, but it seems there are some clear common themes of fear at play here. These themes arise from our own experience, interactions with scholars in the field, and professional research:

> fear of logistics; things could get messy and students could be confused;
>
> fear of attempting multimodal assignments because of the widely held belief that they must be big and bold or complicated;
>
> fear that students will not "get it", that they will not see the connection between the multimodal assignments in their OWCs and their "real-life" writing;
>
> fear of being judged by students and faculty peers for use of multimodal assignments; often the value of multimodal assignments is not recognized and therefore must be defended and explained.

I plan to get past these fears in the near future and begin to implement more multimodal assignments into the course. I've experimented with many low-stakes assignments in my OWCs, and I recently attempted one low-stakes multimodal assignment in an online composition course with success, so there is hope the fear cannot bind us forever. One way of moving past the hesitation is to address these fears individually and evaluate how these fears could actually be hindering real and applicable learning and instructor growth in the OWC.

Fear of the Logistics

Like me, many OWIs really do fear the messy logistics multimodal assignments can present, and this fear is one of the main reasons OWIs are often reluctant to use multimodal assignments in their OWCs. Ball (2014) addresses this reluctance in her piece "Assessing Scholarly Multimedia" (61–68) and again in her piece "Show Not Tell" (2014, 165–69). I am guilty of this fear. In my years of being an OWI, I have learned simple really is better: when the directions are complicated, students get scared; when students get confused, it is hard to calm them down; when things get muddled, it can make instructors lose control of the class. Moe Folk (2013) addresses how instructors take a more traditional approach due to fears that more extensive multimodal projects might not work out successfully (233–34). Multimodal assignments invite chaos because instructors fear the *what ifs*. Many things could go wrong with assigning multimodal work in the OWC, and I am not alone in my fear of the *what ifs*, as Debra Journet (2007) points out in her piece "Inventing Myself in Multimodality," in which she isolates the struggles for "senior" faculty and students when beginning to incorporate multimodal assignments (109–10). Students may already feel isolation, and assigning them a multimodal assignment that includes visual elements or uses software they are unfamiliar with can enhance the stress these students feel. If an instructor does not provide the right tools to assist students' creation of the multimodal assignment, the feeling of isolation is exacerbated. Logistics can be just as big a problem in traditional f2f courses, and I had my share of f2f teaching days on which my ideas or introduction of a technology only caused extra chaos.

However, the challenge with OWCs is that the students do not have visual cues, like my body language and facial expressions, to calm their fears and anxiety if something does not go as planned. They do not have me standing in front of the class saying, "It is going to be okay." Kelli Cargile Cook (2005) addresses this challenge in her piece "An Argument for Pedagogy Driven Online Education" (51), and she is joined by other scholars: Nancy Coppola (2005) in "Changing Roles for Online Teachers of Technical Communication" (89); Beth Hewett (2001) in "Generating a New Theory for Online Writing Instruction (OWI)"; and Patricia Webb Peterson (2001) in "The Debate about Online Learning: Key Issues for Writing Teachers" (360). Another challenge with the logistics of the OWC versus a traditional f2f course is that the entire class is not simultaneously together, ever, except in the discussion boards; the OWC is an environment that by nature is characterized by focused individuals working alone at their own pace. This lack of continual in-person interaction detracts from the peer-to-peer learning that can happen in a traditional f2f course. Another concern is how to help students learn technologies well enough to use them for their multimodal assignments.

This fear is addressed in A Position Statement of Principles and Example Effective Practices of Online Writing Instruction (OWI) (Conference on College Composition and Communication 2013) from the CCCC Executive Committee on Online Writing Instruction, which provides fifteen principles grouped into categories including "Overarching Principle," "Instructional Principles," "Faculty Principles," "Institutional Principles," "Research and Exploration." OWI Principle 2 states, "An online writing course should focus on writing and not on technology orientation or teaching students how to use learning and other technologies." In an f2f course, instructors can dedicate entire classes to teaching a specific technology and troubleshooting issues with the students. In the OWC, instructors are limited to using video examples and linking to website resources to help students learn how to use the technologies; more of the responsibility to learn rests on the students.

Clearly, the logistics present extra challenges in the OWC environment, and they are one of the main reasons OWIs often shy away from using multimodal assignments. But does fear of logistics mean OWIs should omit multimodal assignments altogether and hinder our chance to make an impact on students' definition of composing? Does fear of chaos ensuing mean we should not try to teach our students digital literacy and make them aware that most texts they encounter will be multimodal? No, it means we should understand that the logistics of an OWC are much more complicated than those of an f2f course, and we must account for this complexity in the construction of multimodal assignments. We should locate, for ourselves and our students, the tools and processes multimodal compositions require for completion, and we should make these tools and processes readily available and clear to our students before assigning any multimodal texts.

Fear of the Big and Bold

Another main reason OWIs might fear the use of multimodal assignments is that OWIs are thinking too big. They think a multimodal project must be incredibly complex, involving text, visual images, video, and so forth. This misconception goes back to what Ball and Charlton (2015) note about misunderstandings and gray definitions of multimodality. I was first introduced to the term *multimodal* while I was working on my master's degree, and as someone interested in technology, and more interested in technology than the formal rules of writing, this made sense to me; multimodal writing was the way of the future—it had to be! In the early terms of my master's program, I tried and failed at several multimodal assignments in my composition courses, thinking that the bigger, the bolder, the more exciting, the better. I assumed that if students had to produce something over the top, they would definitely understand what writing involves better than they would if they were working with only words, a thesis, organization, research, and so forth, but I was wrong, and that was why my multimodal assignments failed. Further, I did not have a clear understanding of the rhetoricity of multimodality; I did not understand it or have a clear definition of multimodality, and neither did my students. I thought all multimodal assignments had to mimic the texts of *Kairos*, utilizing alternate patterns of delivery, controlling how the viewer/reader digests or interacts with the text, incorporating audio, video, and images. In other words, I bought into the misconceptions Ball and Charlton (2015) point out: the assumption that all multimodal texts are digital and that the opposite of multimodal is monomodal (42).

Many instructors lack definitions of multimodality, which hinders their ability to utilize the power of these types of assignments. In the OWC, audio/visual features are already worked into the learning management system (LMS) and are clearly present and utilized (at least one hopes) when instructors describe weekly goals, discuss assignment instructions, give feedback, and so on. However, the use of these tools by students is often limited because instructors fear students will run into issues with using the technologies, so it is easier to ask them to do simple, text-based, written work. However, one of the best features of the OWC is that it already has these technologies built into the class, and students are already working in multiple modes and using linguistic, aural, visual, gestural, and spatial ways of making meaning through the sheer nature of interaction with the LMS used for the course content. In a sense, the OWC actually lends itself to successfully incorporating some of the modes but not to going over the top big and bold in the production of texts. Small assignments that combine text and media, such as a photo-journal reflection or a discussion forum that combines audio and text, are great options for starting small with multimodality in the OWC.

Fear Students Will Not "Get It"

One of the main issues with using multimodal assignments is that there is never a guarantee that the students are going to understand that the way they are making meaning (by utilizing multiple modes for a class project) is going to be useful and helpful in their careers; there is no guarantee they are going to draw the connection and assign it value. Yet students do this sort of writing all the time, but the challenge is to connect real-life writing to school writing, as Kathleen Blake Yancey (2009) argues in *Writing in the 21st Century: A Report from the National Council of Teachers of English.* As instructors of writing, one of our main goals is that students take with them a set of skills that allows them to function in future writing situations. One of the fears that persists with OWIs is that, if they choose to use multimodal assignments, the assignments will reduce the potential for learning; they might hinder students' abilities to "get it," to understand that learning to write is learning how to adapt to writing situations, learning what the situation is demanding, who the audience is for that situation, what kinds of elements (besides text) the audience expects to see, and so forth. Takayoshi and Selfe (2007) explain how students actually enjoy multimodal writing because it is more like writing they "do" and "see" daily: "Like the majority of Americans, many students are already active consumers of multimodal compositions by virtue of their involvement in playing and even creating digital music, watching television, shooting home video, and communicating within web space" (4). Students do not automatically understand the connection between multimodal assignments and "real-world" writing; this connection must be clearly drawn.

William Kist explains that NCTE's position statement on multimodal literacies means "students should be able to both read crucially and write functionally, no matter what the medium. In personal, civic, and professional discourse, alphabetic, visual, and aural works are not luxuries, but essential components of knowing" (2005, para. 3). Clearly, reading and writing in various mediums is something that must be taught to students. The nature of the OWC makes teaching this connection between multimodal work and "real-world" writing more challenging due to the lack of lecture time. So, teaching students how to draw connections from what they are producing as authors/designers (Arola, Ball, and Sheppard 2014) of texts to larger concepts and uses in other discourse must be done through lecture pages, video, or the discussion forums in the OWC.

Fear of Judging the Value

Not everyone values multimodal texts or the use of these in first-year writing courses. In A Position Statement of Principles and Example

Effective Practices of Online Writing Instruction (OWI) (Conference on College Composition and Communication 2013), OWI Principle 4 addresses this fear indirectly, noting that "appropriate onsite composition theories, pedagogies, and strategies should be migrated and adapted to the online instructional environment." However, some writing programs across the country, Illinois State University for example, put high value on multimodal composition and spend a lot of time and effort training faculty and developing faculty awareness and understanding of multimodal pedagogy. For those in programs that do not value multimodal pedagogy, defending the value of multimodal assignments might become routine. Many administrators, instructors, and students have been conditioned by a long history of valuing alphabetic texts; the essay is "writing."

The first time I used multimodal assignments in my f2f courses, I remember there were a lot of groans from the students. They did not understand the value of what they were learning by creating multimodal assignments. I was constantly defending my assignment choice to them and explaining that they were, indeed, learning real-life skills. Many of the students were in constant fear because we were not writing five-paragraph essays; instead, we did historical studies that oftentimes ended up as boxes full of artifacts or books akin to a scrapbook. The students were not the only ones questioning my multimodal-assignment selection, either. In my first full-time job at a branch campus of a Big Ten school, I entered a program with very traditional values; essays were taught, thesis statements were carried out, transitions were used. It was a culture shock coming from my work with multimodal assignments, and none of my faculty peers saw value in the multimodal work I'd done with my students and wanted to continue with these new students.

I was all on my own, and I had to justify, often, why I thought these assignments were worthwhile in any teaching context. Blair (2015) reminds us that assigning multimodal projects sometimes depends on reiterating the value of these types of assignments. She states, "Teachers, in collaboration with WPAs and other university stakeholders have a vital advocacy role to play to transform learning outcomes in OWI and f2f writing instruction that continues to privilege alphabetic textual production as the singular mode of rhetorical effectiveness" (489). Fear of being judged by students and faculty peers is real, but fortunately, there is a lot of research that supports the value of multimodal assignments and argues for their place in the first-year writing curriculum.

COST-VALUE ANALYSIS: IS IT WORTH IT?

As outlined above, the all-encompassing hurdle to overcome when incorporating multimodal assignments into the OWC is fear. However, the question remains: Is it worth the challenges and the fear to expand students' understanding of "real-world" composing practices? My answer . . . yes! Even though my experience using multimodal assignments is limited and I continue to experiment with smaller low-stakes assignments, I am confident in stating that the use of multimodal assignments adds value to the OWC. Technology has changed drastically since these arguments (regarding the use of multimodal assignments) were made, and online learning has exploded. A recent report on online education from the Babson Group, "Changing Course: Ten Years of Tracking Online Education in the United States," notes that "6.7 million students are taking at least one course online" (Allen and Seaman 2013, 17). This very large number from this Babson Group report cannot be downplayed, and it must be recognized that, for whatever reason, more and more students are forgoing traditional f2f courses in favor of online ones, so instructors transitioning to teaching composition in an online setting must reconceptualize their courses, as not everything that works in an f2f course works in an online one.

In her CCCC chair's address, Yancey (2004) outlines a moment in composition history that acknowledged the importance of technology and offers definitions of what it actually means to write and how these definitions have changed. She also argues that key differences exist between writing for the academy and writing outside the academy (72). She calls for composition in a "new key," stating that "it becomes pretty clear that we *already* inhabit a model of communication practices incorporating multiple genres remediated across contexts of time and space, linked one to the next, circulating across and around rhetorical situations both in and outside school. This is composition—and this is the content of composition" (72). Yancey's argument is still relevant today, more than ten years later. Composition, as a field, has changed, and the delivery and content of the composition course must change as well. OWIs must consider that "this is composition—and this is the content of composition" (72) and utilize ways to teach students how to write/design both in and outside the academy.

In looking at a simple cost-value analysis, one can see that the online learning space actually offers quite a few benefits that enhance the use of multimodal assignments. The online learning environment is, in and of itself, multimodal. It contextualizes information in multiple modes for students, utilizing the New London Group's five modes of making meaning: linguistic, aural, visual, gestural, and spatial. While the f2f environment is also multimodal, the difference lies in which modalities are emphasized and through which media they are communicated. The online classroom is an ideal place for instructors to show how these modalities work together to make meaning; the connections just have to be clearly drawn for students. While many benefits of using multimodal assignments in the OWC exist, here are a few of the key benefits: less intimidation by technology because most students have a familiarity with the online classroom and/or pick up the navigation easily; a tendency for individuals to make work that is meaningful to them; the features of the LMS (video, audio, and image sharing) that allow for creating meaning beyond alphabetic text; and last, the specific demographic of students who usually take online courses—these students are used to doing multiple things and participate in multimodal communication daily.

Further, the intimidation factor of new technology has already been addressed by the sheer fact that students must learn to navigate the (LMS) in which the course takes place. In addition, if the course is enhanced with multiple modes of communication, students also must know how to navigate the discussion threads, open and upload documents, play videos, view lecture slide shows, and so forth. Another aspect of the online course that yields itself to the use of multimodal assignments is that most students work individually on their assignments; they do not participate in group work (unless it is assigned), and they traditionally do not have study groups that meet regularly. This individual work allows students to figure out what works for them individually: how they digest the information, use it, and grow as scholars. Instructors can take advantage of the isolation of online courses to help students make meaning individually. While students interact with their instructor and their peers, they define and apply their own learning process.

The media-rich environment of the LMS provides a great space to ask students to participate in multimodal compositions. Unlike a traditional f2f course, for which computer classrooms are hard to come by, these students are taking their class on the computer; they have ready access to all these tools in an isolated area. Even though the OWI course happens through a computer, students' multimodal assignments can occur in low-tech ways, too. They can be captured through pictures or videos and shared with the instructor. Student comfort is a big deal, so encouraging students to work with what they are comfortable with makes success more likely. To add to this goal of comfort for students, it should be noted that most LMS platforms are equipped with features that allow for easy creation of audio, video and image/text mixing. Even if students have not used these features yet in the LMS, the features are fairly intuitive and do not take a lot of extra equipment. For example, an instructor can easily make a Jing/Screencast video that shows students how to use these features. Further, thanks to advances in technology, students do not have to be media geniuses or own a lot of equipment to replicate the actions instructors take in their videos.

Last, students who take online courses often take them because it works better for their individual lives; it allows them to work on their school work on their time. These students are busy, as reported in the survey "Grade Level: Tracking Online Education in the United States": "The nature of students in online courses can be very different from those in face-to-face courses. Students might select online because they are not able to attend traditional on-campus instruction because of work, family, or other obligations" (Allen and Seaman 2015, 24). They have families, careers, social lives, passions, and personal interests that drive their devotion to learning and motivate them to be disciplined enough to take online courses. These are the students who are writers on the go; they use their mobile phones to access their online courses, e-mail, social media, and so on. One could argue that these students already participate in multimodal communication daily, which means they already know how to create multimodal texts; they just need direction and connection in order to take what they do and make it work for them in situations they face in school, work, and so forth. Due to interaction with various technologies, students are already thinking in terms of multimodal, whether or not they realize it. It seems as though one of the things we should be teaching in first-year writing is how to combine outside skills with the skills students will need to meet the competencies of their future or current jobs.

Cope and Kalantzis (2000) reiterated this many years ago when they argued that if the mission of education could be defined, it would be that "[education's] fundamental purpose is to ensure that all students benefit from learning in ways that allow them to participate fully in public, community and economic life" (9). Takayoshi and Selfe (2007) add to this argument, indicating the need to explore multimodality with students: "Instructors of composition need to teach students not only how to read and interpret such texts from active and critical perspectives, they also need to teach students how to go beyond the composition of such texts—learning how to compose them for a variety of purposes and audiences" (3). While these arguments were made in 2000 and 2007 respectively, both of them hold true with even more force today, specifically in relation to the OWC. In looking at the unique features offered by the OWC discussed above, one can see there is a lot of potential to teach students how to participate in many facets of a community and compose for multiple purposes and varied audiences. Instructors must consider the use of multimodal assignments in their OWCs because "multimodality reminds us of the richness of all texts. Interestingly, small children—mixing drawing, colors, letters and layout—seem to compose multimodality almost 'naturally.' It may be that engaging in the same kind of 'multimodal play' would benefit many composers: it's often through such 'play' that we see alternative ways of seeing and making meaning" (National Council of Teachers of English 2014). We must remind our students of the richness of texts to get them thinking about expanded definitions of their own literacy (Cope and Kalantzis 2000). We must help them think in terms of the process, not the final product (Lutkewitte 2013), acknowledge themselves as authors/designers (Arola, Ball, and Sheppard 2014), and expand their definitions of what writing is (Yancey 2004); and we must give them the knowledge and tools to support their consumption of the multimodal texts they already digest daily (Takayoshi and Selfe 2007).

A SMALL START: INCORPORATING MULTIMODAL ASSIGNMENTS INTO THE OWC

Based on the honest discussion put forth in this chapter regarding multimodal assignments, it becomes important for me to offer suggestions for incorporating multimodal assignments into the OWC because I truly believe it is doable, and even more so, that these assignments are valuable to OWCs. There is a lot of research and discussion on the misunderstanding of multimodality as *digital*. Multimodal=digital texts is a common misconception and one that hinders many instructors from attempting multimodal assignments in their classrooms. One of the biggest issues instructors face is assuming that to be multimodal, assignments must incorporate digital elements and be elaborate, over-the-top, technology-driven projects. This misconception has been discussed profusely by many (Wysocki 2004; Shipka 2011; Ball 2014), and these scholars have encouraged us to expand our definitions of new media and multimodality. Selfe (1999) argues instead of thinking big, we should consider "small potent gestures" to move us toward new media composing (412). These "small potent gestures" add up and can allow instructors to incorporate smaller multimodal assignments like the one I use (app. A) into their OWCs. Palmeri (2012) argues for this type of small thinking as well, citing Selfe's (1999) "small potent gestures" when he states, "We may not be able to reach multimodal utopia, but we can work together in small ways to begin to change our pedagogies, our universities and our social and political structures" (161). Moving from a big and digital and technology-driven mindset helps instructors and students find a level of comfort in new media writing and focus on the development of practices that can transfer to other writing genres/situations.

Therefore, in the name of "small potent gestures," I offer some basic suggestions for beginning to incorporate multimodal assignments into an OWC (for a more in-depth discussion, I suggest seeing Blair's [2015] aforementioned chapter "Teaching Multimodal Assignments in OWI Contexts" or Tiffany Bourelle, Angela Clark-Oates, and Andrew Bourelle's [2017] piece "Designing Online Writing Classes to Promote Multimodal Literacies: Five Practices for Course Design"):

> The key to starting with multimodal assignments in the OWC is to start small, only one multimodal assignment per term.
>
> Use a trial-and-error approach, capitalizing on your experience as a composition instructor; experiment with low-stakes assignments that do not require an overly complex definition of multimodal writing and do not cost the students too many points if they do the assignment incorrectly. Starting small helps limit the challenges logistics create. If there is not too much to the assignment, there is not a high risk that students could feel overwhelmed or get scared by the unknown.

Another way to start small is to use only one multimodal assignment per term to avoid the earlier mentioned fear trap of assignments being too big or too intense for the OWI context. Takayoshi and Selfe (2007) make this argument in "Thinking About Multimodality," in which they "suggest that teachers start slowly and small—designing courses that make multimodal composition an option for one assignment during a term or creating assignments that make multimodal responses an option *only* for those students who have access to digital equipment . . . and some experience using this equipment" (10). While they are specifically talking about f2f courses, the same can be applied to the OWC.

Here is an example of a small-start multimodal assignment. I began using this assignment in the summer of 2015 in one of my OWCs as a way for students to introduce themselves to the class. This assignment has been adapted from Michael Gonchar's (2014) "What Objects Tell the Story of Your Life?," which was posted to the *New York Times*'s *Learning Network* blog on September 30, 2014. Gonchar got the idea for his assignment from a piece written by Sam Roberts for the *New York Times* titled "Objects Lessons in History" (September 28, 2014). Gonchar's assignment asks students to read Roberts's piece and answer three questions using objects to tell the story of their lives. I took both these pieces (Roberts's 2014 essay and Gonchar's 2014 assignment) and began thinking about what I could do to make this a multimodal assignment. In a sense, Gonchar's was already a multimodal assignment in that it involved tactile, visual, and potentially oral components in the objects students had to isolate. However, I wanted them to produce something both traditional and nontraditional so I would not overwhelm them at the start of the class. I wanted a sort of photo journal, a reflective essay, a mixed-genre representation of them as individuals, so I wrote up the assignment (see app. A).

This assignment has been pretty successful because it relies on something very familiar to students: reflection in the form of an essay or journal entry. The assignment gives students the opportunity to test the waters of designing their text because there are clear directions on how the text should be written or where the media used should go. It also allows them to make authorial choices: which objects they will use and how they will use audio/visual in the text to show the objects. Also, since I use this at the beginning of the semester as an introductory assignment, it allows students to see an expanded definition of personal writing and how elements of a text—their written text and the media they select—work together to create meaning. It allows students to understand a more flexible definition of multimodality and to digest the idea that multimodal texts can take on many forms, utilizing various resources: "The various resources—among them, images, sounds, document design, and graphics—that authors tap to create meaning in all kinds of texts," which "reminds us of the richness of all texts, and the many ways we create meaning" (National Council of Teachers of English 2016).

The students seem to enjoy the project based on their reflections in their essays; they are more detailed and include more analysis of why the objects are meaningful to them. To be sure, they face some small challenges with their "objects" multimodal project, such as how they should incorporate the photos or videos they capture, whether the photos or videos can be embedded, how they can be embedded in Word, and so forth. Some students also struggle with picking a limited number of objects in order to fit into the length of the essay they are composing. Some students have contacted me asking whether they could focus on fewer objects in order to spend more time discussing how their objects connect to Roberts's essay and define their history. Most of the students get very specific in the objects they pick, and their Objects projects turn out to be multimodal in that they combine text, discussion, analysis, and media.

Another very easy and simple multimodal assignment is to ask students to incorporate visuals into their research essay. The OWC is an ideal place to have discussions about images because of the discussion-board feature in most LMSs. Requiring students to find images and use them in their essays also allows many opportunities for learning because students need to understand copyright and citing/giving credit where credit is due when it comes to images. Additionally, they learn how to cite images and use visuals according to a citation style within their essay. Asking students to integrate images into an argumentative text helps them see how the images also serve to help or support their arguments. The students learn to make choices about the images they use in order to produce a desired effect. Smaller assignments, such as discussion boards or a short image-analysis assignment, can work well in the OWC. These types of assignments can further assist in scaffolding the way the students are crafting their arguments. For example, one discussion board could focus on finding credible sources and using sources with specific purposes, and then a succeeding discussion could be on finding powerful images and using images to support the argument. Additionally, due to technologies such as Facebook and Instagram, most students are already pretty adept at analyzing images.

One final example of a multimodal project I've had great success with is having students track their mobile-phone activities and reflect upon their tracking activities (see Borgman and Dockter 2016).

CONCLUSION

Several scholars (Cope et al. 2000; Selber 2004; Cargile Cook 2005) have argued for attention to instruction on multiple literacies, and this seems to be an ever-present concern with the iterative nature of workplaces and the influence of technology. Returning to the National Council of Teachers of English's position statement on multimodal literacies (2005), there is a clear argument that teaching multimodality is simply teaching what we already know and do. One point of the statement makes clear the influence of multiple modes in our daily lives: "The use of multimodal literacies has expanded the ways we acquire information and understand concepts. Ever since the days of illustrated books and maps texts have included visual elements for the purpose of imparting information. The contemporary difference is the ease with which we can combine words, images, sound, color, animation, video, and styles of print in projects so that they are part of our everyday lives and, at least by our youngest generation, often taken for granted." We've seen from scholars, such as Palmeri (2012), that multimodality isn't a new thing; we've always been multimodal, but it's time to acknowledge it and pay attention to it (as others have argued for years) in our writing class-rooms. What better venue than an online classroom (an environment that is already multimodal) to start incorporating more multimodal assignments?

When I began teaching online over seven years ago, it was scary, new, and unfamiliar. I had to participate in years of trial and error before feeling truly comfortable in my capacity as an OWI. Many instructors feel this way, especially those new to teaching writing online, and they go through the same emotions I did during those first few OWCs. The chal-lenges OWIs overcome in order to succeed are many, but with practice, OWIs can become more skilled and experienced. The benefits outweigh the struggles, and by using multimodal assignments in an already multi-modal environment, instructors reinforce what students already engage on a daily basis. Multimodal assignments help students acquire the tools and language to articulate how the texts are functioning and working as pieces of knowledge in our daily lives. This rhetorical knowledge gives students the ability to consider their best options for how to communi-cate their message to an intended audience.

OWI Principle 1 (Conference on College Composition and Commu-nication 2013) reminds us that "online writing instruction should be universally inclusive and accessible," and utilizing multimodal assign-ments that tap into various learning styles is one way of making OWIs more accessible. Yes, there will be challenges, and yes, making multi-modal assignments accessible to students with learning differences or physical disabilities will be an added step. However, as Takayoshi and Selfe (2007) remind us, the joy students get out of alternate methods of composing is worth considering: "For students, such instruction is often refreshing (because it's different from the many other compos-ing instruction experiences they've had), meaningful (because the production of multimodal texts in class resembles many of the real-life texts students encounter in digital spaces), and relevant (students often sense that multimodal approaches to composing will matter in their lives outside the classroom)" (4). Online students should not be denied these benefits because their OWI is too hesitant to incorporate multimodal assignments. As noted throughout this piece, starting with "small potent gestures" and anticipating the challenges can lead online writing instructors to create and use multimodal assignments in OWCs. A potential added benefit just might be more confident student writers and more confident online writing instructors, but only time will tell.

APPENDIX 3.A

TELL ME THE STORY OF YOUR LIFE

In the last few weeks, you've been reading about personal writing. You've learned about personal writing and the modes of narration and description. You've read some example essays from your textbook, but now it is your turn to give personal writing a try!

As you've learned in the last few weeks, writing genres can be mixed; they can include different modes of writing (argumentative, narrative/descriptive, compare/contrast), and they can contain different mediums mixed in with the text (sounds, video, images), so you should think of this assignment as a mixed-genre writing assignment; a reflective journal entry.

To complete this assignment, follow these steps:

1. Go to this site and read the blog post, "What Objects Tell the Story of Your Life?": http://learning.blogs.nytimes.com/2014/09/30/what-objects-tell-the-story-of-your-life/

2. Then read the essay "Object Lessons in History" by Sam Roberts by clicking on the link embedded in the blog post or going here: http://www.nytimes.com/2014/09/28/sunday-review/object-lessons-in-history.html

3. After you read Roberts' essay, begin to think about your own essay and how you'll put together a personal reflective journal entry that answers the prompts in the blog post:

    *   If you had to pick 3–5 objects to tell the story of your life, what would these objects be? If a history museum was doing an exhibit on you, what would be in your exhibit, what would be your object lessons?

    *   After selecting your 3–5 objects, do some reflective journaling on why you selected these objects? Why were they meaningful and how do you feel that define or represent you?

    *   Do you think mixing objects and text is an effective way to tell your history, or the story of you? Do you think that illustrating who you are through the selection of objects is a more intriguing way to share your identity, passions and what you value?

1. Do some pre-writing/brainstorming and then write up a rough draft that addresses the prompts above. Take some time away from your rough draft, then revise and edit it.

2. Take images, videos or sound clips of the objects you've selected and embed these into your text.

3. Use APA Format and be sure to cite any texts you use, such as if you reference Roberts' essay.

4. Submit your Objects Project to the assigned dropbox in the online classroom.

5. Please note: This assignment is based on an idea borrowed from the following site: http://learning.blogs.nytimes.com/2014/09/30/what -objects-tell-the-story-of-your-life/

REFERENCES

Allen, I. Elanie, and Jeff Seaman. 2013. "Changing Course: Ten Years of Tracking Online Education in the United States." http://www.onlinelearningsurvey.com/reports/chan gingcourse.pdf.

Allen, I. Elanie, and Jeff Seaman. 2015. "Grade Level: Tracking Online Education in the United States." http://info2.onlinelearningconsortium.org/rs/897-CSM-305/images /gradelevel.pdf.

Arola, Kristin, Cheryl Ball, and Jennifer Sheppard. 2014. *Writer/Designer: A Guide to Making Multimodal Projects.* Boston, MA: Bedford/St. Martin's.

Ball, Cheryl. 2014. "Show Not Tell: The Value of New Media Scholarship." In *Multimodal Composition: A Critical Sourcebook,* edited by Claire Lutkewitte, 163–86. Boston, MA: Bedford/St. Martin's.

Cheryl E. Ball. 2012. "Assessing Scholarly Multimedia: A Rhetorical Genre Studies Approach." *Technical Communication Quarterly* 21 (1): 61–77.

Ball, Cheryl, and Colin Charlton. 2015. "All Writing Is Multimodal." *Naming What We Know: Threshold Concepts of Writing Studies,* edited by Linda Adler-Kassner and Elizabeth Wardle, 42–43. Boulder: University Press of Colorado/Utah State University Press.

Benson, Alan. 2014. "Review: We Have Always Already Been Multimodal: Histories of Engage-ment with Multimodal and Experimental Composition." *College English* 77: 165–75.

Blair, Kristine. 2015. "Teaching Multimodal Assignments in OWI Contexts." In *Founda-tional Practices of Online Writing Instruction,* edited by Beth Hewett and Kevin DePew, 471–92. Fort Collins, CO: Parlor.

Borgman, Jessie, and Jason Dockter. 2016. "Beyond the Hesitation: Incorporating Mobile Learning into the Online Writing Classroom." In *Mobile Technologies in the Writing Class-room: Resources for Teachers,* edited by Claire Lutkewitte, 148–63. Urbana, IL: NCTE.

Bourelle, Tiffany, Angela Clark-Oates, and Andrew Bourelle. 2017. "Designing Online Writing Classes to Promote Multimodal Literacies: Five Practices for Course Design." *Communication Design Quarterly* 5 (1): 80–88.

Cargile Cook, Kelli. 2005. "An Argument for Pedagogy-Driven Online Education." In *Online Education: Global Questions, Local Answers,* edited by Kelli Cargile Cook and Keith Grant-Davie, 49–66. Amityville, NY: Baywood.

Conference on College Composition and Communication. 2013. "A Position Statement of Principles and Example Effective Practices for Online Writing Instruction (OWI)." NCTE. http://cccc.ncte.org/cccc/resources/positions/owiprinciples.

Cope, Bill, and Mary Kalantzis. 2000. *Multiliteracies: Literacy Learning and the Design of Social Futures.* London: Routledge.

Coppola, Nancy W. 2005. "Changing Roles for Online Teachers of Technical Communica-tion." In *Online Education: Global Questions, Local Answers,* edited by Kelli Cargile Cook and Keith Grant-Davie, 89–99. Amityville, NY: Baywood.

Dunn, Patricia. 2001. *Talking, Sketching, Moving: Multiple Literacies in the Teaching of Writing.* Portsmouth, NH: Heinemann.

Folk, Moe. 2013. *Multimodal Style and the Evolution of Digital Writing Pedagogy.* Boulder: Colorado State Press.

Hewett, Beth. 2001. "Generating a New Theory for Online Writing Instruction (OWI)." *Kairos: A Journal of Rhetoric, Technology, and Pedagogy* 6 (2).

Journet, Debra. 2007. "Inventing Myself in Multimodality." *Computers and Composition* 24: 109–120.

Kist, William. 2005. *New Literacies in Action.* New York: Teachers College Press.

Kress, Gunther, and Theo Van Leeuwen. 2001. *The Modes and Media of Contemporary Communication.* London: Arnold.

Lutkewitte, Claire. 2013. *Multimodal Composition: A Critical Sourcebook.* Boston, MA: Bedford/St. Martin's.

Minter, Deborah. 2015. "Administrative Decisions for OWI." In *Foundational Practices of Online Writing Instruction,* edited by Beth L. Hewett and Kevin Eric DePew, 211–25. Fort Collins: WAC Clearinghouse.

National Council of Teachers of English Position Statements. 2005. "Multimodal Literacies." NCTE. http://www.ncte.org/positions/statements/multimodalliteracies.

National Council of Teachers of English. 2014. "Multimodality." Poster presented at the Conference on College Composition and Communication, Minneapolis, MN, February. http://www.ncte.org/library/NCTEFiles/Resources/Journals/CCC/0653-feb 2014/CCC0653PosterMultimodality.pdf.

Palmeri, Jason. 2012. *Remixing Composition: A History of Multimodal Writing Pedagogy.* Carbondale: Southern Illinois University Press.

Peterson, Patricia Webb. 2001. "The Debate about Online Learning: Key Issues for Writing Teachers." *Computers and Composition* 18: 359–70.

Purdy, James P., and Joyce R. Walker. 2010. "Valuing Digital Scholarship: Exploring the Changing Realities of Intellectual Work." *Profession* 177–95.

Selfe, Cynthia. 1999. "Technology and Literacy: A Story about the Perils of Not Paying Attention." *College Composition and Communication* 50 (3): 411–36.

Selber, Stuart. 2004. *Multiliteracies in a Digital Age.* Carbondale: Southern Illinois University Press.

Shipka, Jody. 2011. *Toward a Composition Made Whole.* Pittsburgh, PA: University of Pittsburgh Press.

Takayoshi, Pamela, and Cynthia L. Selfe. 2007. "Thinking about Multimodality." In *Multimodal Composition: Resources for Teachers,* edited by Cynthia L. Selfe, 1–12. Cresskill, NJ: Hampton.

Wysocki, Anne. 2004. *Writing New Media.* Logan: Utah State University Press.

Yancey, Kathleen Blake. 2004. "Made Not Only in Words: Composition in a New Key." In *Multimodal Composition: A Critical Sourcebook,* edited by Claire Lutkewitte, 62–88. Boston, MA: Bedford/St. Martin's.

Yancey, Kathleen Blake. 2009. *Writing in the 21st Century: A Report from the National Council of Teachers of English.* NCTE. http://www.ncte.org/library/NCTEFiles/Press/Yancey _final.pdf.

SECTION II

4

REVERSING THE PROCESS
Video Composition and the Ends of Writing

Mark Pedretti and Adam Perzynski

INTRODUCTION

Since Donald Murray (2011) exhorted us forty years ago to "teach writing as a process not product" (3), composition studies has been remarkably silent about how and when that process ends. Murray was right to decry the current-traditionalist revolving door of submitted product and "blaming" critique; but, in emphasizing writing as activity, we have somewhat disingenuously neglected the simple fact that academic composition entails a temporal and intentional end, a point at which there is a *something* produced and deemed suitable for submission to an imagined audience for judgment and/or approval. Despite Paul Valéry's (1958) oft-cited maxim that "a work is never complete . . . but abandoned" (140–41), writers do, in fact, make decisions about when a piece of writing is satisfactorily finished—whether for publication, an assignment, or just to get on with the day. As Rob McAlear observed in a March 2, 2015, post to the blog *Another Word*:

> Writing may be an endlessly recursive process, but writing tasks are not. My grocery list is finished, not abandoned. My writing, like my students', has deadlines. In fact, from what I can see, lots of writing gets done every day. Yet teachers of writing are reluctant to talk about stopping writing, and this reluctance is often coupled with the idea that writing is never really finished—a conception observably untrue and discouragingly Sisyphean for our students.

Even as we are used to imagining the writing process as an open-ended, aleatory "exploration" (Murray 2011, 4), the empirical fact that both novice and expert writers complete their writing tasks suggests equally that they use criteria—implicit or explicit, blunt or sophisticated—to determine when a piece of writing has arrived at a satisfactory state to be considered a product (McAlear and Pedretti 2016, 84–87). Such completion criteria might be wholly contingent (as in the hypostasized student

DOI: 10.7330/9781607327974.c004

response "when I reach the requisite number of pages or run out of time"), or intrinsic and complex (e.g., "when I have taken a different rhetorical approach to meet the journal's stated focus and responded to the reviewers' comments by reworking the frame and stakes of my argument"). But because of our reluctance to focus on product, we do not have a nuanced language to discuss these criteria, their relative efficacy, or their propriety for different rhetorical situations and audiences. Instead, we have a model of composition based on "unfinished writing, and [we should] glory in its unfinishedness" (Murray 2011, 4). Process pedagogy may aspire to be a mapping of mental terrain, but it is one with little place for a destination.

Of course, Murray's (2011) "exciting, eventful, evolving" (4) model of the writing process also assumes "composition" entails letters on paper; as composition increasingly refers to the production of meaning in various alphabetical, visual, auditory, and interactive modes, we have the opportunity to rethink the utility and applicability of the process model. In this chapter, we do not rehearse the critiques of process pedagogy that have been leveled on ideological or epistemological grounds (Bartholomae 1986; Harris 2012; Kent 1999). Rather, we contend that multimodal composition—and in particular, video composing—offers a new angle of approach to process pedagogy's elided question of ending. This novelty, however, threatens to be lost under efforts to align these new compositional modes with the process movement; because multimodality requires an overt attention to the technologies of production (Lauer 2009, 36–39), it makes sense that its proponents would insist it is not a return to the product-centric approach of yesteryear. And yet, in that quick homology, multimodal composition risks repeating the same elision of completion criteria that inheres in Murray's process model.

But does an imagination of the finished product *matter* in video composing? To answer this question, we asked undergraduates in their second or third of a three-course composition sequence to comparatively reflect on their processes in composing for video and for paper, and we find that video fostered an awareness of the criteria necessary for making a desired final product in a way that productively shaped their composing processes. It is not that students focused exclusively on the final product, but the medium of video made them more aware of the *relation between* the process and the product. This, in turn, can be analogized to alphabetic composition, suggesting that video composing can serve as a powerful tool to introduce a discussion of the ends of writing—when, how, and according to what criteria a particular composition is considered "done"—into the traditional or blended composition classroom.

We are not arguing for a return to a product-centric approach, but even as a great deal of multimodal scholarship has focused on expanding the range of pedagogical and rhetorical possibilities beyond the alphabetic, we see equal potential for it to reflect *back* on the alphabetic composition process and thus to rethink some of its long-standing axioms.

To do so requires a notion of ending that undoes the process/product dichotomy Murray established. Rarely recognized in the mythology of the process movement—Kathleen Blake Yancey (2004) calls it "the most significant change that has occurred in composition over the last thirty years" (309)—is how Murray (2011) never intended for composition teachers to completely abandon the notion of a finished product in the first place, for the value of process pedagogy lay in its ability to make better products: "The process can be put to work to produce a product which may be worth your reading" (4). How can process and product work together like this? McAlear's (2015) invocation of Aristotelian entelechy offers a productive possibility. For Aristotle (1984), *entelechia* is not the finality of the completed artifact but the *awareness* of finality in the *process* of making; when we make a bowl, we have an image of the completed bowl in our minds that guides our production. *The product is a part of the process*: "For the action is the end [*telos*], and the actuality [*energeia*] is the action [*ergon*]. Therefore even the *word* 'actuality' is derived from 'action,' and points to the fulfillment [*entelecheian*]" (*Met.* 1050a 21–23). This is what Martin Heidegger (1962), in taking up Aristotle's schemata, recognized as the "towards-which [*das Wozu*]" of all purposive human activity: the end is a constitutive aspect for the doer of a task *in the midst of* the doing (99). The product is not an ultimate point to be reached in the future (405) but present during the making (Aristotle 1984, *Eth. Nic.* 1094a 9–16). Heidegger (1962) would describe that teleological presence as a structure of "reference [*Verweisung*]" (97): the criteria by which we determine whether the thing made counts as the kind of thing it is supposed to be—whether it serves the function for which it was intended. If I am making a soup, a table, or an essay, I construct criteria, often *in media res*, by which I judge whether my soup, table, or essay could "count" as the kind of thing it is (for dinner, use, or an assignment). Such criteria need not be goals to achieve, nor need they even rise to the level of intentional mental representation (Dreyfus 1991, 92–93), but they are nonetheless part of the making process and can be brought thematically into view in the mind of the composer. Entelechy thus offers us a way of thinking about product *within* process, without overdetermining it as the locus of evaluation, in a manner far different from the open-ended process pedagogy "that most of us cut our teeth on" (Kent 1999, 1). We contend this is a useful way of understanding students' awareness of ending in the video composing process, which we hope can be brought to bear on the alphabetic composing process as well.

LITERATURE REVIEW

Because completion criteria are not often discussed in traditional process research (McAlear and Pedretti 2016, 73–77), it is not surprising that they are almost wholly absent from theories of multimodal composition as well. Ironically, the foundational work of the New London Group in setting an agenda for multimodality and multiliteracies did not hesitate to recognize the importance of final products. Gunther Kress and Theo Van Leeuwen (2001) define multimodality as "the use of several semiotic modes in the design of a semiotic product or event" (20), placing the emphasis squarely on the end result, which occupies an entelechal relation to the conditions of its design. Likewise, the greater New London Group delight in the "felicitous ambiguity" (Cazden et al. 1996, 73) of the term "design," which can mean the intention of the maker, the structure of the made thing, or the process of making it—an ambiguity Richard Marback (2009) observes also applies to the term "composition" (406). But because the group is trying to articulate a general theory of multimodality, questions of completion criteria for different compositional modes seem far too specific. And while Kress (2005) has argued that any choice of communicative mode is subject to constant reconsideration according to different rhetorical situations, he acknowledges that "each occasion of representation and communication now becomes one in which the issue of my relation to my audience has to be newly *considered and settled on*" (19; emphasis added). *Considering* and *settling* describe a process of ending and imply the need for determining when that process is satisfactorily complete, but Kress gives little indication of how this might take place in any particular compositional mode.

When a discussion of "doneness" does come up, however, it has focused narrowly on questions of technology and audience reception. Dànielle Nicole DeVoss, Ellen Cushman, and Jeffrey T. Grabill (2005), for instance, see the technological limitations of multimodal platforms as a warrant for imagining some version of an end to the composing process: "As with writing, the composer must know something about what the final product will be *before* beginning the process. However, in the case of composing a multimedia video product, the writer must also know what kinds of files will be needed and created to meet the demands of the final product—including types of files and media . . .

and specific forms of media" (23–24). DeVoss, Cushman, and Grabill are right to point out how the digital landscape requires a consideration of product that Donald Murray's eschewal cannot accommodate, but they limit their consideration of ending to what Aristotle would consider to be a material cause (1984, *Phys.* 194b2 3–6), that is, available resources. They do not consider the Aristotelean "final" cause (*Met.* 1013a 33–35), the purpose of an activity, that "for the sake of which" something is done (Falcon 2015). If, for instance, I walk for the sake of my health, it makes sense that I would ask when and how I know I have fulfilled my purpose in becoming healthy. Would the same not be true for a website, an essay, or a film? More interesting is how DeVoss, Cushman, and Grabill take for granted an awareness of entelechy in alphabetic composition without articulating the "something" a writer must know about how and when to end. We contend such an awareness of purposes can move beyond a vague intuition and into an explicit list of completion criteria that participates in students' metacognition of their own composing processes.

DeVoss, Cushman, and Grabill (2005) then link material finality to a notion of rhetorical situation and audience, as composers' technological choices determine "the material and rhetorical realities . . . through which their final products will be produced and viewed" (23). Ultimately, material causes are only germane in relation to the eventual receivers of the multimodal artefact—an audience at a specific time and place. Likewise, Jennifer Sheppard (2009) views the entelechy of a multimodal project (in this case a website) in more traditional rhetorical terms of "reach[ing] target audiences [and] impact[ing] accessibility for users" (123)—which is to say, affecting persuasion. But audience turns out to be a remarkably question-begging criterion for assessing a composer's sense of doneness: how would a writer know they had reached a point where their persuasive intention would be sufficiently fulfilled without a second set of criteria to make that decision? If one is to determine whether a project is complete on the basis of whether it has effectively impacted its audience, what questions could composers ask themselves to make that determination? Because audience response is always a rhetorical effect, it cannot be straightforwardly incorporated into a composer's process calculation of doneness the way meeting the assignment directives, supporting claims with reasons and evidence, or even writing the required number of pages—all criteria students have proposed for knowing when they are done with a paper (McAlear and Pedretti 2016, 79–84)—can. While multimodal composition opens a space for considering ending, that possibility has thus far remained largely unexplored or opaque.

Far more common, however, is for multimodal theorists to align themselves with Murray's process model and thus repeat its elision of completion criteria. The homology between the alphabetic and multimodal is evident, for example, when Claire Lutkewitte (2014) argues, "We can acknowledge Murray-style process theory in order to bridge the past with the present. Murray's quote . . . , for instance, could be referring to multimodal composition if we replaced the word *word* with *mode*, as not all communicative situations involve the search for 'the one true word'" (2). This places multimodal composition squarely in a paradigm insistent on the open-endedness of the composing process. Lutkewitte is so quick to reject any attention to product that, even as she invokes Kress and Van Leeuwen's (2001) definition of multimodal composition given above, she feels compelled to insist, "Though this definition mentions a product or event, implying a certain finality, it also highlights the *act* of composing" (2), even though, as we argue above, the New London Group clearly insists on the final product that guides that activity of its production.

Similarly, Andréa Davis, Suzanne Webb, Dundee Lackey, and Dànielle Nicole DeVoss (2010) argue, "All of the elements of 'good' composing practices carry into digital spaces" (195). They champion a ludic approach to revision: writing and editing entail activities that could be analogously associated in digital spaces with the playful activity of "remixing," such as "delivering a text into a new context; collecting the text with other texts to make a new compilation; adding additional text; taking a new stance toward the existing text; parodying the existing text; transforming an existing image to send a new meaning; etc." (195). These are activities that students of the digital age gravitate towards intuitively but that can also be conceived as unending, subject to infinite variation and reworking, and without final purpose—like Murray's process model. Even as Davis et al. have found *an* analogue for textual editing in the social media practices of today's students, it is not at all clear they have found the most *appropriate* one for meeting the rhetorical demands of academic composing. While a student can play with a project endlessly, as their ludic paradigm suggests, at a certain point, the student must determine when they have played enough, and for that, Davis et al.'s paradigm offers little guidance.

Even when the process paradigm is at least considered to be open for revision in the face of multimodality, completion criteria remain outside the conversation. Jody Shipka (2011), in *Toward a Composition Made Whole*, envisions a unified theory of composition—both alphabetic and multimodal—by expanding the notion of technology to include chalk, slate, paper, desks—all the trappings of the traditional composition classroom alongside emergent digital resources. Shipka (2011) argues for a new phase of postprocess critique, moving beyond an attention to social and rhetorical situation to "the dynamic, emergent, distributed, historical, and technologically mediated dimensions of composing practices" (36). As a result, much like DeVoss, Cushman, and Grabill (2005), she resists "label[ing] a text multimodal or monomodal based on its final appearance" (Shipka 2011, 52), choosing instead to focus on "final products *in relation to* the complex and highly distributed processes involved in the production, distribution, and valuation of those products" (50)—predictably subordinating product to process. In folding the technologies of production into the composing process, Shipka fails to consider how those technologies might impact the quality or determination of ending. Even as she acknowledges the difficulty of determining where, in a student's drawings of their cognition, their "process narrative starts, where it goes, and where and how it ends" (Shipka 2011, 67), she pays no special attention to the student's imagined endings—even though the student's process drawings represent final products several times. As is often the case in process representations, a series of steps is depicted, as is a final result, but Shipka overlooks the relation among them, or their conditions of satisfaction, without comment.

The syllogism thus runs: the alphabetic writing process is open-ended; digital composition is just like alphabetic composition; ergo, digital composition is also open-ended, forever unfinished, and so on. We suggest such a syllogism, at least in the case of video composition, is neither empirically observable nor how students understand that composing process. As a practical necessity, live-action video composing simply *requires* the author/director to envision the end product before they have recorded a single frame; the constraints on time, the availability of actors and locations, and the continuity between scenes requires them to film *everything* they could possibly need up front and then to use the editing process to sort and winnow. Unlike editing a written document (or, for that matter, composing in other modalities like animation, digital design, or the remixing of existing documents), where one's supply of material is theoretically limitless, the availability of cinematic resources determines, in advance, the realm of the rhetorically possible. This is a simple point, and one well known to filmmakers: unless one is making a Hollywood blockbuster, a film's shooting ratio—the relation between film shot and film used—is crucial in determining the production schedule and the amount of prior planning required (Bayer 1989, 206; Bowen and Thompson 2013, 212; Hampe 2007, 43; Jones and

Jolliffe 2006, 282). Preparation and foresight—an imagination of what the final film will look like—are crucial in keeping the shooting ratio low (Goldberg 2011, 51). This principle is illustrated by an old chestnut about Alfred Hitchcock: he was bored with the actual filming of his movies because he had already visualized them so thoroughly in his head (Chandler 2005, 145; Coffin 2014, 57). Even with digital filmmaking, the availability of other resources, like actors and locations, can be equally effective in instilling a sense of entelechy in the composing process. We believe, however, that multimodal composition theory would do well to take notice of this simple point and to use it to introduce completion criteria back into discussions of composing processes across media.

METHODOLOGY

Our inspiration for this line of inquiry comes in part from coteaching an undergraduate writing seminar, Society through Online Video, in which students were asked both to write traditional argumentative essays and to produce live-action video compositions that were uploaded to YouTube. Student perceptions can, potentially, provide evidence of divergence from the process paradigm and offer a distinct vantage to reflect upon the rhetorical value of entelechy in general and across different discursive forms. At the end of the course, we asked students to reflect on their experiences with both compositional modes and to compare the processes they used in each medium. Student narrative reflections can provide rich material for understanding how students learn as opposed to what or why they have or have not learned. We hypothesized that the student narratives would identify themes that challenge the primacy of the open-ended process composition model. The goal of this analysis was to investigate how students view multimodal composition and to describe the implications of their perceptions for writers and educators.

This study involved the qualitative analysis of brief narrative reflections written by seventeen undergraduate students enrolled in an undergraduate seminar at a Midwestern research university. This study met the criteria for exemption by the university's institutional review board. During the final twenty minutes of the last seminar session of a fifteen-week semester, students were asked to complete a paper-and-pencil reflection. The reflection consisted of four questions:

1. How is the process of creating a brief online video like writing an essay?

2. How is the process of creating a brief online video not like writing an essay?

3. In what ways is preparation for creating videos different from preparation for creating an essay?

4. Student videos and essays can be seen as a series of projects. How do the conditions of your life as a student at this particular moment in history shape your projects?

The questions on the self-reflection form were developed with three objectives: (1) eliciting general perceptions of video and essay composing; (2) encouraging students to make comparisons; and (3) providing a safe opportunity for the students to consider their own progress and skill development in the context of a busy semester.

The written reflection forms did not include any identifying information, and responses cannot be tied to a specific student. However, some limited demographics of the class were available. By rank, the class included ten sophomores, six juniors, and one senior. Students' majors were divided among engineering (eight), arts and sciences (four), and management (five). The class was disproportionately male, with fourteen males and three females. All seventeen students completed reflection forms and wrote responses to each of the four questions. Written responses were typed and imported into NVivo qualitative data-analysis software (2012). Word counts were used to understand the raw amount of written text each student contributed to the task. On average, students wrote approximately fifty words in response to each question (see table 4.1).

A thematic constant comparative approach (Boeije 2002) was used to analyze the responses. This began with an initial reading of the responses, followed by the creation of a list of rough thematic categories. Each segment of text was then coded into each thematic category. The initial taxonomy was revised and elaborated after a series of coding sessions, during which similar categories were grouped together. Adam Perzynski conducted the majority of the coding, while Mark Pedretti served as thematic auditor, reviewing the categorization of chunks of text.

The limitations of this research are those common to small, qualitative studies: small sample size, particularity of the institution and assignment, generalizability and representativeness of responses, and coding consistency and reliability, in addition to methodological limitations of constant comparative analysis itself (Fram 2013; Kolb 2012).

FINDINGS

More than thirty themes and subthemes were identified in the iterative analytic process. We report on selected themes that provide preliminary

Table 4.1. Descriptives for narrative reflections

Question	1	2	3	4	Average
Average words per student	50.8	51.8	47.7	67	54.3
Total words per question	865	882	812	1139	924.5
Minimum words per student	25	35	22	33	28.8
Maximum words per student	109	88	84	151	108

evidence of how students think about the relative status of ending in video and alphabetic modes of composition.

Working Conditions Affect the Composing Process in Both Video and Writing

Students were very clear in describing the manner in which a variety of environmental and social conditions influence their creative processes for both video and alphabetic composing. These influences ranged from how the constraints of an academic semester prevented them from undertaking the grand projects they imagined to very clear depictions of how immediate practical concerns apply specifically to video.

> STUDENT 12: If you were to make a video, however, you need to make sure shots remain consistent and the area compliments the mood you are trying to express. . . . With videos you must take into account your environment. You can write a paper whenever you want to and not worry about your surroundings.

> STUDENT 10: Filming is different than writing. You also probably have less control over the details in a video. You can choose what is in your shot but you can't choose what is available.

Planning Is Similar

Students were somewhat divided in their sentiments regarding the similarities and differences of video and essay composition. A unifying theme around which student reflections coalesced, however, was that a vision, idea, and objective are required for both videos and essays.

> STUDENT 1: There is a lot of planning that goes into creating both to make an effective paper or video, you need to outline what you are doing and have a vision beforehand.

> STUDENT 4: The process of creating a brief online video is similar to that of writing an essay because planning is required in order for both the video and essay to have logical substance.

> STUDENT 5: The process of creating a brief online video is similar to essay writing in that it asks us to know what we're going to do before we do it.

Video Composing Requires More Extensive Preparation and Foresight

The students who wrote about differences in video and essay processes tended to focus on the ways in which video preparation was more demanding and less optional. Their sense of planning depends largely on an imagination of the final product they are trying to make.

> STUDENT 9: The preparation for the video actually existed, unlike most of my preparations for essay writing.

> STUDENT 1: In most cases, videos require much more forethought and planning, or else you will make mistakes difficult to fix (poor lighting/audio, missing footage).

> STUDENT 12: They are different in that making a video requires you to plan everything out. Although I know that I'm not supposed to, I find myself perpetually starting a paper without a solid direction. For the creation of a video it really requires you to plan out every shot that you are going to take. Even though we make small changes as the video goes along it's never even remotely comparable to the changes made in writing.

> STUDENT 17: When I plan a video, I visualize shots, character behavior, angles and setting. In my head I play around with different angles and try to look for something interesting. Preparing for writing, I do research and I plan out into sentences and sometimes I think through a paragraph and pick out cool phrases or ideas.

Readiness for Audience as Key Criterion in Both Media

Students also described the common requirement for both videos and essays to contend with and prepare for submission to an audience.

> STUDENT 3: Both forms of media portray a well-developed clean and professional story or idea. Both must have clear beginnings, middles and ends. In both, there is little patience from the audience to deal with wandering, unrelated thoughts.

> STUDENT 15: Making either a video or essay without planning would reveal disparities in the content that makes an audience disinterested and lost in the work.

> STUDENT 5: An audience is much more likely to re-watch a video than reread an essay because the medium takes less energy to absorb. Therefore, problems in the video can be more transparent.

DISCUSSION

Student responses suggest they are aware of the importance of entelechy in both the alphabetic and video composition processes. Several students readily identified it as a point of similarity in compositional modes in response to an open-ended survey question. Sometimes this awareness was expressed as an explicit goal, a form of prospective knowledge—"know[ing] what we're going to do before we do it"—or as an intuitive "vision" of the final product. This awareness of entelechy in turn necessitated "planning," which could be understood as a metacognitive mapping of the compositional process according to the technologies of production. Students typically understood this as "research" and "outlining" in the context of alphabetic composition, while they expressed a more nebulous sense of planning, occasionally tied to the visualization of individual shots, in the context of video composition. This planning could be an informal form of storyboarding, which then entails all the necessary elements to produce the storyboarded shots: locations, actors, props, lighting, time of day, and so forth. The fact that entelechy appears to function as a structuring principle for the video compositional process deserves closer scrutiny. On the one hand, it suggests the need for preproduction tasks that ask students to articulate the steps in their process to get from imagined, storyboarded image to realized shot or scene; on the other, students' sense of visualization offers a nascent completion criterion by which to evaluate their success: have I produced a shot that sufficiently resembles the storyboard? (Hitchcock, reportedly, was happy if he could get 75 percent of what he imagined beforehand [Chandler 2005, 145].)

However, as the students' responses above indicate, they were more attuned to entelechy in the process of video composing, primarily due to the finitude and contingency of visual resources. Because "you can't choose what is available" for particular shots, students felt more compelled to plan ahead in order to maximally utilize the material available for their filming. Students understood that, without sufficient foresight, they were more prone to "mak[ing] mistakes [that are] difficult to fix," and that the options for editing were, unlike alphabetic composition, limited to "small changes." In this regard, they confirm our theoretical postulate that video composition in an academic setting is tightly constrained by both principal photography and students' life circumstances; time, locations, (nonexistent) budgets, and actors' availability make *ex post facto* reshooting extremely difficult. Hence, while an alphabetic essay is subject to infinite revision, and even substantial reconception—discarding large portions, if not all, of a draft—on relatively short notice, in composing for video, many decisions that would otherwise be made in the revision and editing phases of the process must be made, once and for all, prior to the primary compositional activity.

Nevertheless, students in our survey did not seem daunted by this sense of having "less control over the details in a video" but instead understood it as an inevitable entailment of the compositional mode, to be adjusted to accordingly. Rather, they suggest the adoption of what Richard Marback (2009), following Richard Buchanan (1992), calls the "wicked problems" approach to design, in which solutions to design problems are indeed made but recognized as wholly provisional, contingent, and subject to the affordances of the situation: "Things only designed once that could always have been designed otherwise" (Marback 2009, 400). Instead of searching for "the one true word," or even "the one true mode," the video composer must find, with Wallace Stevens (1990) in "Of Modern Poetry," "what will suffice" (174, stanza 1). The preponderance of engineering majors in the survey population may account for this tendency to approach composition problems as design problems, but design may also offer a useful paradigm for conceptualizing the choices students make in multimodal forms (Kostelnick 1989; Kress 1999). A design approach, moreover, suggests ways in which the open-endedness of process pedagogy can be subsumed under a compositional model that incorporates entelechy: final composition/design decisions can be recognized as contingent and theoretically subject to further revision and rethinking, while recognizing that those decisions have been made for good reasons and according to criteria for assessing adequacy and doneness.

Equally interesting is what these survey responses reveal about students' understanding of the alphabetic writing process. Despite respondents having previously taken at least one, if not two, ostensibly process-based writing classes prior to Society through Online Video, their responses in aggregate indicate they are noticeably focused on outcome or product. This confirms the recommendation of McAlear and Pedretti (2016) that lessons in the writing process must be iterative in order to reinforce knowledge and habits that can disappear from one course to the next (85). Students were markedly indifferent to their writing environments—"you can write a paper whenever you want and not worry about your surroundings"—even though the material conditions of a kitchen table, a dorm room, or the subway ride to class would constitute essential "mediational means" (Shipka 2011, 46) that impact the writing activities that take place in them. Students *should* attend to the environments in which they write traditional essays, but they tended to consider this an unimportant factor; however, they recognized its importance when composing in the medium of video. Thus, teachers of composition can and should use the awareness of environment video composing fosters to initiate conversations about the impact of different writing environments. In keeping with Shipka's thesis that the advent of multimedia technologies can relativize our understanding of alphabetic writing practices and pedagogy, video composition brings the mundane technologies of the composing environment to the forefront of awareness, thus affording students the opportunity to consider how their writing environments impact the work they do in those spaces (see also Prior and Shipka 2003).

More surprising is how survey responses indicate that students found the "freedom" of the open-ended process model to be in fact quite paralyzing. Rather than feeling liberated by the "unfinishedness" of writing, students found the prospect of an unfinishable task to be a hindrance to starting: "Although I know that I'm not supposed to, I find myself perpetually starting a paper without a solid direction." This confirms McAlear's (2015) description of open-endedness as "Sisyphean," even a source of guilt. And despite something like Peter Elbow's developmental model of the writing process, in which "making a mess" (Bolker 1998, 34) by freewriting is "a transaction with words whereby you *free* yourself from what you presently think, feel, and perceive" (Elbow 1973, 15), students experience it as precisely the opposite: the paralysis of an empty horizon upon an undifferentiated field. Elbow (1973) acknowledges that the freedom of freewriting can bring "chaos and disorientation which are very frightening" (35) but suggests that any form of prior planning is a sign of bad faith, and that novice writers should simply stare into the abyss. On the contrary, students in our survey found the imagination of the finished film to constitute a "creative constraint" (Biskjaer and Halskov 2013; Damali and McGuire 2013) that enabled, rather than stifled, their progress on the project. Entelechy did not generate an anxiety-ridden expectation for a perfect finished project but offered a clear destination that illuminated the steps necessary to reach it. This is a major departure from the received wisdom of process pedagogy in alphabetic composition. Moreover, students found entelechy to be an actionable way to engage with the project at hand: "The preparation for the video actually existed, unlike most of my preparations for essay writing."

Last, students repeatedly pointed to audience as an important factor in determining the completion of their video projects, but they provided a more nuanced understanding than Sheppard's (2009) notion of simply "reaching an audience." Rather, respondents repeatedly identified imagined audience *scrutiny* as a causal element in defining their perceived need for more extensive preparation. One student, paralleling Marshal McLuhan's (1964) insights on "cool" media (36), felt it easier for audiences to scrutinize errors in video, which logically leads to increased demands for precision and consistency from their creators: "An audience is much more likely to re-watch a video than reread an essay because the medium takes less energy to absorb. Therefore, problems in the video can be more transparent." The perceived fear of "disparities," as another student put it, motivated students to anticipate scrutiny and avoid continuity errors. The imagination of a skeptical, easily distracted audience offers a meaningful way of formulating another completion criterion: one could play a benign version of Elbow's (1973) "doubting game" (147ff.), wherein video composers write down, from the perspective of a highly skeptical viewer of their projects, as many continuity errors, logical and causal flaws, and objections as they can and then use them as a checklist to determine when they have successfully assuaged the skepticism of their imagined viewer.

IMPLICATIONS FOR TEACHING

Student responses to survey questions comparing alphabetic and video composing processes suggest students are implicitly attuned to entelechy in both modes but that they view it as more exigent with video. If educators believe fostering an explicit awareness of the conditions under which a composition project can be considered done belongs to the kind of rhetorical metacognition composition classes regularly attempt to cultivate in other ways—as we believe it does—then building completion criteria into assignment sequences seems a worthy objective. Our aim here is not to prescribe what those completion criteria might be; while students in our survey gravitated towards audience scrutiny as a viable way for assessing a video project's doneness, other students in other composing situations might equally alight on other, equally meaningful criteria. Rather, we believe completion criteria should remain an open question for classroom discussion, to be folded into students' process memos and reflections (McAlear and Pedretti 2016, 88–89) or incorporated into self-assessment rubrics. Students could be asked

- to journal about what their finished projects would look like before recording a single frame;
- to thoroughly storyboard multiple conceivable shots for narrative films; or
- to offer a postproduction analysis of why a composer decided to conclude a project where they did.

Likewise, doneness could be integrated into a rubric by evaluating the conceptual or visual proximity of the finished project with its storyboarded outline (the Hitchcock test) or through a checklist of responses to potential audience critique. Such self-assessments would concretize an assumption in the "statement of goals and choices" used by Shipka (2011) for evaluating multimodal work (113–14) and would be consistent with the "readerly" self-assessment criteria proposed by Cheryl Ball (2006, 393–94) and Chanon Adsanatham (2012, 163–64).

Additionally, we believe these activities all have analogues in the alphabetic domain but that their higher visibility in video offers a novel way to introduce those analogous tasks, and their accompanying rhetorical attention, into more traditional writing assignments. Students' completion criteria for writing will certainly differ from those used in video production, but their incorporation of the overlooked question of ending into all composing modes affords them a revised process paradigm capable of spanning the multimodal curriculum.

REFERENCES

Adsanatham, Chanon. 2012. "Integrating Assessment and Instruction: Using Student-Generated Grading Criteria to Evaluate Multimodal Digital Projects." *Computers and Composition* 29 (2): 152–74.

Aristotle. 1984. *The Complete Works of Aristotle, Vol. 2: The Revised Oxford Translation.* Edited by Jonathan Barnes. Bollingen Series. Princeton, NJ: Princeton University Press.

Bartholomae, Donald. 1986. "Inventing the University." *Journal of Basic Writing* 5 (1): 4–23.

Bayer, William. 1989. *Breaking Through, Selling Out, Dropping Dead.* Rev. ed. Montclair, NJ: Limelight Editions.

Ball, Cheryl. 2006. "Designerly ≠ Readerly: Re-assessing Multimodal and New Media Rubrics for Use in Writing Studies." *Convergence* 12 (4): 393–412.

Biskjaer, Michael Mose, and Kim Halskov. 2013. "Decisive Constraints as a Creative Resource in Interaction Design." *Digital Creativity* 25 (1): 27–61.

Boeije, Hennie. 2002. "A Purposeful Approach to the Constant Comparative Method in the Analysis of Qualitative Interviews." *Quality and Quantity* 36 (4): 391–409.

Bolker, Joan. 1998. *Writing Your Dissertation in Fifteen Minutes a Day.* New York: Henry Holt.

Bowen, Christopher J., and Rory Thompson. 2013. *Grammar of the Shot.* New York: Taylor & Francis.

Buchanan, Richard. 1992. "Wicked Problems in Design Thinking." *Design Issues* 8 (2): 5–21.

Cazden, Courtney, et al. 1996. "A Pedagogy of Multiliteracies: Designing Social Futures." *Harvard Educational Review* 66 (1): 60–92.

Chandler, Charlotte. 2005. *It's Only a Movie: Alfred Hitchcock: A Personal Biography.* New York: Simon and Schuster.

Coffin, Lesley L. 2014. *Hitchcock's Stars: Alfred Hitchcock and the Hollywood Studio System.* Lanham, MD: Rowman and Littlefield.

Damali, Begum Z. Aybar, and Francis A. McGuire. 2013. "The Enabling Potential of Constraints." *Journal of Leisure Research* 45 (2): 136–49.

Davis, Andréa, Suzanne Webb, Dundee Lackey, and Dànielle Nicole DeVoss. 2010. "Remix, Play, and Remediation: Undertheorized Composing Practices." In *Writing and the Digital Generation: Essays on New Media Rhetoric*, edited by Heather Urbanski, 186–97. Jefferson, NC: McFarland.

DeVoss, Dànielle Nicole, Ellen Cushman, and Jeffrey T. Grabill. 2005. "Infrastructure and Composing: The When of New-Media Writing." *College Composition and Communication* 57 (1): 14–44.

Dreyfus, Hubert L. 1991. *Being-in-the-World: A Commentary on Heidegger's* Being and Time, *Division I.* Cambridge: MIT Press.

Elbow, Peter. 1973. *Writing without Teachers.* London: Oxford University Press.

Falcon, Andrea. 2015. "Aristotle on Causality." In *The Stanford Encyclopedia of Philosophy*, edited by Edward N. Zalta. https://plato.stanford.edu/entries/aristotle-causality/.

Fram, Sheila M. 2013. "The Constant Comparative Analysis Method Outside of Grounded Theory." *The Qualitative Report* 18 (1): 1–25. http://nsuworks.nova.edu/tqr/vol18/iss1/1.

Goldberg, Daryl Bob. 2011. *First-Time Filmmaker F*# Ups: Navigating the Pitfalls to Making a Great Movie.* Waltham, MA: Focal.

Hampe, Barry. 2007. *Making Documentary Films and Videos.* 2nd ed. New York: Henry Holt.

Harris, Joseph. 2012. *A Teaching Subject: Composition Since 1966.* 2nd ed. Logan: Utah State University Press.

Heidegger, Martin. 1962. *Being and Time.* Translated by John Macquarrie and Edward Robinson. San Francisco, CA: HarperCollins.

Jones, Chris, and Genevieve Jolliffe. 2006. *The Guerilla Film Makers Handbook.* 3rd ed. London: Continuum.

Kent, Thomas. 1999. Introduction to *Post-Process Theory: Beyond the Writing-Process Paradigm,* edited by Thomas Kent, 1–6. Edwardsville: Southern Illinois University Press.

Kolb, Sharon M. 2012. "Grounded Theory and the Constant Comparative Method." *Journal of Emerging Trends in Educational Research and Policy Studies* 3 (1): 83–86.

Kostelnick, Charles. 1989. "Process Paradigms in Design and Composition: Affinities and Directions." *College Composition and Communication* 40 (3): 267–81.

Kress, Gunther. 1999. "Design and Transformation: New Theories of Meaning." In *Multiliteracies: Literacy Learning and the Design of Social Futures*, edited by Bill Cope and Mary Kalantzis, 153–61. London: Routledge.

Kress, Gunther. 2005. "Gains and Losses: New Forms of Texts, Knowledge, and Learning." *Computers and Composition* 22 (1): 5–22.

Kress, Gunther, and Theo Van Leeuwen. 2001. *Multimodal Discourse: The Modes and Media of Contemporary Communication.* London: Arnold.

Lauer, Claire. 2009. "Contending with Terms: 'Multimodal' and 'Multimedia' in the Academic and Public Spheres." *Computers and Composition* 26 (4): 225–39.

Lutkewitte, Claire. 2014. "An Introduction to Multimodal Composition Theory and Practice." In *Multimodal Composition: A Critical Sourcebook*, edited by Claire Lutkewitte, 1–8. Boston, MA: Bedford/St. Martin's.

Marback, Richard. 2009. "Embracing Wicked Problems." *College Composition and Communication* 61 (2): 385–419.

McAlear, Rob, and Mark Pedretti. 2016. "Writing toward the End: Students' Perceptions of Doneness in the Composition Classroom." *Composition Studies* 44 (2): 72–93.

McLuhan, Marshall. 1964. *Understanding Media: The Extensions of Man.* New York: Signet.

Murray, Donald. 2011. "Teach Writing as a Process Not Product." In *Cross-Talk in Comp Theory.* 3rd ed., edited by Victor Villanueva and Kristin Arola, 3–6. Urbana, IL: NCTE.

NVivo Qualitative Data Analysis Software. 2012. QSR International Pty Ltd. Version 10.

Prior, Paul, and Jody Shipka. 2003. "Chronotopic Lamination: Tracing the Contours of Literate Activity." In *Writing Selves, Writing Societies*, edited by Charles Bazerman and David R. Russell, 180–238. Fort Collins, CO: WAC Clearinghouse.

Sheppard, Jennifer. 2009. "The Rhetorical Work of Multimedia Production Practices: It's More Than Just Technical Skill." *Computers and Composition* 26 (2): 122–31.

Shipka, Jody. 2011. *Toward a Composition Made Whole.* Pittsburgh, PA: University of Pittsburgh Press.

Stevens, Wallace. 1990. *The Palm at the End of the Mind: Selected Poems and a Play*. New York: Vintage.

Valéry, Paul. 1958. *The Art of Poetry*. Edited by Jackson Matthews. Translated by Denise Folliot. Princeton, NJ: Princeton University Press.

Yancey, Kathleen Blake. 2004. "Made Not Only in Words: Composition in a New Key." *College Composition and Communication* 56 (2): 297–328.

5

THINKING BEYOND MULTIMODAL PROJECTS
Incorporating Multimodal Literacy into Composing and Reflection Processes

Tiffany Bourelle, Angela Clark-Oates, Andrew Bourelle, Matthew Irwin, and Breanne Potter

INTRODUCTION

The growing emphasis on multimodal literacy in the field of composition has prompted teachers and scholars to redefine what constitutes composition pedagogy and what counts as an academic text, evidenced by the newest version of the WPA Outcomes Statement (Council of Writing Program Administrators 2014). In the 3.0 version of the outcomes, the introductory section states that "'composing' refers broadly to complex writing processes that are increasingly reliant on the use of digital technologies" (intro. sec., para. 2). Further, the outcomes' authors state, "Writers also attend to elements of design, incorporating images and graphical elements into texts intended for screens as well as printed pages. Writers' composing activities have always been shaped by the technologies available to them, and digital technologies are changing writers' relationships to their texts and audiences in evolving ways (intro. sec., para. 2)." When discussing multimodal composition, scholars typically promote the inclusion of multimodal projects, such as asking students to create websites, blogs, videos, or podcasts (Anderson 2008; Lutkewitte 2014; National Council of Teachers of English 2005; Takayoshi and Selfe 2007; Williams 2007) while emphasizing that rhetorical considerations are a crucial component of multimodal pedagogy (Ball 2012; Borton and Huot 2007; Selber 2004; VanKooten 2013; Wysocki 2004). While we agree with the importance of asking students to create such projects to develop their multimodal literacies and rhetorical knowledge, we do not think multimodal composition should be defined by the limitations of multimedia projects. Specifically, we argue that multimodality should not be limited to a final product; instead,

DOI: 10.7330/9781607327974.c005

instructors can and should promote multiliteracies during various stages of the composing process.

First, we describe how instructors can incorporate multimodal elements into students' composing processes by asking them to create videos or other multimodal drafting during their brainstorming, planning, and early composing stages. In other words, we are advocating for a multimodal approach to composing and inventing. Second, we describe how to incorporate multimodality into the reflection process. Instead of asking students to write text-based reflections, as is common practice, students can create audio or video reflective projects. These strategies expand students' opportunities to acquire and refine multiliteracies while at the same time providing the benefits of text-based metacognitive reflections (Hess 2007; Lauer 2013; Neal 2011; Shipka 2005; White 2005).

Our chapter is meant to be informative. Instructors can adopt or adapt our examples—or use the suggestions as seeds for producing new ideas that can further challenge the borders of multimodal composition. We hope our chapter will prompt teacher-scholars to explore the myriad ways multimodal literacy can enhance and invigorate their pedagogies. As the WPA Outcomes Statement claims, "Digital technologies are changing writers' relationships to their texts and audiences in evolving ways," and we, as the teacher-scholars of this field, must continue to evolve as well.

THEORETICAL BACKGROUND

At the end of *Composition and the University: Historical and Polemical Essays,* Sharon Crowley (1998) argues for a composition classroom in which students critically examine the composing process and practice it in ways that address the rhetorical situation, the exigency for composing, and its relationship to public and professional discourses. Similarly, James Gee (1999), echoing theoretical cords from the new literacy studies movement, asserts that "reading and writing only make sense when studied in the context of social and cultural (and we can add historical, political, and economic) practices of which they are but a part" (1293). This social turn in composition studies (Trimbur 1994) and literacy studies (Gee 1999) challenged practitioners and scholars alike to ask critical questions about what types of texts students were being asked to compose in schools and why they were being asked to compose these texts. While innovative researching, writing, and teaching emerged from these critical questions, inspiring a sort of hacking of the traditional composition curriculum and writing assignments, the influence of technology further inspired the field to reconceptualize literacies as multimodal and prompted pedagogues and scholars to rethink the classroom.

In their introduction to *Multimodal Literacies and Emerging Genres*, Tracey Bowen and Charles Whithaus (2013) assert, "When students are given access to pedagogical spaces and learning opportunities for experimenting with different ways to make meaning, they are drawing on the stuff of everyday social interactions to rethink the shape of written academic knowledge" (2). Much like the social turn, the digital turn in the fields of composition and rhetoric and literacy studies challenged the privileged position of the alphabetic essay in composition classrooms, compelling teachers and scholars to ask how knowledge is created through students' production of multimodal texts (Lutkewitte 2014). And although the field, in the last fifteen years, has participated in shifting the focus of first-year composition curriculum toward a more multimodal focus, as evidenced by books like *Writer/Designer: A Guide to Make Multimodal Projects* and publications like *Digital Writing Assessment and Evaluation*, we have been challenged to also consider the importance of providing students with the opportunity to use multimodal literacies to invent, compose, and reflect to promote the idea that students can use these "new literacies to make and remake media rather than being made by them" (Mills 2010, 257).

Multimodality: A Composing Tool

Although theories and practices of multimodality and multiliteracies have influenced the field's expanded and innovative definitions of academic texts, our chapter focuses on multimodal strategies for composing, what Dànielle Nicole Devoss, Ellen Cushman, and Jeffrey T. Grabill (2005) call "new media composing" (405). Like Bre Garrett, Denise Landrum-Geyer, and Jason Palmeri (2012), we define composing as "a process of making connections, rearranging materials (words, images, concepts) in unexpected ways" (act 1, para. 1). Furthermore, like many rhetoric and composition scholars, we challenge autonomous frameworks for invention. Creativity and invention are sparked by dialogic interactions with the world—words, images, people, sounds—that challenge writers to rethink and reimagine their own experiences, and we believe, like Garrett, Landrum-Geyer, and Palmeri (2012) that "digital technologies open up new possibilities" for inventing (para. 3).

By using multimodal strategies to support the composing of multimodal texts, students have low-stakes opportunities to try on the very tools they will use to construct rhetorically effective multimodal projects and, in the process, build a deeper understanding of the rhetorical capacities of the tool itself. Moreover, in using multimodal strategies, students also engage with what Lauer (2015) calls "multimodal thinking" (para. 1), which allows for more opportunities to interrogate their own ideas and experiences through a variety of modes. As Glynda Hull and Mark Nelson (2005) argue, citing Lev Vygotsky, "Our psychological and material tools . . . are intimately connected with our capacities to think, represent, and communicate" (478). In a study designed to interrogate the overreliance on verbal thinking in professional writing classrooms, Claire Lauer and Christopher Sanchez (2011) showed how the students they labeled as high spatial thinkers designed documents that were much more rhetorically successful by relying on visual language and visual elements, designing a strong, visual focal point, using white space and a hierarchy of information, and integrating words and images in a more unified manner (192). On the other hand, those students who relied much more on verbal thinking alone—"low spatial thinkers"—used visual only to enhance those arguments that had been made verbally. This study, like others, illustrates how "writing with multiple sign systems within technology-mediated environments pushes on systems and established ways of working with a pressure that other ways of writing don't exert" (DeVoss, Cushman, and Grabill, 2005, 407). Similarly, Bill Cope and Mary Kalantzis (2009) write,

> The different modes of meaning are, however, not simply parallel, and this is something we have come to recognise more clearly in the work we have done over the past decade. Meaning expressed in one mode cannot be directly and completely translated into another. The movie can never be the same as the novel. The image can never do the same thing as the description of a scene in language. The parallelism allows the same thing to be depicted in different modes, but the meaning is never quite the same. In fact, some of the differences in meaning potentially afforded by the different modes are fundamental. (14)

Simply put, composing the university (Werner 2015) multimodally means using new modes for inventing it.

Multimodality: A Reflective Tool

Reflection is an integral learning strategy in most writing classrooms, a foundational assessment practice of most writing programs, and a key element of many teacher-education and professional-development programs (Dewey 1910; Schön 1984; White 2005; Yancey 1998). Despite the ubiquity of these practices of reflection in classrooms, Blaine E. Smith and Bridget

Dalton (2016) argue that "little research has examined how youth reflect on their multimodal composing processes or how they do so through multimodal digital formats" (1). Working from this premise, then, our chapter also contributes to the dearth of research on multimodal reflection.

Much like our belief that multimodal composing provides learning opportunities that stretch rhetorical understanding for students designing multimodal projects, using a variety of modes to mediate students' reflective practices stretches students' meaning-making capabilities. In their study of learning resources from 1930 to 2005, Jeff Bezemer and Gunther Kress (2008) indicate that "modes can be used to do different kinds of semiotic work or to do broadly similar semiotic work with different resources in different ways" (237). Kress (2005) argues that "new media make it possible to use the mode that seems most apt for the purposes of representation and communication. . . . Aptness of mode to the characteristics of that represented is much more a feature now—it is a facility of the new media" (298). Although writing has always been shaped by technologies, in the practices we describe in this chapter, we were deliberate about asking students to select a variety of modes for their reflective practice. In doing so, we sought to understand how rhetorical agency during the reflection process would impact the relationship among mode, metadiscourse, and the learning process. As Cope and Kalantzis (2009) posit, "Reading and viewing, in other words, require different kinds of imagination and different kinds of transformational effort in the re-representation of their meanings to oneself" (14). And if reflection is about disrupting the connection between writer and text so writers can critically examine the relationship between themselves and the text (Sommers 2011), multimodal reflection has more potential than paper and pen for re-presenting and remixing the imagination.

In the sections that follow, we offer various ways instructors can incorporate multimodal strategies within the composing processes of invention and reflection. Like scholars before us, we suggest instructors first become aware of students' learning styles to guide their teaching (Felder and Silverman 1988; Keefe 1979; Kolb 1984). To this end, we encourage instructors to consider our examples of multimodal composing and the ways in which they account for students' learning styles and preferences, using and adapting the examples for their own classrooms as they see fit.

MULTIMODAL COMPOSING

In this section, we discuss three ways composition instructors can introduce multimodal strategies into the writing process: video storytelling, photo essays, and crowdsourcing. The strategies are beneficial because they help teach composition to students with various learning styles, they engage students with extracurricular digital tools, they give students tools to think critically about their own work, and they treat writing as a dialogic process that not only considers but also includes audience. Ideally, these processes take place in a low-stakes environment in which students can feel free to experiment and make mistakes.

Video Storytelling

The first strategy for introducing multimodality into the writing process is actually an adaptation of a classic one. In *On Writing Well*, William Zinsser (2006) observes that writing students tend to linger around the sentence level and that new and young writers often don't know how to organize their thoughts for long assignments. In order to help students focus on the process of writing rather than on a completed project, Zinsser came up with the radical idea of teaching a writing course in which no writing was actually required. Over the course of a semester, he asked his students to stand in front of the class and tell their stories. Each session, he pushed them to go deeper, and the other students commented on aspects of the stories they found interesting or about which they wanted to know more.

A basic adaptation of Zinsser's assignment turns the structure of his course, titled People and Places, into a four-video process. First, in groups of three or more, students make a two- to three-minute video in which they talk about a place that is important to them. They explain *why* that place is important and *how* they want to write about it. Then, they post their videos to a discussion board or other online forum (such as the Facebook group discussed in the section on crowdsourcing below) and respond to the other students in their groups. Students explain what the "author" is saying about their place and ask two questions about that place or the author's approach. Instructor and peer feedback on the first video is especially important, as many students rely on platitudes to explain the importance of their places. For instance, a student might say, "My hometown is the most amazing place I have ever been. It is so beautiful. Everyone I love is there. My family is so supportive, and they have made me the person I am today." An instructor can try to avoid such generalizations by giving examples of vivid details within assignment prompts, but we have had more luck using students' own examples to help them think beyond such limited responses. The instructor can choose two or three videos from students to post to the discussion and give suggestions for improvement, and these examples can then guide peer feedback. (See the section on crowdsourcing for more on intervening.)

For the next video assignment, students provide more intimate details on their important places. Zinsser (2006) writes that after hearing his students tell their stories, he realized they had given a lot of facts but not conveyed much sense of urgency (255). Therefore, for the second two- to three-minute video, students look for connections between themselves and the places about which they write. Instructors can ask them to recall memories, people, sensations, events—anything that comes to mind. In their responses to one another and in their self-critiques, they should explain what they find interesting about each other's stories and should zoom in on memories that make the audience want to know more.

In the third video, students explore a wider context for their stories, things to which their readers might relate. Zinsser (2006) gives the example of a woman who writes about the decline of small towns by writing about her small town in Iowa; he also describes a man who writes about the state of soccer today by remembering how soccer was the cause of a lifelong friendship among the guys with whom he played (256–59). Before they explain the wider context, however, students briefly recap their stories, focusing on the memories, people, and events their peers found interesting. In the feedback, students explain how they connected to each other's stories and provide self-critiques that explore other possible contexts.

For the last video, students prepare loose outlines to present their four- to five-minute stories. Students who take the rhetorical situation seriously tend to be more detailed, so we suggest instructors provide rhetorical context, asking students to think of the video as a pitch they might make to a publisher or book agent: they have five minutes to tell this person about their ideas. Students who think of the assignment this way might begin their final video with a brief introduction of themselves and why they are pitching the idea, whereas students who thinks of the exercise as merely a class assignment might just jump right into the pitch without providing much-needed context.

At the end of the four-video sequence, students are prepared to write place-based memoirs, but the exercise also encourages them to develop their own voices, critique themselves, adapt to feedback, and hone in on and connect the most interesting and important details of their work. Students who have taken the self-critique seriously have often changed the direction of their memoirs, having shifted their train of thought from "Will my professor find this interesting?" to "Do I find this interesting?" The exercise works just as well for research papers and other writing assignments. However, instructors may want to group students more strategically based on their topics and research interests.

Photo Essays

The next strategy for incorporating multimodality in the writing process is the photo essay. Photo essays are low-stakes assignments for students who already regularly use media, as well as others who feel intimidated by traditional composing strategies. As Ben Lauren and Rich Rice (2012) suggest, students use media-rich spaces to invent themselves and their identities; therefore, incorporating the photo essay as a multimodal composing strategy embraces students' "'natural' media reading experiences and visual rhetoric expertise to develop both technological literacy and academic discourse" (para. 2). In essence, we argue that photos act as unedited blocks of content that help students outline and structure their writing, while the photos themselves provide an opportunity for instructors to talk about writing vivid descriptions (e.g., showing, not telling), developing perspective, creating a sense of place, and potentially making an argument with just the mode of image. For example, a student might take a wide-angle photo of a doctor's waiting room. The instructor can "read" the image for the student, suggesting *zooming in* as a way to both take better photographs and write better descriptions. For instance, "The waiting room had four soft-colored walls with colorful paintings and a coffee table with assorted magazines" could be "I focused on the out-of-date magazines on the coffee-table and wondered how popular culture and everyday life move at different speeds, as if this trip to the dentist prevented me from aging, if only for an hour." This type of feedback can help students think more critically about the level of detail they add to their writing.

To introduce the photo-essay strategy, instructors can first design a minilesson to foster a discussion on how photos can stand alone to make an argument, or they can tell a story by bringing in examples of photo essays in popular culture. The online version of *Time* magazine often features "The Best Photo Essays of the Month," in which the editor showcases various photo essays (published in multiple venues) with dramatic scenes and narration from the photographer or the editor of the magazine or newspaper where the essay was first published. Typically, there is little context for each essay, as the photos tell the story or make an argument by themselves. For instance, the photo essay "See What

Undocumented Immigrants Carry Across the Border," published in *Time* in 2015, showcases pictures of immigrants' belongings in an attempt to illustrate the personal struggles immigrants face when leaving their home countries (Laurent 2015). Instructors can use examples such as this to illustrate how an argument can be made through pictures alone, prompting students to do something similar with photo essays, working up to telling a story with pictures and text. Students can also bring in examples of photo essays they find in popular culture for the class to analyze. Ideally, their examples use text in different ways, but it is a good idea for instructors to have a few of their own photo essays as a backup. Instructors can use these examples, for instance, to emphasize the difference between captions (which contextualize photos by adding details that aren't necessarily apparent) and narrative entries that connect the photos together.

When students begin their photo essays, they should take and gather many more photos than they think they will need. For memoirs, they take their own photographs, but photos from friends and family are also useful. For literary analyses, students can search online for photographs relevant to the themes they are developing. Images of places are an obvious example. For reviews, they ask questions about audience and purpose by not only photographing the subject of the review—an artwork, for instance—but also by looking at the venue and the attendants. These photos construct a visual record of details the observer might have missed, and photo essays act as visual outlines, which, like written outlines, require students to organize and structure their thoughts, create transitions, add definitions, and recognize areas that need further development.

Crowdsourcing, or The Facebook Writers' Room

In *Crowdsourcing*, Daren Brabham (2013) describes crowdsourcing as a process by which businesses, nonprofits, and government agencies "regularly integrate the creative energies of online communities into day-to-day operations" (xv). However, crowdsourcing is also a trend we see embraced by individuals in the form of a "writers' room" on Facebook. Facebook users who count writers, journalists, performers, or other artists among their friends may recognize this phrase as a call to order—in other words, someone is working on a project and is asking for help on Facebook. The resulting thread opens a writer's process to the *public*, constructing opportunities for feedback from friends and followers interested in their topic or just interested in helping. For instance, instructors can showcase author Jeff Goins's Facebook page, on which the author encourages his social media community to post stories of their work and family life that are similar to the stories he provides in his book, *The Art of Work* (Goins 2015). Some commenters in writers' crowdsourcing social media pages post links to other stories, some post gifs or memes, but all of them react to the original statement or question in ways that are useful to the writer. Instructors can imitate similar social media communities in the classroom by setting up a Facebook group and encouraging students to post questions about their writing and to receive feedback or ideas via the class community.

With video storytelling, photo essays, and crowdsourcing, instructors must discuss rules and requirements for citing people, photos, and crowdsourced ideas. They can measure the effectiveness of these strategies through student reflections, making adjustments as they see fit. We have found, for instance, that instructors may have to spend more time helping students make the theoretical connection between photo essays and written composition. Similarly, some students might prefer not to use social media for schoolwork, and others might resist multimodal composing strategies altogether. We suggest that instructors address these potential issues in syllabi and in classroom discussions, putting special emphasis on the *public* nature of the class. Although we suggest coming up with alternatives for students concerned about privacy, in our experience, students tend to embrace multimodal strategies for composition. A number of our students have said in reflections that they had fun with the assignments and ended up thinking about writing as a process that includes digital tools with which they are already familiar.

Multimodal Reflection

In this section, we discuss how our students used multimodal strategies and digital tools during the reflection process. We argue that students can incorporate multimodality into the reflection process without forfeiting all the benefits of text-based reflection. Reflection requires students to develop a metacognitive habit toward their learning, examining their position and processes as the author. Refining this habit of mind in the writing classroom encourages student to ask themselves how they moved from the beginning to the end of the composing process, why they chose to include particular modes (e.g., sounds, images, words), or how they crafted ideas and selected evidence. In this way, students become self-aware of their writing process. Research has shown that inserting the self into learning increases academic motivation, eagerness to learn, enjoyment of learning-related activities, and belief that education and knowledge are important (Liu, Ye, and Yeung 2015; Vansteenkiste, Lens, and Deci 2006). In this section, we describe three ways students create their metacognitive message, including through screencasts, oral reflections, and video.

Screencast Reflection

Tony Croft, Francis Duah, and Birgit Loch (2013) suggest that "students who create screencasts will 'learn by doing' and gain deeper understanding through the exposition they give in their screencasts" while simultaneously developing "their technical, personal, organizational, and also communication skills" (1047). When preparing screencasts, students must make decisions regarding the purpose and organization of the media, including what they want the viewer to see and how they want to structure the modes within. One student might choose to create a PowerPoint presentation, with some slides showing screenshots or images of certain points within their composition and other slides displaying a modest amount of text that will help the viewer follow the student's speech. Another student may choose to capture their composition itself so they can manipulate it live, bringing the viewer to specific points in the composition as they explain it. Whatever students choose to display on their screens, they discover the importance of carefully selecting the content they want to cover in their screencast reflection; they think critically about the visual evidence they use to support their oral claims; they see the need to follow an organized outline in order to keep the viewer focused on what they hear and see; and they learn to coordinate the images on the screencast and their oral explanation so the viewer can easily follow along.

Lessons surrounding screencasting often involve asking students to download free software such as Screencast-O-Matic or Jing to first create low-stakes screencast projects. For instance, students can create a short video that screen captures their desktop on their computer, walking the instructor through how the files are organized. Once the students familiarize themselves with the software, the instructor can introduce writing projects, such as producing minilessons for other students by creating and narrating a PowerPoint that explains certain concepts in the course. We suggest that the instructor pair such lessons as these with a discussion regarding the reasons a student might choose screencasts over other reflective mediums; for instance, some students may feel more comfortable reflecting on their work in an interactive way that allows them to focus on and highlight specific areas of their coursework. Discussions of audience may also be relevant, as a screencast can easily bring the viewers' attention to specific points within students' writing while they narrate their reflection. Students who feel uncomfortable standing in front of an audience—or a camera—often prefer this medium.

Oral Reflection

Oral reflection is another multimodal reflective strategy that allows students to supplement projects that are less visual in nature and are often useful for students who prefer thinking out loud. In "The Movement of Air, The Breath of Meaning: Aurality and Multimodal Composition," Cynthia L. Selfe (2009) argues that a "single-minded focus on print in composition classrooms ignores the importance of aurality and other composing modalities for making and understanding the world" (617). Selfe discusses the history of aurality, its prevalence in diverse cultures, and its persistence in English composition courses, and she includes a link to various autobiographical, audio essays to illustrate how oral compositions share and even exceed the depth, complexity, and creativity of text-based compositions.

In our classrooms, we have incorporated audio essays created by experts who reflect on their work. One such podcast comes from *This American Life*. For example, in "Play the Part," radio personality Ira Glass has a conversation with television-show producer Bill Langworthy in which Langworthy talks about his work as a producer and how he considers his audience at each point of production (Glass and Murdock 2012). The podcast proceeds, with Glass interweaving reflections from other actors that highlight their experiences on stage doing the exact opposite of what they would normally do in real life. One of these actors is Louis Ortiz, an Obama impersonator, and in the podcast, Ortiz details his thoughts on his work, how it feels to appease an audience, and how it feels to impersonate a persona of someone as important as the president of the United States. This example of reflection within a medium of podcast can illustrate for students how oral reflection is used within our everyday lives, much like Selfe (2009) suggests.

After listening to these individuals share their experiences producing their own kinds of compositions, we ask students the following questions: What was thought provoking about this podcast? What effect did hearing the individuals' voices have on you, and how was it greater than reading the transcript might have been? Why was this medium chosen for this particular story? We share how *This American Life* introduces each episode: "This American Life is produced for the ear and designed to be heard, not read" ("Note" n.d.). Students can specifically reflect on how audio projects, which are purposefully designed to be heard and not read, influence their rhetorical decisions. These types of discussions can encourage students to see how they can use mediums to reflect in a personal and meaningful way, allowing them to understand the power of aurality in reflection that cannot be replicated by text alone.

Video Reflection

Similar to screencasts and sound projects, video reflection can provide opportunities for students to bring in their literacies from outside the classroom. As Kathleen Blake Yancey (1998) notes, "Including students' literate practices in our curricula provides a place from which they can speak, an opportunity for them to exercise an authority that comes with and from knowledge worth having, a knowledge that is at the heart of literacy. Put simply, it allows us to *foreground that which they do know and ask them to share it with us* (173; italics in original)." Indeed, our students' literacies are shifting, with many students interacting with, creating, and commenting on YouTube videos on a daily basis. As Lauren and Rice (2012) point out, during the month they wrote their article on incorporating photo essays into basic writing courses, YouTube welcomed over one hundred million unique visitors, indicating that students "clearly inhabit these media-rich spaces and use them constantly" (para. 2). For this reason, we suggest instructors connect students' extracurricular literacy practices, like video creation, to the classroom.

One way students in our classes have used video reflections is by hybridizing screencasts with videos. The student might choose to appear on the screen side by side with their work. By doing so, they are able to highlight specific parts of their composition, explaining sections they're pointing to in greater detail. This method allows them to show their writing and tell about it simultaneously, using facial expressions and hand gestures to further express their thoughts. As Lillian Spina-Caza and Paul Booth (2012) write, "Unlike other visual media, video can come closest to writing not only because it can reflect what and how we are thinking, but also because of its immediacy and visibility" (para. 14). Video reflection allows for this window into the students' experiences as they reflect on their work.

We suggest instructors use examples of video reflection in pop culture to teach students how and when to use video reflection. Director's commentaries for films are excellent examples of this. When students see directors reflect on their work, the students are more likely to grasp how the medium can be used effectively for reflection. For example, in the director's commentary of the 1975 film *Jaws* (Zanuck, Brown, and Spielberg 1975), Steven Spielberg, the director, and John Williams, the film-score composer, together reflect on the film's musical theme. Through their discussion, the viewer learns that the composer repeated just two notes at the beginning of the theme song, two notes that are very low and only a half-step apart—a musical interval that evokes fear and anxiety in the hearer. Williams also indicates the combination of music, speech, and visual effects make the entire experience of viewing films moving for an audience, and this discussion of the various modes used in *Jaws* can be used to broach the topic of using different modes to appeal to an audience for a specific purpose. Using a video clip of experts reflecting on their composing process illustrates for students that reflection can be done in many different mediums, including video.

Instructors can introduce each medium—screencast, oral reflections, and video—by showing a few examples from past students' work or from the Internet; these examples can guide students in a critique of the multimodal texts, modeling for them what to do and what not to do in their own reflections. After introducing examples to the class, students can analyze each medium. To guide critical analysis, we ask our students these questions: Why did the author reflect in this way? What are the affordances inherent to reflecting in this medium? What are the limitations? How would this reflection have been different if delivered in a different medium? Can you see yourself reflecting in this way? Why or why not? By answering these questions, students learn the advantages of reflecting multimodally. They often discover an affinity toward a certain medium based on their learning styles and preferences of delivery.

As students experiment with reflecting through one or all the mediums presented above, they learn more about the reflective process and see it as "a mode of behavior indicative of growth of consciousness" (Yancey 1998, 4). Students see their writing change and grow as they reflect on it in multiple ways. Giving the option to reflect multimodally through the various media we describe can open doors for students who prefer to express themselves through talking about or showing something rather than through composing in an alphabetic text; in addition, providing students autonomy in choosing their medium of reflection shows students we see them "as agents of their own learning" (5). Offering a variety of modes in which students can reflect also opens doors for diverse language learners who may come from cultures in which oral communication or visual communication is more personal and expressive than text-based communication.

CONCLUSION

In her introduction to *Multimodal Composition: A Critical Sourcebook*, editor Claire Lutkewitte (2014) states that "multimodal composition offers us the opportunity to discover other ways of knowing and communicating ideas besides the ways we know and communicate through traditional print-based writing" (11). If what Lutkewitte states is true, there is no reason these ways of knowing should not be expanded to encompass all steps of composing processes so our students can, in fact, "discover other ways of knowing and communicating ideas besides the ways we know and communicate through traditional print-based writing" (11). In this chapter, we attempt to uncover ways in which instructors can adopt and adapt strategies that encourage students to communicate multimodally during the composing process, not just in the finished product. Specifically, we illustrate a variety of ways in which multimodality can be used in both the composing process and in reflections after the process is complete. Through our discussion, we suggest that a curriculum that incorporates multimodal composition at all stages of the writing process can deepen the students' learning of multimodal concepts, including the rhetorical considerations of audience, purpose, and medium—concepts important for entrance into a community of literate twenty-first-century citizens.

What we present in this chapter is by no means an exhaustive list of ways in which an instructor can incorporate multimodality into the composition classroom. However, our chapter starts the conversation of using multimodal composition during the composing process and offers examples of how to do so effectively. The examples we provide here can be used as a starting point for multimodality or as exercises that complement an existing curriculum. The field of composition is just beginning to understand the implications of adopting a multimodal pedagogy, and as we argue, there is much to be gained by turning the conversation from the finished product to the process of composing. As such, we encourage our readers to use our ideas, learn from them, and build upon them in their own classrooms while simultaneously adding to the existing conversation surrounding multimodal composition within our field.

REFERENCES

Anderson, Daniel. 2008. "The Low Bridge to High Benefits: Entry-Level Multimedia, Literacies, and Motivation." *Computers and Composition* 25 (1): 40–60.

Ball, Cheryl. 2012. "Assessing Scholarly Multimedia: A Rhetorical Genre Studies Approach." *Technical Communication Quarterly* 21 (1): 61–77.

Bezemer, Jeff, and Gunther Kress. 2008. "Writing in Multimodal texts: A Social Semiotic Account of Designs for Learning." *Written Communication* 25 (2): 166–95.

Borton, Sonya, and Brian Huot. 2007. "Responding and Assessing." In *Multimodal Composition: Resources for Teachers*, edited by Cynthia L. Selfe, 99–111. Cresskill, NJ: Hampton.

Bowen, Tracey, and Carl Whithaus. 2013. "Introduction: 'What is Else is Possible': Multimodal Composing and Genre in the Teaching of Writing." In *Multimodal Literacies and Emerging Genres*, edited by Tracey Bowen and Carl Whithaus, 1–12. Pittsburgh, PA: University of Pittsburgh Press.

Brabham, Daren. 2013. *Crowdsourcing*. Cambridge: MIT Press.

Cope, Bill, and Mary Kalantzis. 2009. "'Multiliteracies': New Literacies, New Learning." *Pedagogies: An International Journal* 4 (3): 1–30.

Council of Writing Program Administrators. 2014. "The WPA Outcomes Statement for First-Year Composition (3.0)." http://wpacouncil.org/positions/outcomes.html.

Croft, Tony, Francis Duah, and Birgit Loch. 2013. "'I'm Worried About the Correctness': Undergraduate Students as Producers of Screencasts of Mathematical Explanations for Their Peers—Lecturer and Student Perceptions." *International Journal of Mathematical Education in Science and Technology* 44 (7): 1045–55.

Crowley, Sharon. 1998. *Composition and the University: Historical and Polemical Essays*. Pittsburgh: University of Pittsburgh Press.

DeVoss, Dànielle Nicole, Ellen Cushman, and Jeffrey T. Grabill. 2005. "Infrastructure and Composing: The When of New-Media Writing." *College Composition and Communication* 57 (1): 14–44.

Dewey, John. 1910. *How We Think*. New York: D. C. Heath.

Felder, Richard, and Linda Silverman. 1988. "Learning and Teaching Styles in Engineering Education." *Engineering Education* 78 (7): 674–81.

Garrett, Bre, Denise Landrum-Geyer, and Jason Palmeri. 2012. "Reinventing Invention: A Performance in Three Acts." In *The New Work of Composing*, edited by Deborah Journet, Cheryl Ball, and R. Ryan Trauman. Logan: Computers and Composition Digital Press/Utah State University Press. https://ccdigitalpress.org/book/nwc/chapters/garrett-et-al/.

Gee, James. 1999. "The New Literacy Studies and the 'Social Turn.'" *United States Department of Education*. https://files.eric.ed.gov/fulltext/ED442118.pdf.

Glass, Ira, and Ryan Murdock. 2012. "Play the Part—458." *This American Life*. Podcast audio, February 17. http://www.thisamericanlife.org/radio-archives/episode/458/play-the-part.

Goins, Jeff. 2015. "Jeff Goins Shares His Strategy for Publishing a Best-Selling Book." *Write with Impact*, June, 14. http://www.writewithimpact.com/jeff-goins-shares-his-strategy-for-publishing-a-best-selling-book/.

Hess, M. 2007. "Composing Multimodal Assignments." In *Multimodal Composition: Resources for Teachers*, edited by Cynthia L. Selfe, 29–37. Cresskill, NJ: Hampton.

Hull, Glynda, and Mark Evan Nelson. 2005. "Locating the Semiotic Power of Multimodality." *Written Communication* 22 (2): 224–61.

Keefe, James W. 1979. "Learning Style: An Overview." In *Student Learning Styles: Diagnosing and Prescribing Programs*, edited by James W. Keefe, 1–18. Reston, VA: National Association of Secondary School Principals.

Kolb, David A. 1984. *Experiential Learning: Experience as the Source of Learning and Development*, Vol. 1. Englewood Cliffs, NJ: Prentice-Hall.

Kress, Gunther. 2005. "Gains and Losses: New Forms of Texts, Knowledge, and Learning." *Computers and Composition* 22 (1): 5–22.

Lauer, Claire. 2013. "Examining the Effect of Reflective Assessment on the Quality of Visual Design Assignments in the Technical Writing Classroom." *Technical Communication Quarterly* 22 (2): 172–90.

Lauer, Claire. 2015. "Invention Strategies for Visual and Multimodal Projects." Digital Media and Composition Institute. http://www.dmacinstitute.com/wp-content/uploads/2015/05/DMAC-Invention-Handout.pdf.

Lauer, Claire, and Christopher A. Sanchez. 2011. "Visuospatial Thinking in the Professional Writing Classroom." *Journal of Business and Technical Communication* 25 (2): 184–218.

Lauren, Ben, and Rich Rice. 2012. "Teaching Style in Basic Writing through Remediating Photo Essays." *Basic Writing eJournal* 10 (1). https://bwe.ccny.cuny.edu/Laurenand RiceRemediatingPhoto.html.

Laurent, Oliver. 2015. "See What Undocumented Immigrants Carry Across the Border." *Time*, February 1. http://time.com/3647891/undocumented-immigrants-bags/.

Liu, Elaine S.C, J. Ye Carmen, and Dannii Y. Yeung. 2015. "Effects of Approach to Learning and Self-Perceived Overall Competence on Academic Performance of University Students." *Learning and Individual Differences* 39: 199–204.

Lutkewitte, Claire. 2014 Introduction to *Multimodal Composition: A Critical Sourcebook*, edited by Claire Lutkewitte, 1–16. New York: Bedford/St. Martin's.

Mills, Kathy Ann. 2010. "A Review of the 'Digital Turn' in the New Literacy Studies." *Review of Educational Research* 80 (2): 246–71.

National Council of Teachers of English. 2005. "NCTE Position Statement on Multimodal Literacies." http://www.ncte.org/positions/statements/multimodalliteracies.

Neal, Michael. 2011. *Writing Assessment and the Revolution in Digital Texts and Technologies*. New York: Teachers College Press.

"Note." N.d. *This American Life*. All episode transcripts.

Schön, Dan. 1984. *The Reflective Practitioner: How Professionals Think in Action*. New York: Basic Books.

Selber, Stuart. 2004. *Multiliteracies for a Digital Age*. Carbondale: Southern Illinois University Press.

Selfe, Cynthia L. 2009. "The Movement of Air, the Breath of Meaning: Aurality and Multimodal Composition." *College Composition and Communication* 60 (4): 616–63.

Shipka, Jody. 2005. "A Multimodal Task-Based Framework for Composing." *College Composition and Communication* 57 (2): 277–306.

Smith, Blaine E., and Bridget Dalton. 2016. "Seeing It from a Different Light." *Journal of Adolescent & Adult Literacy* 59 (6): 719–29.

Spina-Caza, Lillian, and Paul Booth. 2012. "Video Unbound: Have You Vlogged Lately? Infusing Video Technology in the Composition Classroom." *Basic Writing eJournal* 10 (1). https://bwe.ccny.cuny.edu/BoothHaveYouVlogged.html.

Sommers, Jeff. 2011. "Reflection Revisited: The Class Collage." *Journal of Basic Writing* 30 (1): 99–129.

Takayoshi, Pamela, and Cynthia L. Selfe. 2007. "Thinking about Multimodality." In *Multimodal Composition: Resources for Teachers*, edited by Cynthia L. Selfe, 1–12. Cresskill, NJ: Hampton.

Trimbur, John. 1994. "Taking the Social Turn: Teaching Writing Post-Process." *College Composition and Communication* 45 (1): 108–19.

VanKooten, Crystal. 2013. "Toward a Rhetorically Sensitive Assessment Model for New Media Composition." In *Digital Writing Assessment and Evaluation*, edited by Heidi McKee and Dànielle Nicole DeVoss. Logan: Computers and Composition Digital Press/Utah State University Press. http://ccdigitalpress.org/dwae/09 vankooten.html.

Vansteenkiste, Maarten, Willy Lens, and Edward L. Deci. 2006. "Intrinsic Versus Extrinsic Goal Contents in Self-Determination Theory: Another Look at the Quality of Academic Motivation." *Educational Psychologist* 41 (1): 19–31.

Werner, Courtney L. 2015. "Speaking of Composing (Frameworks): New Media Discussions, 2000–2010." *Computers and Composition* 37: 55–72.

White, Edward M. 2005. "The Scoring of Writing Portfolios: Phase 2." *College Composition and Communication* 56 (4): 581–600.

Williams, Bronwyn. 2007. Foreword to *Multimodal Composition: Resources for Teachers*, edited by Cynthia L. Selfe, ix–xiii. Cresskill, NJ: Hampton.

Wysocki, Anne Frances. 2004. "Opening New Media to Writing: Openings and Justifications." In *Writing New Media: Theory and Applications for Expanding the Teaching of Composition*, edited by Anne Frances Wysocki, Johndan Johnson-Eiola, Cynthia L. Selfe, and Geoffrey Sirc, 1–41. Logan: Utah State University Press.

Yancey, Kathleen Blake. 1998. *Reflection in the Writing Classroom.* Logan: Utah State University Press.

Zanuck, Richard, David Brown, and Steven Spielberg. 1975. *Director's Commentary of* Jaws. Los Angeles, CA: Universal Studios.

Zinsser, William. 2006. *On Writing Well: The Classic Guide to Writing Nonfiction.* 30th anniversary ed. New York: HarperCollins.

6

ARCHIVING DIGITAL JOURNALING IN FIRST-YEAR WRITING

Steven Alvarez

INTRODUCTION

Incorporating digital journals into first-year writing (FYW) composition courses opens a type of socially connected, fast, and revisable multimodality. Understood as an electronic journal and portfolio, digital journals are a way for students to compose for purposes of both play and discipline while also thinking of writing as revision. Multimodal journaling opens a digital space for intense practice of transmodal literacy practices, and such compositions address students' questions about writing differently for different purposes and audiences in a digital world (Berry, Hawisher, and Selfe 2012; Delagrange 2011; Guzzetti and Gamboa 2005; Horner, Selfe, and Lockridge 2015; Takayoshi and Selfe 2007; Tarsa 2015). Incorporating the multimodal journaling element of "open writing" as informal writing to build upon academic English is an important element that engages FYW students with writing as a pleasurable experience in day-to-day practice. This type of social media communication promotes various creative expressions, such as embedding videos and images, formal and informal texts, and comments between students, while it also promotes so-called necessary elements of academic writing. In this article, I argue that the multimodality, visual rhetoric, and levels of formality of digital journals intersect with literacy activities in which students navigate the capabilities and restraints of the blogging platform while they use technology to learn more about genres of academic-styled prose.

Several recent studies of multimodal literacy practices (Ball 2013; Berry, Hawisher, and Selfe 2012; DeVoss, Cushman, and Grabill 2005; Gee 2007; Horner, Selfe, and Lockridge 2015; Pacheco and Smith 2015) have theorized about the shifting reading and writing habits and the kinds of texts students cultivate in their day-to-day changing social contexts. Exclusive attention in multimodal literacy research has focused on

DOI: 10.7330/9781607327974.c006

reading paths, the agencies and constraints of texts, semiotics, and how modalities interface with our literacy learning. With this background in my research and pedagogy, two central questions emerged: (1) How does online learning change the teaching of writing? and (2) How can FYW instructors use digital platforms to align with standardized registers while maintaining students' voices?

These questions I asked myself as I began as a writing instructor, and the narrative about arriving at digital journals in my pedagogy begins in this essay with my lived experience from my first years of teaching. On one level, I theorized about multimodality, digital literacies, and archives. On another level, I theorized about all this as I lugged across campus the projector I picked up from the audiovisual office before teaching my two biweekly early-morning FYW courses at Municipal College (MC), a four-year commuter college located in the northeast United States. I also carried my own laptop, which I plugged into a data projector and speakers, loaned to me by MC since the classroom I taught in was not technologically equipped. Fortunately, the AV folks prepared a projector, speakers, and an extension cord for me for each semester, ready twenty minutes before I started teaching for the day, all of which I had reserved at the beginning of each term for the dates I taught. Often, I projected my computer screen onto a whiteboard or wall, and sometimes onto a projector screen. Instead of making copies or erasing chalkboards, I spent my time on the extra effort of hooking everything up and putting things away. The classrooms at MC were one reminder that teaching with digital journals in classrooms literally changed how I taught writing, as MC expected me to teach writing in a more "traditional" way, which I learned to defy. MC's classrooms' few power outlets did not meet the tech expectations of FYW students who brought their laptops. This sense of practice, and the practical, became part of the conversation in my theorizing, blending into the practice of lived experience. Nevertheless, the mobility of online navigation for engaging literacies outweighed the difficulties of making a pop-up tech classroom for each class.

When I had set the equipment up in my FYW courses, I projected our class homepage. On our class homepage, I archived the course syllabus, the password-protected course readings, and a class-composed Interview Release form to be signed by any student participating in research. Figure 6.1 is from a spring 2011 FYW course, and this blog became the digital workspace for the class.

This lugging of equipment worked for me for six years as I was developing my own emerging literacy pedagogy, when I dared to experiment

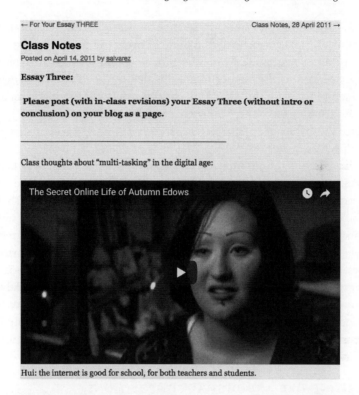

← For Your Essay THREE   Class Notes, 28 April 2011 →

Class Notes

Posted on April 14, 2011 by salvarez

Essay Three:

Please post (with in-class revisions) your Essay Three (without intro or conclusion) on your blog as a page.

Class thoughts about "multi-tasking" in the digital age:

The Secret Online Life of Autumn Edows

Hui: the internet is good for school, for both teachers and students.

Figure 6.1. FYW class blog, spring 2011. The course homepage includes the most recent course notes published.

with FYW assignments I felt connected to students' own lived experiences and multimodal literacies. The constraints and differences of teaching writing with technology, from not having a fully equipped classroom to unfamiliarity with technology, all became sources of student and instructor literacy interactivity. Incorporating digital journals as student workspaces and archives became fundamental to how I designed an FYW pedagogy that was both interactive and process oriented. For MC students, writing for the web engaged graphic design while they composed with different levels of formality. I also used the blog to record the in-class dialogue as my own notes to each day's class.

After each discussion, I also updated a running blog of class notes. I posted videos or sound clips for students to listen to in addition to what was covered in class. I also began each class with the syllabus, and if I made changes, I made them in front of the class and gave them the reasons for those changes. This negotiation in class and reasoning for making disruptions to the "contract" was done in person. I was held accountable for where the course moved. Students' experiences with blogging platforms varied, from extensive use to no use. Students became better acquainted with the blogging platform as the semester progressed and as they experimented with it more. The literacies they practiced to navigate the capabilities and restraints of the platform modeled their use of technology in their everyday lives.

Since those days of pop-up tech classrooms at MC, using digital technology in my classrooms has become the basis of my multimodal pedagogy. I both experimented with improvising tech spaces and learned to link more formalized registers of academic English with FYW students' literacy practices online, such as searches, making videos and photographs, sharing media, commenting, and reading. In the process of making and reflecting on what they made, students used their digital journals for developing ideas and practicing research and as digital archives of their writing processes. I believe that in utilizing these process functions for writing, workspace, and archive, writing instructors can organize multimodal FYW assignments that look to the process of journaling online to generate informal writing that is revised into more formal registers of student-centered research writing exploring lived experiences with digital tools.

M_WRITING.ORG AND DIGITAL COMPOSITIONS: ARCHIVED MULTIMODAL LITERACIES

It is important to understand the literacy strengths students bring to classrooms, which influence how they compose academic writing, as well as how students practice critical and creative thinking. My early FYW courses used M_writing (a WordPress blogging platform) to organize formal and informal class writing while also interacting with classmates and sharing writing. Students in those courses used M_writing digital journals that archived formal and informal course writing assignments, which they composed in multiple media and genres. Throughout the semester, the M_writing blog process archived writers at different stages of development in various genres and media, and as such, also facilitated the flow of revision. These practices model multimodal and rhetorical genre scholars' calls for merging revision techniques found in process-based composition studies (Alexander and Rhodes 2014; Ball 2013; Banks 2011; DeVoss, Cushman, and Grabill 2005; Horner, Selfe, and Lockridge 2015; Shipka 2005; Van Kooten 2016; Wysocki 2004). FYW students at MC posted topics on their digital journals ranging from research for their assignments, rough drafts, and freewrites to advice about classes and college life. This social media type of communication

Essay #2 - College's Postiche Representation (revised)

College's Postiche Representation

There are many different colleges. Each college presents themselves as having certain unique qualities. Some say they are small and personal, while others pride themselves on career based curriculums. No matter how the colleges portray themselves, they can never really capture what it is like to be there. It's the view of actual students at each college that gives one a real understanding of how the college runs. In this essay we will explore three different representations of college and test them against the reality of my college experiences thus far.

The first college representation comes from Blame Society Productions. In 2006 Blame Society Productions created a character named Chad Vader. Chad Vader became an instant favorite among hundreds of viewers. On one particular episode, Chad Vader attempts to get accepted to community college. "Chad Goes to Community College" is a humorous depiction of community colleges. In the video, Chad is required to take an

Figure 6.2. FYW student blog, spring 2011. This student's composition focuses on how community college is represented in the short film Chad Goes to Community College.

promoted various interactive expressions such as simply changing a visual theme to embedding videos and images to formal and informal texts and video comments between students.

Using digital journals in composition opens fields of digital composition, or a type of socially connected, fast, and revisable writing. Students connect with one another about writing, and they also find similar points of interest. I've noticed the level of formality depends on whether the audience is understood to be contextual or judged to be more or less formal. Because the students understood the blog as an electronic journal and portfolio, students changed tones when they knew they had to sound academic. This allowed them to compose for purposes of both play and experimentation.

Though play is important for the pleasure of practicing multimodal literacies, play alone does not challenge the strict assessment standards that allegedly measure the abilities of students.

Mark B. Pacheco and Blaine E. Smith's (2015) research exploring multimodal journal writing with emergent bilingual adolescents surveyed a class of students learning how to cope with academic standards of literacy. Pacheco and Smith argue that students mesh linguistic and modal resources to reach diverse audiences, convey ongoing thinking through multimodal composing, and voice lived experiences. Pacheco and Smith examine journaling as an individual and group-forming practice of informal language use, or personal use, and they note that journaling opens up questions for students about writing in different ways for different uses and audiences across languages, registers of speech, and modes. Incorporating the journaling element of expressivity as informal, multimodal composing to build upon is an important element in engaging students with writing as a pleasurable experience in day-to-day lived practice. The FYW student from MC below in figure 6.3, though recently emigrated from China and by his own standards not fluent in English, used his blog to experiment with English by crafting a poem.

Pacheco and Smith's (2015) multimodal pedagogy asks instructors to build on students' confidence through informal writing. Following Pacheco and Smith's research leads to questions about how technology and journaling can not only enhance the multimodal potential for emergent bilingual students but also benefit students who identify as monolingual because they gain experience thinking across languages, genres, and media. Through the use of digital journals, media in pedagogy, and student interactivity between formal and informal writing within electronic platforms, writing takes on a different significance for students. Digital journals encourage different avenues of connectivity, research, and expression. Students build on "traditional" writing forms while also creating a digital space for writing to grow, encompassing an online arena where error, language play, and invention are not only accommodated but actively incorporated. Digital journals are a surprisingly straightforward way to negotiate the tensions of error and encourage editing, sharing, and commenting. Digital journals also add a new platform for writing that increases opportunities for student-driven expression, facilitates and energizes the processes of collective brainstorming and peer review, stimulates creativity and class community, and supplements more traditional platforms for writing without supplanting or detracting from them. Students today write more but in less conventionally academic ways. They enter academic writing with certain multimodal literacies that are a result of their practice with various texts and modes of communication in their day-to-day social interactions.

Untitle

April 1, 2011 at 12:51 am · Filed under Uncategorized

In the gray raining day.

You talk to me in the bitter way.

I don't want to you go away.

But you can't stay.

I have nothing to say.

You know I love you everyday,

I just can't say.

I just try,

Try to stop you say good bye,

I know you want to fly,

Fly in the sky.

I don't want to cry,

I know I tell the lie.

You turn and go somewhere,

I can't stop you, my dear,

I am really fear,

Fear that you aren't here.

I look at you until you disappear,

Figure 6.3. FYW student blog, spring 2011. This student had immigrated to the United States two years previously. He used his journal extensively to practice writing, often using YouTube videos in his home language to inspire freewriting sessions.

My research into sociolinguistics and literacies has influenced my willingness to engage writing with technology. I try my best to structure composition course assignments so they engage with multimodal literacies (Alexander and Rhodes 2014; Berry, Hawisher, and Selfe 2012; Delagrange 2011; Stein 2008; Tarsa 2015; Van Kooten 2016). Many scholars favor the multimodal character of learning and literacy over the notion of literacy and learning as a primary linguistic accomplishment. By illustrating how a range of modes contributes to the shaping of knowledge and what it means to be a learner, a multimodal literacy framework provides conceptual tools for a fundamental rethinking of literacy and learning. What I examine here are the forms of literacy, not solely writing but also hybrid forms that combine literacies of different media and technologies. These literacies focus on the agencies and constraints of written and visual forms and how different media expressions interface with audiences.

It was obvious that the daily lives of MC students—like students of all ages—were immersed in hundreds of multimodal literacy events conducted in all varieties of electronic media for different audiences. Walking down MC's halls between classes and observing students with phones, laptops, tablets, and, yes, paper, offered sufficient proof. Consider all the varieties of literacy events individuals produced on a daily basis, including PIN numbers, lists, e-mails, signatures, notes, math problems, phone numbers, computer documents, and text messages on cell phones. It is important for educators to tap into the writing public, and one such way is to evolve pedagogical innovations for connecting what students know with the distinctive ways of knowing we value in the academy. Not only will students transition to academic literacies more easily if their academic spaces make use of multimodal potential for literacy and research, but students and teachers alike will benefit from remaining open to reconsiderations of what constitutes academic writing both in terms of style and of what subjects students write about. The new relationships and alignments affect literacy education because they create new kinds of opportunities for advancing the substances of students' lives.

Opening up the familiar discourses and literacies students experience in daily exchanges to the academic circle of discourses and literacies is an ongoing process. Being open to considerations from the academic perspective is the purpose of pedagogical research into methods for teaching writing, focusing on the dialogic interaction between the differences in literacies students practice on an everyday basis outside school and those students experience in K–12 and universities. With regards to academic literacies, ideological claims of language for certain audiences command that "good" language be written with confidence, purpose, and precision and any other number of prescriptive terms that evaluate students.

Certainly, students do own their language when they think of it as "fun," but I would argue that students rarely have that sense of ownership with "college" language because it is not fun since it is written at—and for—school. Using digital journals in conjunction with the technology in the classroom, and the classroom as space for self-reflexive discussions of the use of technology, "redraw[s] routes of access to public expression that precede our classrooms, driving new kinds of students into academia, and challenging us to develop pedagogies that accommodate and empower them as intellectuals who may take part in the dominant social debates" (Smith 2008, 46–47).

Students must eventually familiarize themselves with the "fun" languages of their respected majors or disciplines; the essays they, without a doubt, will rush to complete for a college-course deadline will, once complete, fall to the wayside—such is the metabolism of undergraduate student prose. FYW students especially benefit from writing about their educational and college experiences and from critically engaging with what it means to be a college student at such an early point in their studies. The importance of articulating what they are studying in college, what their goals are for the future, and how they will get there cannot be overstressed, especially if they are ever to look back on what they wrote as an historical artifact.

WRITING ABOUT COLLEGE, STUDYING COLLEGE

I have persistently sought to organize assignments in processes or sequences that align with departmental writing goals and make connections between college students' writing and appropriate self-reflective, socially themed texts. In my FYW courses, students applied critical reflection to readings about education in multiple media genres, including student-written admissions statements, web searches, online newspapers, online magazines, images, online journal articles, blogs, YouTube videos, and social media profiles. The theme for one FYW course unit dealt with exploring what I term *multimodal representations* of "college culture" on different search engines, including MC's advertising campaign, and students conducted these searches in class.

MC students also studied the writings of their classmates and engaged in group work via their M_writing digital journals. In one FYW course I taught using the theme of education for the semester, students critically examined and explored their subject positions as students at a commuter campus of a large, public, urban university, as well as some history of MC (for this project, students practiced researching articles on the university library's online database) and also theories and models gleaned from online readings in sociology and anthropology of education. MC student interactions with these texts and with one another all led to questions about what it meant to be meritorious—or how scholastic merit functions individualistically and how it fosters forms of structured inequality.

When writing and drafting their schooling narratives, students examined their relations to the languages they spoke and wrote, and this activity intertwined with the previous essay unit they had completed dealing with literacy in practice. Student compositions combined video, text, images, and sound, and they were able to share and comment immediately. As one in-class exercise, students "translated" articles gathered from different newswires into text-message code, and these "translations" were traded with classmates and retranslated back into journalese. Formulating assignments that tested student skills by

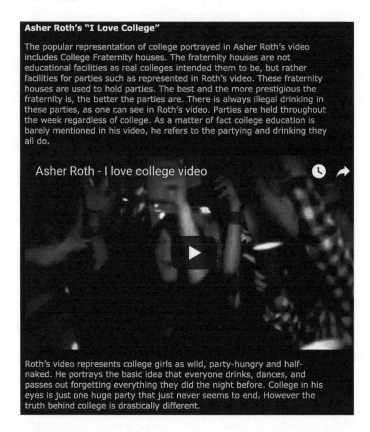

Asher Roth's "I Love College"

The popular representation of college portrayed in Asher Roth's video includes College Fraternity houses. The fraternity houses are not educational facilities as real colleges intended them to be, but rather facilities for parties such as represented in Roth's video. These fraternity houses are used to hold parties. The best and the more prestigious the fraternity is, the better the parties are. There is always illegal drinking in these parties, as one can see in Roth's video. Parties are held throughout the week regardless of college. As a matter of fact college education is barely mentioned in his video, he refers to the partying and drinking they all do.

Asher Roth - I love college video

Roth's video represents college girls as wild, party-hungry and half-naked. He portrays the basic idea that everyone drinks, dances, and passes out forgetting everything they did the night before. College in his eyes is just one huge party that just never seems to end. However the truth behind college is drastically different.

Figure 6.4. FYW student blog, spring 2011. This essay explores the "misrepresentation" of college in Asher Roth's I Love College.

critically engaging students in their own multimodal literacy habits by asking them to gather information and rewrite it in informal prose required an examination of the ways writing for different audiences and purposes can function differently in social contexts. One example is that their literacy biographies included the ideological assumptions underlying the standard English mythos, such as text-message language is a nongrammatical form of language—a typical "prescriptive" manner of diagnosing the presentation of grammar. The 2011 inclusion of *LOL* and *OMG* (Brown 2011) and the 2015 inclusion of the Face with Tears of Joy emoji in the *Oxford English Dictionary* (*Oxford* 2015) may perhaps point to a shift of written vernacular into legitimate usage.

There is a descriptive grammar to the complexity of the text-messaging code, but there is also a social effect of the language, and one instance of this effect is that young people maintain a form of language that excludes adults (though how this shall develop as these youth age will be interesting to follow). Another instance is the code's exclusion from the academy. Its exclusion is not solely because the code is senseless to the many professors and administrators who are not able to decipher it but also because the difficulty of this code, reserved for a select audience privy to its conventions, is supposedly not of the same difficulty as the dense language of academia, also reserved for a select audience. So-called academic English claims its legitimacy through its highly polished rhetorical constructions. Throughout my teaching, I have studied how my students' relations to the intimidating genre of academic writing have varied, from ease and comfort in handling "college-level" writing for some to the dread and conflicting anxieties— Pierre Bourdieu, Jean-Claude Passeron, and Monique de Saint Martin's (1996) "rhetoric of despair" —that writing generates for others.

FROM INFORMAL TO FORMAL

The journal-writing aspect of the course was composed of multiple low-stakes, in-class writing assignments, initially written in class by hand and later transferred to type and posted as digital journals. Students began with these handwritten compositions and later typed them as journal entries, sometimes adding to them by embedding clips from YouTube, original photographs, images from texts, or sound clips. Typically, at this stage, students edited their writing as well or returned later to add details and information.

For formal writing assignments, I encouraged FYW students to compose texts generated from their informal writings. On these separate pages of their digital journals, students revised texts from archived, informal writing and different media gathered through journal posts. Students also added information with additional research, including research into correct Modern Language Association citation conducted online in class and outside class through the Purdue OWL (http://owl .english.purdue.edu/). The M_writing blog thus became one method of utilizing an informal virtual space where writing developed and grew through levels of formality and structure. Students used their formal writing by researching their informal writing for ideas and media to develop and stitch together with new ideas and media. These formal features of creating and manipulating texts included building skills in the collection, storage, and analysis of multimedia texts, increasing awareness of social and cultural contexts, and working to build confidence persistence of dance—their dream. Compared to them, I feel so ashamed. I had ever attended the school dance team, but I escaped finally as a shameful "deserter" because of the fear of the hard and boring training. I also took part in the interest group of piano; but I was afraid of the painful of practicing, and then gave up again. There were so many similar situations in my life; so until now I don't have any specialty. I didn't find the reasons until I saw the "Thousand-hand Kwan-Yin". After that, I realized my idleness and that what I lacked were the persistence to do things and the courage to conquer difficulties. If I could try my best to do everything I thought as the deaf girls rather than care about the hardships at first, I would be succeed many times.

Thanks to these deaf girl for teaching me that there are not hills full of difficulties I couldn't master. What I need is to believe in my dream and never fear the hardships I will meet, just tell myself I can do it and persist. In the end, I will claim up the hill as the girls.

Figure 6.5. FYW student blog, spring 2011. Notice the two comments to the post about Thousand-Hand Guan Yin.

and voice (Berry, Hawisher, and Selfe 2012; Dressman 2007; Shipka 2005; Van Kooten 2016). The last formal assignment for the course was an exercise in voice, or ethos.

Marisa A. Klages and Elizabeth J. Clark (2009) perpetuate one misconception about the "process-less" writing that happens digitally. They write that "the virtual world is process-less: writing becomes an act of moving from immediate composing to instant publishing" (33). Addressing this concern about instant publishing, they rhetorically ask,

> How do we teach process in a process-less world of digital media? How do we engage students and help them to value process as a necessary tool for becoming more articulate in their writing? How can we engage students so that they can navigate both digital and traditional writing? How do we help students to code switch between their use of technology with friends and its use in academic and professional situations? (33)

Klages and Clark conceive of the instantly published as not malleable or as somehow skipping process altogether. However, conceiving of revision as stages of publication is a much better model that presents digital journals as resources for both formal and informal writing, both public and personal.

Klages and Clark's (2009) organization of blogs as portfolios looks to "develop rich multimodal ePortfolios characterized by an intensive use of visual rhetoric to complement their written and oral productions" (39). Klages and Clark overlook the potential for combining digital journals and portfolios, rather than simply creating portfolios. As in mathematics when instructors ask students to show their work, digital journals archive these "scratch pages" that demonstrate the process of arriving at more polished texts. Combining an element of process is important to digital journals, and the generation of a vast amount of informal writing to be used later in formal, ePortfolio composition is the best way to get students writing and to value their multimodal literacies as tools of expression. Smith (2008) uses a similar method in arranging journaling assignments to be composed as process compositions on digital journals. Smith arranges small-stakes, informal entries that serve as "meditations," which can be polished and used in later writing. The structured, informal writing assignments lead up to the three longer, formal essays (41). Smith argues for user-friendly compositional practices as ways of getting students familiar with both the multimodalities of the blogging platform and the strengths of their voices. Blogging is one such user-friendly compositional practice in the multimodalities of literacies in play. Using YouTube videos, for example, can inspire students to generate freewritings about the clip or aspects of it that explain or express critical ideas. YouTube Editor can also be important for students creating and uploading videos of their own.

TOWARD COMPOSING WITH STRENGTHS

I have offered arguments in favor of online journaling for process orientations to FYW, a bridge between multimodal literacies and sequencing archived writing assignments that build upon one another and extend students' multimodal repertoires. The examples of MC students' M_writing digital journals respond to formal writing prompts that align with standardized registers of academic language meeting departmental guidelines. These digital journals built on the aspects of practicing and experimenting with writing digitally while building on archived, informal writing that explored different critical and creative aspects of students' research and interests that became part of their more formal writing. Blogging platforms like M_writing offer FYW instructors a pedagogical tool that deserves further attention. In this brief piece, I document one method I have used. With documents on their M_writing digital journals, in addition to other formal assignments, students put to practice multimodal text-building skills used outside the academy to strengthen their formal, academic compositions. There are, of course, countless ways to use digital journals in classrooms, all with intentions to improve student writing.

The formative days of developing my FYW pedagogy created an indelible mark in how I approach literacy learning for students at all levels. More of the classrooms I'm around these days, fortunately, have technical equipment available, though I often still use my own laptop anyway. I continue to experiment with methods of organizing FYW blog assignments that use multimodal writing to help students explore their sociohistoric subject positions at their university. More recently, students in my FYW courses have been using Instagram to compose journal entries, or ethnographic "field notes," reflecting on what they understood college to be for, what they expected from college, and what they understood their college expected of them, using common hashtags to archive and share their texts. Students share their informal field notes and later revise from them in order to generate more formal written essays performing cultural analyses of their everyday experiences. I am in favor of digital journals for developing student ideas and also as archives of development. In utilizing these functions for writing, workspace, and archive, I believe writing instructors of all levels can look toward organizing assignments that see the processes of digital journaling on different platforms as ways to generate informal writing to revise into formal writing. To this end, academic writing instructors have the responsibility to reinforce the importance and power of students' voices and students' ethos as an avenue for recognizing and cultivating students' rights to their own language. After all, college English is not the first language for any college student. The qualities proponents attribute to digital journals—student expression, authorship and ownership, and interactive engagement with audiences—naturally resonate with many writing instructors.

REFERENCES

Alexander, Jonathan, and Jackie Rhodes. 2014. *On Multimodality: New Media in Composition Studies.* Urbana, IL: NCTE.

Ball, Cheryl E. 2013. "Multimodal Revision Techniques in Webtexts." *Classroom Discourse* 5 (1): 1–15.

Banks, Adam. 2011. *Digital Griots: African American Rhetoric in a Multimedia Age.* Urbana, IL: NCTE.

Berry, Patrick W., Gail E. Hawisher, and Cynthia L. Selfe. 2012. *Transnational Literate Lives in Digital Times.* Logan: Computers and Composition Digital Press/Utah State University Press.

Bourdieu, Pierre, Jean-Claude Passeron, and Monique de Saint Martin. 1996. *Academic Discourse: Linguistic Misunderstanding and Professorial Power.* Translated by Richard Teese. Cambridge: Polity.

Brown, Mark. 2011. "OMG! *Oxford English Dictionary* Adds LOL to Its Pages." *Wired.* https://www.wired.com/2011/03/omg-oxford-english-dictionary/.

Delagrange, Susan. 2011. *Technologies of Wonder: Rhetorical Practice in a Digital World.* Logan: Computers and Composition Digital Press/Utah State University Press.

DeVoss, Dànielle Nicole, Ellen Cushman, and Jeffrey J. Grabill. 2005. "Infrastructure and Composing: The When of New-Media Writing." *College Composition and Communication* 57 (1): 14–44.

Dressman, Mark. 2007. "Theoretically Framed: Argument and Desire in the Production of General Knowledge about Literacy." *Reading Research Quarterly* 42 (3): 332–63.

Gee, James Paul. 2007. *What Video Games have to Teach Us about Learning and Literacy.* New York: Palgrave Macmillan.

Guzzetti, Barbara, and Margaret Gamboa. 2005. "Online Journaling: The Informal Writings of Two Adolescent Girls." *Research in the Teaching of English* 40 (2): 168–206.

Horner, Bruce, Cynthia Selfe, and Tim Lockridge. 2015. *Translinguality, Transmodality, and Difference: Exploring Dispositions and Change in Language and Learning.* enculturation. http://intermezzo.enculturation.net/01.htm.

Klages, Marisa A., and Elizabeth J. Clark. 2009. "New Worlds of Error and Expectation: Basic Writers and Digital Assumptions." *Journal of Basic Writing* 28 (1): 32–49.

Oxford Living Dictionaries. 2015. "Word of the Year 2015." http://blog.oxforddictionaries.com/press-releases/announcing-the-oxford-dictionaries-word-of-the-year-2015/.

Pacheco, Marko B., and Blaine E. Smith. 2015. "Across Languages, Modes, and Identities: Bilingual Adolescents' Multimodal Codemeshing in the Literacy Classroom." *Bilingual Research Journal* 38 (3): 292–312.

Shipka, Jody. 2005. "A Multimodal Task-Based Framework for Composing." *College Composition and Communication* 57 (2): 277–306.

Smith, Cheryl C. 2008. "Technologies for Transcending a Focus on Error: Blogs and Democratic Aspirations in First-year Composition." *Journal of Basic Writing* 27: 35–60.

Stein, Pippa. 2008. *Multimodal Pedagogies in Diverse Classrooms: Representation, Rights, and Resources.* New York: Routledge.

Takayoshi, Pamela, and Cynthia L. Selfe. 2007. "Thinking about Multimodality." In *Multimodal Composition: Resources for Teachers,* edited by Cynthia L. Selfe, 1–12. Cresskill, NJ: Hampton .

Tarsa, Rebecca. 2015. "Upvoting the Exordium: Literacy Practices of the Digital Interface." *College English* 78 (1):12–33.

Van Kooten, Crystal. 2016. "Identifying Components of Meta-Awareness about Composition: Toward a Theory and Methodology for Writing Studies." *Composition Forum* 33. http://compositionforum.com/issue/33/meta-awareness.php.

Wysocki, Anne F. 2004. "Opening New Media to Writing: Openings and Justifications." In *Writing New Media: Theory and Applications for Expanding the Teaching of Composition,* edited by Anne F. Wysocki, Johndan Johnson-Eilola, Cynthia. L. Selfe, and Geoffrey Sirc, 1–42. Logan: Utah State University Press.

SECTION III

7

BLOGGING MULTIMODALLY
A Multiyear Study of Graduate-Student Composing Practices

Kathleen Blake Yancey

For a decade, I've used blogs as required, integral discussion spaces (Yancey 2002) for several graduate courses, including Rhetorical Theory and Practice, Composition Theory, and Digital Revolution and Convergence Culture. An analysis of these blogs—eleven in number, used from 2006 to 2013—demonstrates self-sponsored changes in composing practices, which have occurred in three waves. First, blog postings were word-only responses to instructor posts; then during a second wave, posts included both words and images; and then, in a third phase, posts become fully multimodal, including words, images, and multimedia. Moreover, these changes did not come at the cost of words: the number of words in these posts, over time, did not decline and in some cases increased. Of interest is (1) why, in the absence of a requirement, such changes in composing practices occurred and (2) what they suggest about how to encourage fully multimodal composing more generally.

COMING TO TERMS: MULTIMODAL COMPOSING AND (WE)BLOGS

Since the advent of digital composing, writing studies has increasingly attended to what we call *multimodality*. Often, we are influenced by work like Gunther Kress's (2010), which identifies modes as resources allowing us to make meaning, in print, for example, through font style and size, page layout, **boldfacing**, *italics*, and underlining. These modes are especially available with digital technology, of course, as are other modes like visuals (e.g., photographs, graphs), audio files, and video files. The availability of such modes for the everyday composer is, however, a relatively recent phenomenon; even fifty years ago, everyday composers had access to almost none of these modes, as they typed on a conventional typewriter offering only pica, elite, and underlining. At the same time, a

DOI: 10.7330/9781607327974.c007

kind of multimodality, even if sometimes rudimentary, has always charac-terized writing, regardless of medium, as Lester Faigley (1999) explains:

> Images and words have long coexisted on the printed page and in manu-scripts, but relatively few people possessed the resources to exploit the rhetorical potential of images combined with words. My argument is that literacy has **always** been a material, multimedia construct but we only now are becoming aware of this multidimensionality and materiality because computer technologies have made it possible for many people to produce and publish multimedia presentations. (175)

Here, I trace both kinds of multimodality as they inform the writing of students composing short homework assignments on a class blog. In the first wave of words-only, students' multimodality was of the conventional kind without which we cannot make meaning; even for our words to make meaning, we must have spaces between the letters of one word and those of another, as we see here. In the second and third waves, the students' composing becomes what I am calling *fully multimodal*, initially through the addition of images and then, progressively, through the ad-dition of multiple media.

As to weblogs, or blogs, according to *Wikipedia*, they are distinguished by three features: (1) they are online sites; (2) they are published on the web; and (3) they include discussion or information, usually "in discrete entries ('posts') typically displayed in reverse chronological order (the most recent post appears first)." Developed originally in the 1990s, blogs became ubiquitous in the early twenty-first century, and as Laura Gurak, Smiljana Antonijevic, Laurie Johnson, Clancy Ratliff, and Jessica Reyman (2004) argue, they seem to offer a new kind of compos-ing space:

> [Some] understand [blogs] to have revolutionized the way we receive information and connect with each other in online environments. Enthusiasts claim that blogs allow anyone's voice to be heard and resist hierarchical modes of information dissemination and communication. While this idealist egalitarian model of the Internet has often been criti-cized, we find value in the power of blogs to forego the institutionalization of communicative practices and offer spaces for writing that are more collaboratively constructed than other online spaces, as bloggers freely link to, comment on, and augment each other's content. In this way, blogs allow for the possibility of developing new cultural practices of online communication in relation to previously established modes of ownership, authorship, and legitimacy of content and access to information. (2)

It was exactly the possibility of developing new cultural practices of on-line communication that motivated me to design a blog for my courses, although there was a learning curve for all of us, as I explain below. And such a learning curve was required in spite of the fact that I had previously incorporated online spaces in teaching. In other words, it's not that I hadn't already used online spaces in my teaching: listserv conversations, for example, had been a staple of my courses for several years. On one of my typical listservs, students responded to writing prompts in a kind of communal digital substitute for personal print journals; we also invited scholars to join us on the listserv so they could talk with students about course topics. In such a course, blogs were in some ways redundant: just another online space. What I liked about them, however, and what I saw in them regardless of some disciplinary disappointment with them as a teaching tool (e.g., Krause 2004), was their ability to provide students with a capacious space to record their thoughts through words and more: students, and visiting scholars, could link, comment on, and respond to their peers' posts; could link to material outside the course, including but not limited to scholarly material; could incorporate multimedia into their posts; and could thus compose in a more fully multimodal, interactive, networked way. At the same time, like many faculty, I didn't plan a definitive shift from listservs to blogs; I thought, quite simply, that I would design blogs into my course and see how well they supported learning.

THE FIRST WAVE: AN OVERVIEW AND THE INITIAL EXPERIENCE

When I began with blogs, I wasn't entirely sure how I would use them, and that uncertainty—which over time shifted into a clear sense of purpose for the blog and ways it would be incorporated into the course—is reflected in some of the data I have collected about different kinds of participation. As the numbers suggest, in the first course in which I used blogs, there were only two posts and only 130 page views. Clearly, the blog didn't provide the capacious site for writing I had initially envisioned: it was not a central activity for writing, reading, or learning. As the visual suggests, though, and as I became more informed about how blogs might work and more strategic in my assignments, the numbers changed over time; in 2009, three years later, in the Convergence Three course, for example, there are 126 posts and 2,448 reading views, a ratio of posts and reading views that stays fairly constant over time. What's as interesting in terms of multimodality, of course, is what work the posts did and how.

In my initial offering in 2006, the blog was available in a comp theory class as a place serving two purposes: (1) to think about composing as we composed and (2) to discuss course topics. To begin the process of blog

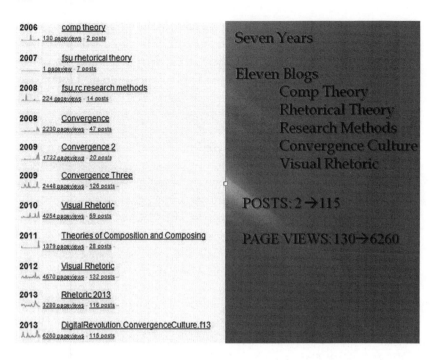

Figure 7.1.

composing and discussing, I suggested students use the blog as a place to respond to a query about the role of assessment in any composition theory. Using the reply feature exclusively—which was their only choice since I had not made students coadministrators of the blog—everyone replied to my post using the multimodality characteristic of print since, of course, this is all the reply function permits. Moreover, from the very first post, it was clear that my goal for an interactive, back-and-forth response wasn't being realized, either: students simply replied to my post without acknowledging or making use of others' responses. Consequently, as the screenshot indicates, I tried to define what I was looking for in this kind of composing, which I identified as an *interactive responding,* one located in responses connecting to earlier replies. Later in the term, Jody Shipka visited with the class on the blog, and her visit motivated a genuinely interactive exchange: students posted questions, with Jody replying to and discussing them. In addition, Jody shared a link with students pointing them to a site hosting student work. In sum, that exchange demonstrated that blogs, as teaching tools and thought spaces, could enrich a course, especially where there is an authentic exigence.

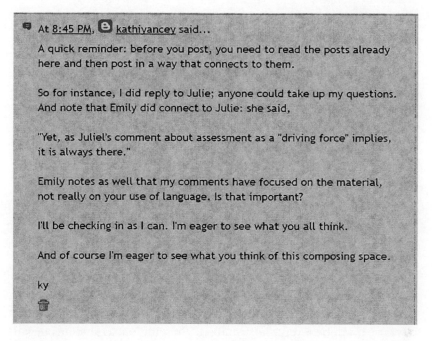

At <u>8:45 PM</u>, kathiyancey said...

A quick reminder: before you post, you need to read the posts already here and then post in a way that connects to them.

So for instance, I did reply to Julie; anyone could take up my questions. And note that Emily did connect to Julie: she said,

"Yet, as Juliel's comment about assessment as a "driving force" implies, it is always there."

Emily notes as well that my comments have focused on the material, not really on your use of language. Is that important?

I'll be checking in as I can. I'm eager to see what you all think.

And of course I'm eager to see what you think of this composing space.

ky

Figure 7.2.

In our rhetoric/composition program's course in research methods, which I taught soon after Composition Theory when I was still in the process of exploring how a blog might enhance learning, I used our course blog for a different twofold purpose: as a site where we could (1) revisit and reinterpret extant studies and (2) think together about how to design research studies. In this course, then, the blog acted to authorize our composing and thinking together about tasks that had immediate relevance. The first task I set for the class responded to an inquiry on the WCENTER listserv: "One of our consultants is wondering about research on the practice of reading the paper aloud at the beginning of the tutoring session. While it's a practice we advocate, different consultants choose different techniques and sometimes adapt them to the writer. Has anyone looked into this in a formal way?" My question to the class: "Let's assume you wanted to research this. How would you go about it?" The students found the question nicely aligned with the course material, and of course it was a genuine question; our answers, if shared, could help another consultant. As important, in replying, and without my prompting, students connected their thinking to that of their peers. One student, for example, began her reply by noting that she was contributing to what had been previously posted: "I am going to attempt to build on Ruth's ideas. What if the question was: During a tutoring session, who should read the student writing aloud? The wording is not very clear, but what I am getting at is should the tutor read the writing or should the student read the writing?" Another student took the same approach, explicitly observing the connection between previous contributions and her new one: "Like Kara and Ruth, I would have to do preliminary research, because I don't know much about this practice other than what I did in my own classroom as a middle school teacher." A third student, in beginning to design a research project based on the query, raised another question that moved in a somewhat different if related direction: "Do writing center tutors ask their tutees to read their papers aloud during writing center consultations, and if so, what are tutors' rationales for such practice?" My replies to the students focused on helping them think about the implications of their research questions and nascent designs. In responding to the question about writing center practices, for example, I praised it as I issued a caution: "*ok, a clearly focused question, though you'd better hope the answer to Q1 is yes, or it will be a very short study ;)." In addition, as students began articulating and designing research projects keyed to this inquiry, they also problematized the emerging designs:

> Here is a thought that occurred to me as I was re-reading all of the posts. . . . If studying the use of the read aloud tutoring strategy, would it matter if the student had poor reading skills? How would this impact your study if a student was asked to read her writing out loud and the reading was so painful that by the time she was finished reading, neither the tutor nor the student had any clue as to what had been read. Hm? Could this be handled during participant selection? Should it even be considered?

In sum, the task itself and the space where it was addressed seemed very generative.

Given that, I introduced a second task, one taking advantage of an open data set developed in connection with a CCCC-sponsored research project. In 2004, the Conference on College Composition and Communication began the CCCC Research Initiative; among the first grantees was a large group—Daniel Anderson, Tony Atkins, Cheryl Ball, Krista Homicz Miller, Cynthia Selfe, and Richard Selfe—who developed a survey for national distribution so as to learn if and how multimodality was being incorporated into writing programs. The team produced an article on the project, "Integrating Multimodality into Composition Curricula," published in *Composition Studies* in 2006, accompanied by an online database (available here: https://www.uc.edu/journals/composition

-studies/issues/cccc-data.html) providing both survey and results. Working in groups, the class took up two tasks. First, having interpreted the results on their own, they inquired into whether their interpretations matched those provided in the article. Second, they considered how they might revise the survey were they to use it in a new piece of research. In engaging with these processes, each group raised at least one question the class could discuss. One group, for instance, focused on how survey questions are worded: "What we found interesting was that while both question 137 and 138 asked for resources, the responses in 137 were mostly names in the field. But the responses in 138 were rarely names, which we attributed to the two examples provided in the question. . . . The examples predispose the respondents to think in terms of two materials ('everyday texts' and 'examples')." When the students had completed this exercise, we considered their observations and used them as a basis for making a list of practices to consider when researching. When the class concluded and I was reviewing the student evaluations, what the students volunteered in the comments stunned me: over half of them commented that the blogging activities, which supported our making knowledge together, were the most important class activities for their learning. Of course, it's fair to observe that these activities could have been conducted in class, but then there would have been no record of them; and they could have been conducted on a listserv, but then there wouldn't have been a common space to which students could return. The class blog, in other words, provided a continuing host for and record of activities students evaluated as helpful.

THE SECOND WAVE: COMPOSING MORE MULTIMODALLY

At this point, I wanted to move beyond a blog of verbal replies, but I also wanted to keep students engaged, and I appreciated that—as indexed by several factors, among them the number of words; access to new materials made available by visiting scholars; the course evaluations; and the kinds of discussions—these course blogs were supporting learning in new ways. In that sense, they were succeeding; in the first iteration in Composition Theory, for example, the eleven students in the class wrote seventeen thousand words, ten thousand of which were produced in the discussion with Shipka. Put as an observation, a single prompt could generate considerable online discussion. To support that kind of engagement, I began including on the syllabus specific encouragement for what I called *a responsive reply*, now not in the reply function but

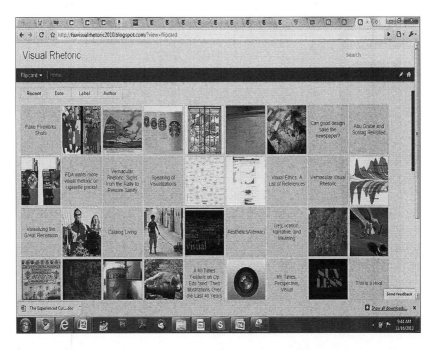

Figure 7.3.

rather in a post itself, which would also permit inclusion of multimedia. I called the posts *shares* and identified what sharing on a blog meant: "responding on the blog=provide context; connect your observations/ post to earlier ones and to readings; help us all see anew." Initially, as the definition demonstrates, I neither required nor encouraged inclusion of media in the posts: my focus was largely on interaction as a kind of social construction. At the same time, however, thought of in Kressian modes, there was the opportunity for students' composing to become fully multimodal since once they were allowed to post, rather than simply reply, they could draw on other resources to make meaning; all this became clear when I taught Visual Rhetoric.

The first blog assignment for Visual Rhetoric had a twofold goal: help students begin thinking about the content of the class as they also brought into class their own prior knowledge. More specifically, students began with an image so as to use it as the basis for analysis:

→ share: (1) choose an image you like; (2) share it with the class; (3) identify why you like it, including in your explanation the tradition it draws from; and (4) identify questions the text raises for you. Please also respond to at least two members of the class.

KRESSIAN MODES

	KY	Students
Layout	yes	some
Visuals	11	21 (but 15 required)
Links	7	8
Video	0	3
Audio	0	0
Tweet	0	barely invented

Figure 7.4.

Completing this task, then, required composing in both image and word, and it also required that students respond to the images posted by two of their peers. Moreover, during the course of the term, as the chart indicates, students began composing more multimodally: all students included images, as did I; six students included an image again; some students used layout in composing; I included seven links while students collectively included eight, and—unlike me—three students included video.

In sum, students were beginning to compose more multimodally, and a good question is why now? Nine factors, I think, played a role—both individually and collectively. First, my syllabus, which was filled with images, signaled that composing multimodally, and especially with images, was going to be normal practice in this course. Second, the first blog assignment asked students to begin with what they knew visually, that is, to identify images of their own, to post them to the blog, to comment on them (as explained above), and to reply to others' images. Moreover, this protocol, coming first thing in the term, reiterated the tacit message in the syllabus, communicated with images, about how we defined normal composing practice in that setting. Third, this protocol also signaled that in Visual Rhetoric, we would not only study visual rhetoric but also practice the visual rhetoric we were studying. Fourth, the favorable responses from others encouraged students to continue, and several of them continued voluntarily, posting images from outside the class because they thought we would find them relevant; one student, for example, pointed us to a URL showing how the FDA was requiring a new visual rhetoric in the packaging of cigarettes. Fifth, in the course of this iterative blog posting and responding, students developed new multimodal responding patterns that seemed kairotic, that is, appropriate for the genre (Miller and Shepherd 2004). Sixth, perhaps in response to my posting of links, students too began using links to point us to

July, 2010: In the latest figure quoted on the company's webpage, Facebook has over 500 million active users.

24th September, 2010: The Social Network, a film claiming to protray the story of Facebook founder Mark Zuckerberg, is released in the US; the film, which was a subject of much controversy, went on to gross an estimated $50 million at tje box office. The Social Network has been nominated for six Golden Globe awards and is highly tipped to win an Oscar in 2011

8th November, 2010: Queen Elizabeth II — TIME magazines' person of 1954 - joins Facebook, with a page titled 'The British Monarchy', which at last count is 'liked' by 295,044 Facebook users.

December, 2010: Facebook creator and CEO Mark Zuckerberg is named TIME magazine's person of the year, beating Julian Assange Hamid Karzai, the Chilean miners and the Tea Party to the top spot.

Figure 7.5.

relevant material outside the course. Seventh, the cultural moment may have also unintentionally authorized multimodal composing, and here I am thinking specifically of Facebook, which was in ascendance in the fall of 2010 when the course was offered. More specifically, during this time, Facebook—a site designed for posting commentary, images, links, and so on—was being used by five hundred million people, among them these students, and Facebook itself, given the movie *The Social Network* and the designation of Facebook founder Mark Zuckerberg as *Time*'s person of 2010, was identified as something of a phenomenon. Put another way, the composing students did on Facebook could have normalized and naturalized multimodal composing in other sites as well. Eighth, all these factors, I think, communicated to students that the composing on the blog was both institutional practice and noninstitutional composing, at least as we ordinarily conceive of it. On the one hand, this composing was certainly institutional in that most of the blog posts were composed to satisfy a course requirement. On the other hand, the composing on the blog differed considerably from the seminar paper that inhabits many graduate seminars. And ninth but not least, the students were composing in a common space; they were not isolated, nor did they have to decide if such composing was acceptable; they were composing separately together, much like toddlers in parallel play, each composing in the (sometimes virtual) composing company of others. And it was a composing they found valuable: members of the class continued posting for over a year after the class concluded.

THE THIRD WAVE: ANOTHER BLOG DESIGN

Although my course blogs seemed to support the new composing space I had hoped for, I decided that if I made a simple change to the blog—moving from all posts being single authored to some being collaboratively authored—I could achieve several goals at once. First, in the collaboratively authored posts, students would need to talk to each other about the task before posting; in this way, the blog assignment would sponsor more interaction. Second, with multiple kinds of authorship available, we would all see authorship as more flexible, including (the conventional) single authors but also collaborative teams. Third, with these changes, the blog could function as a site for composing *and* as a hub for authorship and interaction. I also thought that while multimodality does not ordinarily refer to multiple authorship, other twenty-first-century-oriented models of composing do. For example, the NCTE's Definition of 21st Century Literacies (National Council of Teachers of English 2013) includes such collaborative composing:

> Literacy has always been a collection of cultural and communicative practices shared among members of particular groups. As society and technology change, so does literacy. Because technology has increased the intensity and complexity of literate environments, the twenty-first century demands that a literate person possess a wide range of abilities and competencies, many literacies. These literacies are multiple, dynamic, and malleable. As in the past, they are inextricably linked with particular histories, life possibilities, and social trajectories of individuals and groups. Active, successful participants in this twenty-first-century global society must be able to develop proficiency and fluency with the tools of technology; build intentional cross-cultural connections and relationships with others to pose and solve problems collaboratively and strengthen independent thought; design and share information for global communities to meet a variety of purposes; manage, analyze, and synthesize multiple streams of simultaneous information; create, critique, analyze, and evaluate multimedia texts; attend to the ethical responsibilities required by these complex environments.

In sum, by adding a collaborative composing process to the blog, I thought I could achieve several goals.

In designing this new blog-composing assignment, I thought in terms of—and remediated—a print homework assignment I have used in both undergraduate and graduate classes, which I call *summary, respond, and reflect,* or *SRR* for short. When I designed the one-page SRR as a homework assignment in the 1990s, my purpose was to help both students and me see what students thought they had read; I often used the SRRs as a mechanism for beginning class; and I could spot-check the SRRs to see how well students were reading the texts in question. I also knew how useful summary writing could be for later, more formal work incorporating summaries. The SRR thus asked students to use one-third of the assignment as a space to summarize the reading. The second third of the SRR is designed for response, by which I mean react—did you like it or not? was it confusing or troubling or affirming?—in large part because, as I've learned from students, sometimes they cannot engage with the reading until they have processed and articulated their own reaction to the text, especially if it's less than a positive one, and often in the course of that processing, students create a very different meaning of the reading. And the last one-third of the SRR is for reflection, which in this case is linked to connection: connect this reading, I ask, to other course readings, to class discussion, to reading and discussions in other classes, to life: make sense and meaning of the reading through reflection.

Since I first used SRRs, however, I have elaborated them from a single genre into a family of genres. One is an SRR, typically in print, in which students summarize readings and connect them to other class readings, class discussions, material from other classes, and/or relevant material from outside school; they are turned in to me, and I respond. The second genre is the blog SRR, which is a single-authored post responding to a focused assignment with its own directions: I don't reply to this genre, typically, although sometimes I ask students to reply, and sometimes I bring work from the blog into class. The third genre is the new one I designed for the blog, the collaborative SRR, which tends to focus on how students read a given text or on what reading across two or more theorists or texts helps us see; again, I don't reply to this genre, but I often cite insights from it in class discussions.

The course hosting the collaborative blog was Digital Revolution and Convergence Culture, a course I created for our rhetoric and composition graduate program, which is required for all doctoral students and which focuses on writing, reading, and the making of knowledge and on how all three change given shifts in technologies:

> Using several frames of reference, ENGL 5933-04 will explore two related questions. First, what difference does technology, especially digital technology, make in the ways that we read, the ways that we compose, and the ways that knowledge is made, sanctioned, and shared? Second, what do the changes related to digital technology mean for those of us who teach

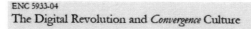

ENC 5933-04

The Digital Revolution and *Convergence* Culture

Kathleen Yancey (kyancey@fsu.edu)

M 6:45-9:30
Fall 2013
Hours: Mon 4-6 and by appointment
Williams 223B
Phone: 645-6896

<u>Purpose</u> Using several frames of reference, ENGL 5933-04 will explore two related questions. First, what difference does technology, especially digital technology, make in the ways that we read, the ways that we compose, and the ways that knowledge is made, sanctioned, and shared? Second, what do the changes related to digital technology mean for those of us who teach reading, literature, and composing? To answer these questions, we will consider briefly the relationship between literacies and technologies, marking the shift from manuscript culture to print culture; and from models of private knowledge to mass consumption of knowledge abetted by mass media and the role of politics, economics, and ideology in each shift. Our focus, however, will be on the changes that are occurring now. What are they? What do we make of them? How are societies and public institutions reacting? As scholars and teachers, how do we respond to them?

After completing this course, you'll be able to discuss in depth significant questions in play around digital culture (in several of its manifestations), especially those related to the circulation, distribution, and control of information, particularly from the perspective of the composer and composition. You'll also be able to cite key works in, and

Figure 7.6.

reading, literature, and composing? To answer these questions, we will consider briefly the relationship between literacies and technologies, marking the shift from manuscript culture to print culture; and from models of private knowledge to mass consumption of knowledge abetted by mass media and the role of politics, economics, and ideology in each shift. Our focus, however, will be on the changes that are occurring now: What are they? What do we make of them? How are societies and public institutions reacting? As scholars and teachers, how do we respond to them?

After completing this course, you'll be able to discuss in depth significant questions in play around digital culture (in several of its manifestations), especially those related to the circulation, distribution, and control of information, particularly from the perspective of the composer and composition. You'll also be able to cite key works in, and thinkers commenting on, changes in what and how we know and how we represent and circulate that which we think we do know.

I designed nineteen weekly assignments; seven of these were print SRRs; five were individual blog posts; two were blog posts composed by a smaller collaborative group, a pair of authors; and five were collaborative blog posts composed by teams of five students. Through such different groupings, students would, I hoped, gain experience with, and be

MORE KRESSIAN MODES

	KY	Students
Layout	yes	yes
Visuals	9	37
Links	5	32
Video	0	7
Audio	0	1
Tweet	0	1

Figure 7.7.

able to reflect upon, different composing and authoring experiences; and over the course of the term, they would have the opportunity to compose with every other student in the class. In addition, while the early SRRs asked for summaries of single texts, the collaborative SRRs asked for analysis, interpretation, and evaluation in response to questions still in search of answers. For example, one individual blog post asked students, "What is the role of technology in reading and writing, and how important is that role?," while another asked "What is the function of school in a democracy, and what is the appropriate use of technology in school?" Paired collaborative posts asked questions like "What evidence is there that we are not in a convergence culture? Alternatively, is a/the convergence culture more inescapable than ever?," while collaborative posts included "Reading across these texts, what do they propose as the new work of composing? And do you agree? Is this the new work of composing?" and "What's a network, and what role does it play in literacy?" In other words, students were composing multimodally about composing in many ways, including multimodally.

As this tally suggests, in Digital Revolution and Convergence Culture, students again composed multimodally, though in this course both individually and collaboratively; and in this course, students' Kressian contributions were more numerous than mine, and in some cases they included materials I did not. We all used layout, as the tally suggests, but their visuals outnumbered mine by a factor of four; they had six times as many links; and they included video, audio, and a tweet I did not. In addition, some students *created* multimodal materials for their posts, especially to illustrate ideas and relationships. Not least, through some of their comments, it became clear that students were borrowing from each other; for instance, in introducing a post, one group commented on their process, noting they were borrowing it from another group:

"Early in our collaborative process, we decided to work via Google Docs in a dialogue, much like some of our colleagues did in the last share. The space of the Google Doc turned out to work not only as forum for ideas, but, at times, case and point for our conversation." In addition, students were, as they observe, using new sites for composing, like Google Docs, "not only as forum for ideas, but, at times, case and point for our conversation." This kind of contextual comment tends to confirm my sense, expressed above, that one key to fostering multimodality without requiring it is to provide a common space for it; here, the blog functions as a kind of sandbox for play, which over time can widen the repertoire of composers' writing strategies.

Over time—and admittedly, the period of time addressed here is years—students' composing on the blog has grown in both kind and degree. In terms of the number of words, the sum has increased from seventeen thousand for a single class to over one hundred thousand for the class, or from one thousand words per student to over five thousand words per student. In terms of visuals, the increase is from none to at least two per student, both visuals imported from other sites and student created. In terms of other modalities, the increase is, again, from none to many, among them links, videos, audio files, and tweets. In terms of authorship, students write in print, and they write for the web—individually, in pairs, and in larger teams. As important, in composing with multiple modalities, students tend to draw on their own knowledge from other sources, knowledge they share with their peers on the blog and that they synthesize with the knowledge from the course. Currently, for example, I'm teaching Visual Rhetoric again: one student included an image of Legos to make a point; another, working juxtapositionally, included an image of Donald Trump standing in a very ornate Trump Tower next to an image of an impoverished family from the Walker Evans, James Agee book *Let Us Now Praise Famous Men* we are reading for class. Interestingly, another student in the class is intentionally using visual design in writing her print SRRs; in this case, the print SRRs, like their cousins the blog posts, are also an exercise in Visual Rhetoric. Which reminds us that all composing participates in an ecology (Edbauer 2005): what we learn in one site we are likely to take with us to another.

CODA

My claim is that without a specific mandate or requirement, without direct instruction, and without any monitoring, students have, over time, found in the course blog a site for developing multimodal composing.

That claim is supported by empirical data showing that students do compose more multimodally—as times change, as assignments become more intuitive, as students bring what they already do to the blog. As outlined here, it's a slow process, but it's also a process that seems to take hold. Partly, students' composing multimodally is a function of curricular design, as is detailed here; beginning with conversational replies, students over time began to add images, then other multimodal elements, first as novel exercises, then more routinely. Partly, as explained earlier, it's a function of multiple interacting factors—sometimes, the zeitgeist of the moment; syllabi that are intentionally multimodal; an early invitation to include a personally meaningful image on the blog and tell the class about it in terms of the content of the course; the modeling students provide for each other; the kinds of questions students are asked to engage, individually and collaboratively; the blog-as-sandbox giving us all permission to compose in new and novel ways. The blog, in other words, is a website hosting composing for the screen and the web, a site supporting many and multiple kinds of conversations that are essayistic in bridging high and low. The blog, with its space and multiple affordances, is an environment for expressing, representing, and connecting what we are learning (together), a site where we compose the way we do now: in a fully multimodal, hyperlinked, conversational writing that doesn't have a predetermined end and that occurs in a shared learning space where we make meaning together.

REFERENCES

Anderson, Daniel, Anthony Atkins, Cheryl Ball, Krista Homicz Miller, Cynthia Selfe, and Richard Selfe. 2006. "Integrating Multimodality into Composition Curricula." *Composition Studies* 34 (2): 59–84.

Edbauer, Jenny. 2005. "Unframing Models of Public Distribution: From Rhetorical Situation to Rhetorical Ecologies." *Rhetoric Society Quarterly* 35 (4): 5–24.

Faigley, Lester. 1999. "Material Literacy and Visual Design." In *Rhetorical Bodies*, edited by Jack Selzer and Sharon Crowley, 171–201. Madison: University of Wisconsin Press.

Gurak, Laura, Smiljana Antonijevic, Laurie Johnson, ClancyRatliff, and Jessica Reyman. 2004. "Introduction: Weblogs, Rhetoric, Community, and Culture." In *Into the Blogosphere*, edited by Laura Gurak, Smiljana Antonijevic, Laurie Johnson, Clancy Ratliff, and Jessica Reyman. Minneapolis: University of Minnesota Press. http://hdl.handle.net/11299/172840.

Krause, Steve. 2004. "When Blogging Goes Bad: A Cautionary Tale About Blogs, Emailing Lists, Discussion, and Interaction." *Kairos* 9 (1).

Kress, Gunther. 2010. *Multimodality: A Social Semiotic Approach to Contemporary Communication.* London: Routledge.

Miller, Carolyn, and Dawn Shepherd. 2004. "Blogging as Social Action: A Genre Analysis of the Weblog." In *Into the Blogosphere*, edited by Laura Gurak, Smiljana Antonijevic, Laurie Johnson, Clancy Ratliff, and Jessica Reyman. Minneapolis: University of Minnesota Press. http://hdl.handle.net/11299/172840.

National Council of Teachers of English Position Statements. 2013. "The NCTE Definition of 21st Century Literacies." http://www2.ncte.org/statement/21stcentdefinition/.

Yancey, Kathleen Blake. 2002. "The Pleasures of Digital Discussions: Lessons, Challenges, Recommendations, and Reflections." In *Teaching Writing with Computers*, edited by Brian Huot and Pam Takayoshi. Belmont, CA: Wadsworth

Yancey, Kathleen Blake. 2013a. Digital Revolution and Convergence Culture Course Description.

Yancey, Kathleen Blake. 2013b. Digital Revolution and Convergence Culture Syllabus.

8

WHEN MULTIMODALITY GETS MESSY
Perception, Materiality, and Learning in Written-Aural Remediation

Jennifer J. Buckner

INTRODUCTION

After weeks of anticipation, students transition from writing researched, argument papers to designing a creative, multimodal project. Everyone shows for class the first day of the workshop, anxiously glancing at one another while their professor demonstrates how to record voices in Audacity. Then she walks the aisles, distributing headphones and microphones to students from a recycled cat-litter container. Digital sound projects are still fairly new to this campus, so technology is simple, open source, and recycled. She resumes her place at a teaching station, shifting to independent practice, and waits for a show of enthusiastic hands as students ask questions. Students click through Audacity's interface, glancing at screens on either side. Finally, when there are no more icons to click, they reluctantly slide headphones on, pulling them over their ears like a hoodie at sundown. Hunching over microphones, students record in goofy voices, sing silly songs, make cartoon voices, or comment on the act of recording. Almost all look around as soon as they click stop, eyebrows raised and eyes darting to see who witnessed their recording. Immediately, many delete their recordings. Some never play them back. Several, who cannot stop squirming in their chairs, open a new window and surf the Internet for background music until class chatter reaches a dull roar, loud enough to hide their second attempt.

Such a scene can be difficult to understand as a teacher, especially when last week's announcement of shifting to multimodal projects was greeted with smiles and nods. Multimodal composition, touted as a method for engaging students with existing media practices, should be easy. But sometimes it is not. Playing with Garageband on your brother's laptop to make a silly remix about his ex-girlfriend is not like creating an audio essay for a freshman composition class. Multimodal composition

DOI: 10.7330/9781607327974.c008

invents worlds, technologies, and individuals in ways that are complex and shifting. And, often, students find themselves in intersections, lacking any map to navigate further.

Composing, itself, is a complex act of semiosis, a process of understanding and utilizing a variety of signs in communication whereby composers must negotiate a variety of material, cultural, and social resources. Academic writing, for example, requires that students understand various material signs for digital composing, signs they can use in immediate social contexts while drawing from their histories and larger cultural understandings about what signs students should reproduce to produce "academic writing." As toddlers, we are socialized to recognize a variety of semiotic resources, such as alphabetic signs that constitute acts of literacy. In response, literacy has been primarily associated with alphabetic, print-centric writing tools with a problematic, yet present, assumption that also privileges academic writing as a primary means to analytical thinking (Welch 1999, 16). Teachers introducing new tools or signs present students with a developmental task in which their understandings of literate signs are challenged by unfamiliar tools and forms of mediation. In response, students engage in a "long series of developmental events" by which they interact with tools in socially rooted and historically influenced activities (57).

Though this interaction can be a struggle, many students grow familiar with conventions of traditional, written discourse and are able to navigate its demands. In contrast, multimodal composition challenges students to bring a range of materialities into academic settings that may seem contradictory. For students, this happens when using new technologies in multimodal composition, such as digital sound editing software. Through this process, students understand unfamiliar signs, negotiating among histories of use, immediate cultural contexts, and social interactions. Though some students may excel in creating media-centric texts circulating in popular culture (e.g., memes, podcasts, video mashups), they can be confused when those modal worlds conflict with ideologies of academic settings. And what of the challenges faced by students who lack experience creating multimodal texts at all?

Historically, one type of multimodal composition that has garnered much scholarship in writing studies is transformations between speech and writing, especially as speech has been theorized as a means of improving writing. This disciplinary attention to speech and writing has fostered a variety of pedagogical practices that incorporate activities with speech in invention or revision stages to polish a written product (e.g., writing groups, talk-aloud protocols, writing center tutor practices, and logography). More recently an emerging subfield within composition studies, self-identified as *sound studies* or *soundwriting*, features scholars attending to composing with digital sound materials (Ahern 2013; Comstock and Hocks 2006; Halbritter 2006; Selfe 2009; Whitney 2008).

These new practices incorporating digital sound into first-year composition include dramatic shifts in sound materiality when compared to practices in our disciplinary roots. Studies of literacy should not be separated from studies of materiality. Materials employed in composition impact language, shaping conditions of their production and consumption by capturing language in "mass or matter and occupying physical space" (Haas 1996, 4). Digital sound may seem less material when compared with a conventional pen-and-paper sense of writing's materiality, yet oral composition introduces a variety of material tools into composing practices. Traditional contexts for live speech (e.g., conversations, lecture halls) take place in material settings with material tools but often do not result in tangible artifacts unless the speech is archived with a recording device (4). New media technologies shift the nature of speech by transforming embodied voices into digital sound bites that often exist in elusive, online spaces. Gadgets, gestures, and spaces employed in digital audio composing processes differ starkly from those of traditional contexts of speech, whose materialities are situated in physical rooms with perceivable, present audiences. Students record their voices using mobile devices, computers, microphones, and headphones; use a mouse and screen to edit sound into layered tracks of imported sounds and music; and publish remixed sound files within online networked communities for others to interact with on their smart phones, mp3 players, or computers.

In addition to shifts in materiality, today's sound scholars reflect a more complex perception of the nature of composing with sound. Traditionally, we've conceived of a linear relationship between writing and sound whereby these distinct modalities are perceived ends of an exclusive, cognitive, and compositional spectrum. By this tradition, I'm referring to scholarly work, such as that of Walter Ong (1982), that bifurcated orality and literacy by constructing "great-leap" histories of shifts from orality to writing without accounting for relationships between them (McCorkle 2012, 21). These histories and distinctions serve as terministic screens that inhibit our ability to recognize overlaps among writing and speech (Palmeri 2012, 15). Alternatively, Paul Prior, Jody Shipka, Julie Hengst, and Kevin Roozen (2006) reframe multimodality through their concept of semiotic remediation, and, in doing so, account for more complex, situated examinations of literate practices.

Prior et al.'s use of the term "semiotic remediation" accounts for more than a shift in mediums during composing because, as Irvine (2010) explains, they emphasize repurposing, an "emphasis on social and semiotic process, on ever-emergent social relations, and on the ways semiotic forms can serve as resources for social agents" (236).

Such an approach utilizes empirical methodologies that value language as signs of students' shifting perceptions of their composing practices and materialities. These signs function as chronotopic utterances, capturing students' perceptions in a specific instance, revealing how resources gain meaning and capturing sign significance in a dialogic relationship between immediate contexts and histories of use. Prior's (2009) work characterizes the "temporalities of semiosis" because "utterances do not achieve their sense and function in a moment" but in "the histories that lead to an utterance, the unfolding events of its use, the imagined projections of its future and ultimately the way it is in fact understood, taken up, replayed and reused in near and perhaps more distant futures" (21). In the case of first-year composition, students bring their histories and attitudes about academic performances to a writing class, influencing language they use when characterizing signs they encounter. Introducing nondominant forms of composing in multimodal forms can complicate students' ability to understand, take up, and replay multimodal signs when situated in laminations of their histories, present contexts, and distant futures. In addition, when invited to participate in reflection, students may also recognize themselves as signs in a material world (i.e., bodies involved in multimodal ensembles) when engaged in remediation practices with a heightened awareness of semiotic resources that impact their own development.

RESEARCH DESIGN

To better understand students' complex negotiations when engaged in multimodal composition, I examined the attitudes, experiences, and practices of seven first-year writing students enrolled in an Honors Composition II course at a private, liberal arts institution in the South. Although these participants varied in many ways in their histories, practices, and attitudes, they did share some commonalities. All these students (1) received advanced placement (AP) college credit, placing out of composition I and into a composition II course their first semester of college, (2) entered college with an honors-program designation, (3) performed exceptionally in standardized placement exams, (4) ranked in the top 10 percent of their class, (4) and had GPA of 3.8 or higher.

The professor of this honors composition II course, themed around the topic of sound, asked students to engage in a mixture of oral and written practices to produce a range of multimodal written-aural assignments. In their final assignment, she asked students to revise an earlier written assignment into a digital audio composition. These participants shared a history of access to technology, having all owned and used personal computers for schoolwork prior to college, and only one student expressed any dislike or discomfort using new technologies. Five of the seven participants were familiar with the idea of sound-editing technology, and though they had no experience digitally composing sound, they demonstrated a self-efficacy in their click-and-figure-it-out approach. Though their background might lead one to assume a multimodal sound project would go smoothly, I had witnessed many classes like this in the past in which students struggled through similar tasks; I considered this an opportunity to study how students work through composing with new modes. In studying this group, I was interested in learning (1) how students negotiate materials when asked to complete an unfamiliar composing task; (2) what students' reflective discourse reveals about their understanding of semiotic resources associated with digital sound and writing; (3) and what student perceptions reveal about relationships between technology, remediation, and self.

While popular theories of aurality and writing by scholars such as Kathleen Welch (1999), Walter Ong (1982), and the New London Group (1996) have been powerful conceptualizations, I felt that as a heuristic for analysis they may limit the potential to discover unrecognized phenomena in students' use, characterization, and understanding of semiotic resources. As Barney Glaser and Anselm Strauss (1967) argue, existing theories have "not provided enough theories to cover all the areas of social life" (10–11), in this case, that of digital sound remediation. Therefore, I chose to use grounded theory to provide a rigorous, recursive, and reflexive approach to analyzing data, composing categories, and refining existing theories about sound and writing as influenced by students' histories, immediate contexts of social interaction, and evoked cultural worlds.

In this study, students submitted a variety of artifacts to their professor as part of their audio revision including (1) a written annotation of their previously written draft, (2) an MP3 file of their digital audio, (3) and a written reflection. In addition, I conducted pre- and postinterviews with each student lasting thirty to forty-five minutes each. Initial interviews sought to understand students' experiences and attitudes regarding their perceptions of writing, speech, and technology. I also asked

students to bring to our final interview an illustration of their composing process, using a method from Paul Prior and Jody Shipka (2003),
that included interactions with other people, texts, and technologies
during different stages of working on their audio revisions. Follow-up
interviews took place after students submitted their final projects, and
interviewers asked students to play and describe their perceptions of
their audio projects, explain their illustrations, and reflect any shifts in
their attitudes towards written and aural modalities. Student discourse
in these final interviews was critical in understanding the significance
they associated with such a range of aural, visual, and written signs in the
wide body of work associated with their projects.

Using grounded-theory methods (e.g., memoing, open coding, cat-
egorizing, diagramming, and theoretical sampling), I examined their
perceptions and practices through a fine-grained analysis of students'
discourse, characterizing their material practices and cognitive learning while negotiating an unfamiliar remediation task. As a framework
for theoretical coding, Charles Bazerman's (2004) conceptual levels
of intertextuality provided my heuristic for examining participants
balancing "originality and craft" within "specific situations, needs, and
purposes" while "rely[ing] on the common stock of language [they]
share[d] with others" (83). These intertextual references revealed patterns across data about how students negotiated, especially through
social interaction, when multimodal composition gets messy.

WHEN FUN BECOMES FRUSTRATING AND FOREIGN

Based on what the initial interviews revealed, neither the students nor
I anticipated the level of frustration that would arise once they started
working on their audio revisions. Once they began, enthusiasm waned
as students became incredibly frustrated working sound-editing devices
and software. Student frustrations started with technical glitches in the
campus computer lab, illustrated by one student's drawing of a Dell
computer as a T-Rex (see fig. 8.1). While students certainly found ways
to work without campus machines because they had access to personal
computers, their initial attitudes about this project are well represented
in John's[1] illustration, in which visual metaphors of scribbles and annoying flies reflect his level of frustration, setting the tone for his process.
In addition, the open-source audio-editing software, Audacity, posed
additional challenges for some students, who perceived having to download software as adding "clutter" to their machines; some downloaded
malware to their machines, requiring technology-services help.

Figure 8.1. Frames 1 and 2 of John's process illustration

Student histories, grounded in formal academic discourse, also influenced how they perceived and valued audio revisions. When prompted to describe their histories as writers, participants described formal academic experiences in high-school advanced-placement English (AP) classes that established their attitudes and practices. In those initial interviews, all participants' shared histories in these classes seemed to influence students' intertextual references to writing as "correct, analytical, and formulaic." While they found AP's formality unappealing to produce, they bragged of their mastery, often through narratives of struggle, identifying strongly with genres such as literary analysis.

Having never composed with digital audio as an assignment, students questioned the nature of the assignment when it was introduced to the class. On the day the professor introduced the assignment, one student, Mikala, blurted, "So, we just revise what we wrote, record it, and put music in it? What's the catch?" Others in the room nodded.

In our interviews, participants struggled to characterize digital sound. Beth called the audio revision "definitely different" and said she wasn't "completely sure of everything," didn't have "a definition yet" of what she was doing. Several students, including Kathryn, indicated their perception that writing was valued more than sound composition because writing was graded. Kathryn said, "The sound [is] just kind of like a fun new exploration kind of thing. But I know some people really like it because it is technology and it's kind of modernizing English class." Following this logic, almost all students indicated that writing was *serious* while sound was *fun*.

Many students characterized their recorded voices by comparing them with their written voices. In this pairing, students used written voices as a measure for recorded voices, judging qualities of their recorded, mediated voices with features they favored in written discourse. Focusing on issues of arrangement, John described his mediated voice as "choppy," "more systematic," and "a bit less organized" when compared with his thoughts "coming down easier in writing." As a result, he valued his written voice for having what he described as "more weight to it" than his audio recording. Anna also preferred her written voice for its confidence, describing her recorded, spoken voice as "a really girly voice which isn't a bad thing because I'm a girl, but. Um. But I think that's what I think about my voice. [In writing,] I feel like it's just like stronger and more like. It's clear. And people are able to understand what I'm trying to say better." She later explained a "girly voice" was "soft" whereas her writing voice had "more of a punch behind" it, communicating her sense that her written voice was superior. Her confidence with her written voice highlighted her seasoned history with academic writing, especially in academic genres such as analysis, that awarded her assertiveness. In contrast, she perceived her recorded voice as weak or vulnerable.

Students were most uncomfortable listening to their recorded voices during in-class workshops and our follow-up interviews. When first recording in class, student postures were hunched, hugging microphones; they pulled off headsets in disgust during playback or deleted recordings without even listening to them. Rena described the recording as feeling "weird coming out of my mouth, like I stumbled over my words." All students commented that the sound of their voices, resonating in their bodies, had shifted in sonic quality when digitally captured. Several students characterized this strangeness by pointing to differences in pitch and tone. For example, Megan likened her unfamiliar, recorded voice to "a six-year-old boy . . . awkwardly deep, but not" and "nasally and annoying." Her disgust was so great that she admitted, "I wouldn't want to listen to my voice."

These students, accustomed to being confident in a writing class, seemed disoriented by shifts in their voice when it was captured in digital audio. They repeatedly described their audio-revision voices as "out there," and, in doing so, they discursively separated voices from bodies, which contrasted with their descriptions of written voices as internalized. John also talked about how his "speaking came out," creating a sense that speaking starts within until separated from the body through mediation. For John, this separation served as a kind of catharsis, "getting out what was weighing down [his] heart." For others, this separation was disconcerting and disembodying.

In Kathryn's experience, recording her piece with audio-editing software heightened her awareness of her disembodied voice. Kathryn's process illustration characterized listening and recording in different ways with respect to her body and mind, differentiating her perceptions of hearing other's voices and her voice when recorded (see fig. 8.2). Kathryn's illustration begins with a thought bubble, representing her thinking of a topic for her audio revision. Her second frame features only part of her body, an ear and a corner of her glasses, listening to Judy Garland's song "Have Yourself a Merry Little Christmas." This very close shot emphasizes an intimate, internal relationship with the music. Frame three creates distance by zooming out to show her recording, words visually coming out in a dialogue balloon. In our follow-up interview, she described this image as getting "all of her thoughts out there." Kathryn is absent in the next two frames, replaced by a thought bubble, an Audacity icon, and two emoticons, representing her editing stage. In this stage, her body is absent in the composing process and not present again until the final frame, where her final product is considered pleasing when it "seem[s] to convey purpose to others." Her illustration suggests an ideological distance between her as composer and digital sound processes, which were only reconciled when her project was affirmed by others.

FRAMING THE STRANGE WITH THE FAMILIAR

Students employed a range of strategies to understand and orient to this new multimodal composing task, drawing from their writing histories. Early in their introduction to sound composition, these students made intertextual references to visual constructs commonly used in writing pedagogy to understand audio composing, framing sound as

Figure 8.2. Kathryn's process illustration

it related to familiar features of writing. During one class session, the professor shared a sample podcast titled "Colors" from National Public Radio's show *RadioLab*. When she prompted students to describe the multimodal sound, students described the choir track as "illustrating" or "showing you what they were talking about," and they described two speakers as "one body." In addition to implicating visualization with listening, students borrowed the term *showing* from writing pedagogy, which says to writers, "Show, don't tell."

Later, all participants referenced visual cues common to written discourse when talking about their audio revisions rather than emphasizing audible sound features. In her final reflection, Beth pointed to her audio revision as her favorite piece from Composition II: "[I especially liked] the last of each paragraph because I feel they are the heaviest with meaning. I feel like someone can read that and connect it to something in their lives. I also really enjoyed writing it." When describing her audio revision, Beth's references to paragraphs, reading, and writing revealed her conceptualization of her audio revision through writing constructs. There are no paragraphs in an audio recording, yet she intertextually borrowed this visual construct as a means of understanding parts of her audio project.

While several acknowledged that writing and digital sound had varied purposes and formality, six of the seven students began their audio project by writing a script. Two students, Rena and Kathryn, used writing and sound throughout their composing process. Rena recorded sound effects to accompany her stream-of-consciousness representation of a typical day in her mind, including her journaling. She laughed when sharing that she "spent like five minutes scribbling on paper to get the right sound for that." Materially, she used writing to sonically remediate, or repurpose, the act of writing through a different mode. Similarly, Kathryn's practice revealed a simultaneous multimodal process. She explained, "I've never had to 'write for the ear' before, except when planning a speech or something along the same lines, so I tried to read aloud as I wrote to see how it sounded." Kathryn read her writing, remediating a visual text as temporal speech to anticipate how listeners would perceive her digital products. By "talking aloud while writing," Kathryn explained, she could "see if it flowed easily when [she] spoke." Kathryn's approach to this novel assignment reveals a complex and conflated remediation of modalities: writing while speaking in order to visualize sound.

While recording was a private act, students sought responses from others to gauge their success. Without audience interaction, many students would have remained ambivalent about the nature of their digital sound compositions. Five of the seven student participants shared their audio revisions with others prior to submission. One day in class, Rena pulled up video logs of her riffing "drafts" during a workshop. She noticed a peer beside her looking on, clicked play, and watched her friend carefully. When her friend laughed, Rena exhaled a bit and began smiling. In her follow-up interview, she explained how that moment helped her realize she wanted her revision to be funny and not "dry and boring and whatever." Her friend's positive response confirmed her decision to sing the songs as if "in her head" rather than dubbing in original tracks of music. Others' responses to their audio revisions influenced student decisions in composing and also their overall sense of whether or not their audio revisions were successful.

Kathryn's audio revision became something of legend, as participants referred back to it, without my prompting, in all eight follow-up interviews. An overwhelming response of approval situated her project as a benchmark for audio-revision standards. Anna—who admitted to not valuing her audio-revision experience—called Kathryn's audio "really good . . . it sounded like it meant a lot to her." Students were amazed that the professor cried when Kathryn shared her project with the class, assuming this show of emotion meant it was meaningful. Kathryn was surprised by her professor's response as well but felt that affective response confirmed her (Kathryn's) intent, relieved her vulnerability, and gave her a sense of closure (see fig. 8.2).

Ironically, one phenomenon that emerged from students' growing more comfortable with digital sound was the change in their attitudes towards writing, revision, and their role as writers. In addition to broadening their notions of what constituted writing—now including multimodal compositions—students' ideas about revision evolved throughout the study. Prior to audio revision, students admitted to never revising their work other than intentionally putting "mistakes" in their writing so they would have some mechanical error to fix during in-class workshops. Juxtaposing different materialities in a written-aural revision helped students realize revision is not limited to sentence-level polishing. As part of their audio revision, students were forced to make substantive changes to their early drafts; as a result, many indicated their willingness to invest time in fine-tuning their personal "voice" and writing style. For example, Kathryn became more aware of her use of formal writing structures, and, as a result of her audio revision, practiced "'loosening up' [her] writing by keeping the sound aspect in mind." Mikala also aimed to write with an auditory sensibility, indicating that her writing was growing "less robotic" and "more natural."

In their process of reenvisioning ideas about sound and writing, students also tuned their learning towards themselves. During their composing process, two students in particular found clarity about goals, clarity that emerged in revising through sound. John's audio revision, focused on his history leading music worship, prompted a late-night Skype conversation with a distant friend in which he decided to change his major from music education to music ministry. He called his audio revision a "reflection," and said, "So, I think this part of the reflection itself, kind of guided my mind a little bit towards the way I should be thinking in terms of my future." Kathryn had a similar experience. She claimed in her final reflection, "This semester has been revolutionary not only in my writing, but in my life as well, developing my awareness to reflect and even deciding my major for right now." The same week Kathryn submitted her final reflection, she declared English as her major, empowered by others' responses to her project.

DISSONANCE, SEMIOTIC SYNAESTHESIA, AND RESONANCE

Student processes and discourse suggest that encountering unfamiliar composing tasks—such as revising writing into digital sound—involves learning as a relationship between distancing from and drawing closer to a range of semiotic resources. Student frustrations mark moments of discord or dissonance. In this analysis, I use the term *dissonance*, drawing from a sonic metaphor that refers to sounds marked by discordant chords, which are perceived as harsh and unresolved, created in *pairings* of sounds that are discordant. In this remediation task, students encountered semiotic systems and practices that were dissonant with their past experiences in academic writing and/or present attitudes and practices, and those new systems and past experiences were catalyzed by the introduction of digital sound as a means for composing.

Student discourse exhibited dissonance when students expressed their distance from audio-revision materials and practices, highlighting discord between paired histories and practices in academic writing and those in digital sound composition. These participants were well attuned to crafting formal, written discourse in ways that had ensured their work would be acceptable by authority figures, who represented larger ideologies of academic writing (e.g., preference for formal genres of writing, choice of fast writing over revision, formulaic writing that would get an *A*). Therefore, this task of creating audio revisions displaced participants, creating discord between novel sign-making tools and ways they had learned to recognize and reproduce written, academic discourse. Materially, this meant many students were unfamiliar with digital-editing software, sound tracks, and sound dynamics and were unfamiliar with software-specific signs, such as editing icons, required to manipulate Audacity. When replaying audio revisions during their follow-up interviews, many students framed their responses by saying, "I meant to include . . . but I was unable to because I didn't know how to . . ." All participants communicated some level of discontent with their completed audio revisions when their product failed to match their goals for their audio revision. In doing so, they discursively paired a completed revision with an imagined revision, communicating a kind of material dissonance.

In addition to dissonant materials, students also communicated that audio revision was a strange genre, especially when situated in an honors college composition course. As many genre theorists point out, genres do more than shape texts; genres shape composers by affording desires and actions in a combination of material, cultural, and social features. Anis Bawarshi (2003) argues that genres are "discursive and ideological sites of action" that provide writers agency in adopting or resisting activities, relations, and subjectivities bound up in a genre's features (54). If genres invent the writer, then a student whose history is deeply entrenched in formulaic, academic writing has developed a subjectivity as a writer closely tied with the kinds of precise, text-centered ideologies that support AP-like curricula. Digital sound presented students with activities and texts they perceived as less stable than genres such as literary analysis. Further, this remediation task required that they use unfamiliar, material resources of digital sound that had an impact on their perception of their subjectivity as composers. For example, students could no longer rely on projecting a polished subjectivity shaped by careful syntax and sophisticated diction, which made it difficult for them to perceive their presence in the composing activity.

Students also characterized dissonant moments when, through metacognitive discourse, they discursively separated mind and body, setting their inner voices apart from their recordings (e.g., "my words came out," "that doesn't sound like me"). This discursive disembodiment captures a disconnect between students' material experiences and embodied perceptions, especially as bodies listening to their prerecorded voices in digital sound, copresent with a self situated in a different time. Digital sound, as an audible-inscription technology, challenges new sonic composers accustomed to experiencing their voices only resonating in live, temporal moments of speaking. Frances Dyson (2009) writes, "Recorded sound cannot claim the so-called authenticity of direct, live transmission, since the recording is no longer tied to the here and now of the sonic event" (143). Students' disembodiment illustrated a "troubling moment" of body effects in which the "organic whole" of aurality (143) becomes virtually embodied, creating discord between a recording and a listening body. Further, students perceived their recorded voices as discordant with their inner voices and/or imagined voices when listening to audio files. They explained that their voices sounded "strange" in contrast to their inner voices. At some point in this study, all student participants communicated a sense of their own mind-body bifurcation, yet no listener ever discursively separated another student's recorded voice from their body, instead indicating that peers' recorded voices seemed true to themselves. This pattern suggests that instances of disembodiment were unique to students' perceptions of self.

Temporally, disembodied listening reflected students' struggles to reconcile a confluence of voices present in their audio recording: a recorded past self, a present listening self, and an anticipated future audience. In digital sound, our perception of voices is challenged when captured and replayed in inscribed files, providing infinite playback access to the past as if still present. This copresence of voices created a crisis for the student listeners. Dyson (2009) also explains that virtual audio is "'spatialized' sound" whereby digital sounds signal an atemporal presence, creating a sound space where voices exist in timeless ways (138). And when someone listens to virtual audio, technology admits "the listening body to the interface" while it also functions as a sound source with an "independent, autonomous identity" (139). This phenomenon is, perhaps, best understood by reconsidering Mikhail Bakhtin's notion of utterance in light of student recordings. Adapting Bakhtin's (1981) concept of heteroglossia to digital sound, authentic environments of student utterances [i.e., digital audio recordings] are "dialogized heteroglossia" (272), at once drawing from histories of cultural assignments, immediate social contexts, and individual concrete accounts. Aural recordings create a kind of embodied heteroglossia when students recognize—or at least are disoriented by—the influence of time on remediated speech. When listening back to these sound utterances, students are faced with sound bites they must resolve as listeners with knowledge of ways their various roles (e.g., subject, student, listener) are projected and complicated in this new composition, challenging their perception of self when historical, social, and cultural identities are copresent and potentially conflicting.

In response to this dissonance and disembodiment, students returned to what was familiar, conceptually and materially using writing to help them compose. In doing so, they blended practices and perceptions of writing and sound, bringing different signs together and blurring sensory distinctions as a method of understanding and shaping unfamiliar resources. Materially, students employed a range of visual-spatial resources (e.g., outlining, drafting, and annotating), and conceptually, they framed perceptions of digital sound using discourse drawn from perceivable features of writing (i.e., visual-spatial features of writing). In doing so, students remediated modal resources through one another, shaping signs and learning through a practice I call *semiotic synaesthesia.*

In the context of this study, I use the term *semiotic synaesthesia* to characterize instances when students describe or approach one modality through discursively employing features or practices from another modality. These students engaged in semiotic synaesthesia when they materially and conceptually repurposed and shaped digital sound affordances through their perceptions of it as a form of writing. L. S. Vygotsky (1978) calls this learning through "categorical rather than isolated perceptions," whereby users assimilate unfamiliar tools with familiar ones (33). In doing so, students remediated their historical and cultural sensory perceptions of modalities as a strategy for repurposing their written text into an audible form. Through these moments of semiotic synaesthesia,[2] students did more than sequentially remediate modalities; they simultaneously blended situational practices and semiotic signs from multiple modalities in an attempt to resolve dissonant sign systems.

Student perceptions of their written-aural revisions as meaningful relied on their ability to recognize personal or social connections with others and themselves. While participants were familiar with ways to create written texts they considered deep and meaningful in academic cultures, they were not familiar with ways to use digital sound's sign-using principles. For this reason, remediation processes were developmental, growing in students' evolving material and social interactions with sound resources, creating resonance with semiotic resources. *Resonance*, as a sonic term, refers to audible sounds perceived as "deep, full, and reverberating" and is often used as a metaphor to describe something that can evoke lasting images, memories, and emotions (*Oxford*, "resonance"). In this study, I use resonance as a concept to highlight (1) material reverberation, sounds resonating in chambers of and between sounding bodies upon vocalization and (2) metaphorical reverberation, practices and values participants recognize as deep, full, and lasting.

Many students only recognized resonance in their audio revisions after receiving a response from someone else, which determined their sense of it as deep and meaningful or cursory and lacking. Social interactions influenced the degree to which audio revisions functioned as a semiotic resource that could resonate between people, or, from a physics perspective, as synchronous reverberations from neighboring objects (*Oxford*, "resonance"). In the case of this study, "neighboring objects" constituted composers and their audience. Students who shared their work—albeit hesitantly—with others expressed their satisfaction after hearing another person connect with their ideas and emotions. These acknowledgements validated projects, and by extension, composers.

While many compositionists have emphasized the value of reflection in writing pedagogy, few have emphasized the value of inviting students to consider the impact of materiality such as technologies on their composing practices (Haas 1996, 5). Rather than simply advocating for multimodal texts as a means for capturing student identity, scholars must first examine how students understand various materials through which they compose and are composed. These participants were actively engaged in metacognitive inquiry (e.g., interviews, assignment reflections, class discussions) as part of their audio-revision assignment and my research protocol, which served as a catalyst for their learning. In their reflections and practices, students recognized and shaped sign meanings through their characterizations of semiotic resources, exhibiting what I call *reflexivity*. The term *reflexivity* implies more than simply reflecting or looking back. I use *reflexivity* to refer to students' understanding of a cause-and-effect relationship between their perception of an object and its impact on their perception of self. In this analysis, I specifically refer to instances when students recognize the significance of a semiotic resource, and in turn, understand its influence on their attitudes or practices. In this way, reflexivity as a concept provides a way to recognize students as signs (i.e., bodies) involved in and shaped by remediation.

To understand relationships between materials and self, Marshall McLuhan's concept of narcosis frames this problem through a metaphor of a mythical man extended by technologies he is numb to recognize. Narcissus's tragic flaw is his failure to recognize materiality. To avoid his tragic numbness, Narcissus must recognize he is looking at water with reflective properties that create a mirror image of himself. Such a numbness, McLuhan (2003) argues, is the result of the central nervous system performing a kind of self-amputation, whereby the body psychologically ignores technological extensions in order to foster progress and acceleration (63–65). By extension, students in this study failed to recognize ways their long-assimilated technologies for writing were influenced by materialities, metaphorically ignoring their technological extensions. For these students, academic writing fostered progress when measured in advanced-placement credits, honors-program status, and higher grades; they loved their reflection in the AP English pool. Through the course of written-aural semiotic remediation, however, students recognized ripples in the pool and could no longer recognize their reflections. Students employed a variety of material resources whose dissonant meanings and practices jarred them in ways that rippled their narcotic reflections, drawing their attention to otherwise numb technologies. Metaphorically, they noticed the pool that is materialities of writing and digital sound as an extension of themselves.

Students developed a duality of presence when describing various instances of dissonance and resonance, characterizing and experiencing self as a listening present and recorded past. Dissonance, disembodiment, and metacognition worked symbiotically to create an essential distance for looking inwardly at their thoughts and outwardly at their past and present perceptions of materials and situations. When students discursively disembodied their mind from body, they separated their perceptions from materials that shaped their ideas (e.g., recording devices) and developed reflexivity about materials impacting their perceptions of self. This metacognition afforded students a way to pair recorded voices with imagined voices, describing how an archived representation was discordant with a present interiority.

As witnesses, students reframed these archived attitudes or experiences with language that conveyed new realizations. For example, in Anna's case, participating in research provided her an opportunity to distance herself from her experience in an ongoing class conflict. While listening to her audio revision in our follow-up interview, she paused the sound and launched into a ten-minute commentary on the "truth" behind her audio revision. In doing so, she simultaneously remediated several out-of-time selves through intertextual references to (1) her angry self in a class conflict as narrated in the audio revision, (2) a student-composer reluctantly creating an audio revision, and (3) a research participant providing raw, angry responses to the other two selves. In the course of her surprising tirade, Anna recognized she was unhappy with her submissiveness in the past and her drive to perform for grades, a point she blatantly admitted. Finally, she resolved that she wanted to reframe how she performed in class environments, socially and academically. In this unscripted remediation, Anna discursively drew her chronotopic selves together, resulting in a transformation in the way she understood herself as a student.

Composers who were disoriented by virtual representations of their voices physically sensed what Dyson (2009) calls a "body effect" in the audible, tangible vibrations of their recorded voices during playback. Students rejected these harsh, unfamiliar representations of their voices and, as a result, developed the essential distance to recognize digital sound as a material shaping their perceptions. Even in this essential distance, students recognized that recordings *were* their voices. The materiality of virtual audio prevented listeners from a comprehensive fragmentation with "self," as they recognized a unique "phenomenal field wherein sound and the body can recover ground lost to reproduction, simulation, and mediatization" (143). Through embodied responses, students sensed that discordant sounds were still grounded in their past, material selves. While disconcerting, this virtual fragmentation of self was essential to fostering students' perceptions of signs involved in remediation. Such a paradox of presence drew users' attentions to the materiality of digital sound resources. Ultimately, what seemed to be an exercise in frustration and failure turned out to be an intense moment of introspection and learning. Material and conceptual duality were discordant, providing an essential distance for students to remove self from technology and subsequently recognize the impact of materiality on ways they composed and were composed, developing reflexivity.

CONCLUSION

I've come to expect a certain level of frustration from students when asking them to compose multimodally, especially if a task involves working with new technologies. Frustrations are often present, though they're often indicative of much more than just learning toolbar icons on new software applications. Though frustrations may start with slow processing speeds of dinosaur lab machines, they often escalate because multimodal composition is a process of understanding and shaping a shifting body of resources. Students' frustrations with negotiating new composing tasks, as perceived in unfamiliar materials and genres, highlight our need to attend to materiality when asking students to work with nondominant modalities. Pedagogically, framing those experiences through familiar practices and resources may bridge student attempts to encounter and use new resources.

In this study, learning did occur because these instances of *dissonance* coexisted with moments of resonance when students perceived semiotic resources as deep, full, and lasting. These moments that juxtaposed discord with connection were essential in fostering learning, distancing students enough to recognize a resource before drawing them closer to shape its significance. It was essential that students experience and struggle with these resources in order to understand and use them. Their recognition, in metacognitive discourse, represents yet another sign, one that illustrates ways remediation also impacts the student through metaphorically remediating self.

Our disciplinary language functions as a sign that shapes our perceptions of multimodal composition and its affordances. These potentialities, in turn, inform our pedagogies through theories about composing practices and material affordances. Given this, our theories of remediating sound and writing are actualized and limited by the language scholars and teachers provide to frame those experiences. Inadequate, decontextualized linguistic stores may fail us when framing new experiences, such as those of digital sound composition. Also, we must consider the implications when studying novel composing experiences for which students and teachers lack language to frame their experiences. In order to move past unstable signifiers (e.g., terms such as *speech, writing, voice*), participants must be prompted to characterize their perceptions of remediated composing and modal affordances through rich descriptions of experiences in specific contexts (e.g., social interactions, composing histories, cultural contexts).

For this reason, I invite fellow scholars to move away from using disciplinary terms in empirical studies to accurately capture student perceptions and learning. Of course, studies of participant perceptions still rely on student use of a linguistic form (i.e., words) that is not "stable and always self-equivalent signal, but that . . . is always changeable and adaptable sign" (Voloshinov 1973, 68). Such a paradox is complicated even more when considering studies of composing practices when students remediate texts with unfamiliar modalities. Still, our drawing from discipline-adopted signs (i.e., terms for concepts) almost certainly limits our ability to understand how students understand and use unfamiliar materials as terms become generalized in extended use. And, honestly, who wouldn't prefer a drawing of a Dell computer as a T-Rex over stodgy, academic speak?

REFERENCES

Ahern, Katie. 2013. "Tuning the Sonic Playing Field: Teaching Ways of Knowing Sound in First-Year Writing." *Computers and Composition* 30 (2): 75–86.

Bahktin, Mikhail. 1981. *The Dialogic Imagination.* Austin: University of Texas Press.

Bawarshi, Anis. 2003. *Genre and the Invention of the Writer: Reconsidering the Place of Invention in Composition.* Logan: Utah State University Press.

Bazerman, Charles. 2004. "Intertextuality: How Texts Rely on Other Texts." In *What Writing Does and How It Does It*, edited by Charles Bazerman and Paul Prior. New Jersey: Lawrence Erlbaum. Kindle edition.

Comstock, Michelle, and Mary E. Hocks. 2006. "Voice in the Cultural Soundscape: Sonic Literacy in Composition Studies." *Computers and Composition Online.* http://cconline journal.org/comstock_hocks/index.htm.

Dyson, Frances. 2009. *Sounding New Media: Immersion and Embodiment in the Arts and Culture.* Los Angeles: University of California Press.

Gee, James P. 2008. *Social Linguistics and Literacies: Ideology in Discourses.* 3rd ed. London: Taylor & Francis.

Glaser, Barney G., and Anselm L. Strauss. 1967. *The Discovery of Grounded Theory: Strategies for Qualitative Research.* Chicago, IL: Aldine.

Haas, Christina. 1996. *Writing Technology: Studies on the Materiality of Literacy.* New York: Routledge.

Halbritter, Bump. 2006. "Musical Rhetoric in Integrated-Media Composition." *Computers and Composition* 23 (3): 317–34.

Irvine, Judith T. 2010. "Semiotic Remediation: Afterword." *Exploring Semiotic Remediation as Discourse Practice*, edited by Paul Prior and Julie Hengst, 235–42. New York: Palgrave/ Macmillan.

McLuhan, Marshall. 2003. *Understanding Media: The Extensions of Man.* Critical ed. Edited by Terrence Gordon. Berkeley, CA: Gingko.

McCorkle, Ben. 2012. *Rhetorical Delivery as Technological Discourse: A Cross-Historical Study.* Carbondale: Southern Illinois University Press.

New London Group. 1996. "A Pedagogy of Multiliteracies: Designing Social Futures." *Harvard Educational Review* 66 (1): 60–92.

Ong, Walter. 1982. *Orality and Literacy.* New York: Routledge.

Oxford English Dictionary. s.v. "resonance." Accessed Sept 14, 2013. www.oxfordreference.com.

Palmeri, Jason. 2012. *Remixing Composition: A History of Multimodal Writing Pedagogy.* Carbondale: Southern Illinois University Press.

Prior, Paul. 2009. "From Speech Genres to Mediated Multimodal Genre Systems: Bakhtin, Voloshinov, and the Question of Writing." In *Genre in a Changing World*, edited by Charles Bazerman, Adair Bonini, Debora Figueiredo, 17–32. Fort Collins, CO: Parlor.

Prior, Paul, Julie Hengst, Kevin Roozen, and Jody Shipka. 2006. "'I'll Be the Sun': From Reported Speech to Semiotic Remediation Practices." *Text and Talk* 26 (6): 733–66.

Prior, Paul, and Jody Shipka. 2003. "Chronotopic Lamination: Tracing the Contours of Literate Activity." In *Writing Selves/Writing Societies: Research on Activity Perspectives,* edited by Charles Bazerman and David Russell, 235–42. New York: Palgrave/Macmillan.

Selfe, Cynthia L. 2009. "The Movement of Air, the Breath of Meaning: Aurality and Multi-modal Composing." *College Composition and Communication* 60 (4): 616–63.

Voloshinov, V. N. 1973. *Marxism and the Philosophy of Language.* Cambridge, MA: Harvard University Press.

Vygotsky, L. S. 1978. *Mind in Society: The Development of Higher Psychological Processes.* Edited by Michael Cole, Vera John-Steiner, Sylvia Scribner, and Ellen Souberman. Cambridge, MA: Harvard University Press.

Welch, Kathleen E. 1999. *Electric Rhetoric: Classical Rhetoric, Oralism, and a New Literacy.* Cambridge: MIT Press.

Whitney, Allison. 2008. "Cultivating Sonic Literacy in the Humanities Classroom." *Music, Sound, and Moving Images* 2 (2): 145–48.

9

ENTERING THE MULTIVERSE
Using Comics to Experiment with Multimodality,
Multigenres, and Multiliteracies

Rebecca Thorndike-Breeze, Aaron Block, and Kara Mae Brown

INTRODUCTION

Though multimodal instruction is often associated with the digital, analog compositions—like making comics with pencil, pen, and paper—elegantly demonstrate how multimodality makes meaning through image, text, and design. As Jody Shipka notes (2011), a number of scholars argue "that there is, technically speaking, no such thing as a monomodal text" because visual design elements, such as "color, quality, and texture of paper," are inherent in "even print-linear alphabetic texts," (13; see also Kress 2009; Prior 2009; Wysocki 2003). When comics creators write about how they view their craft, they often emphasize this same semiotic synthesis. According to Chris Ware, creator of *Jimmy Corrigan, the Smartest Kid on Earth* and *Building Stories,* "'Cartooning is not really drawing at all, but a complicated pictographic language to be read, not really seen'" (quoted in Brunetti 2011, epigraph). And Ivan Brunetti (2011)—known for the dark humor and simple style of *Schitzo,* his series of autobiographical comics—emphasizes the importance of compositional choice and craft in the development of that language: "Cartooning is built upon the Five Cs: calligraphy, composition, clarity, consistency, and communication, each reinforcing the other" (25).[3] Instructors have begun turning to comics because, as Dale Jacobs shows (2007a; 2007b; 2013), they demonstrate with such elegance how multimodality makes meaning while also sponsoring students' multiliteracies. For years the field of writing studies has known that teaching pop-culture texts, like comics, helps students connect their own interests to public life and institutional expectations (Finlay and Faith 1980), and the practice of multimodal literacy with comics draws upon what Juan Guerra (2008) calls student "learning incomes," the literacies, content knowledge, and other strengths "students bring with them when they

DOI: 10.7330/9781607327974.c009

come to school" (296). Brunetti (2011) inadvertently hits upon the connections among making comics, student "learning incomes," and multimodal literacy when he writes, in *Cartooning: Philosophy and Practice*, "What is cartooning, ultimately, but a consistent and identifiable system of communicative marks expressing our unique experiences of life?" (15). While Brunetti is clearly biased toward autobiographical comics and comic stories derived from real life (as his body of work demonstrates), reading and making more fantastical comics can also capitalize on this synthesis of multimodal learning potential. Indeed, if we conceive of comics as a medium, then the possibilities for stories and arguments that can be conveyed in comics form are endless.

Quite recently, we have seen an increase in publications about comics' value in teaching multimodal composition. In 2013, Elizabeth Losh, Jonathan Alexander, Kevin Cannon, and Zander Cannon published *Understanding Rhetoric*, a composition textbook in comics form, that encourages creating comics in the classroom; and in spring 2015, *Composition Studies* published a special issue, edited by Dale Jacobs, dedicated to exploring how the study and creation of comics can enhance multimodal composition instruction. The three authors of this chapter agree with these scholars that comics and graphic novels offer students opportunities to consider multimodality both as an object of study and as an approach they might take to composing their own texts. Further, comics give instructors an opportunity to experiment with multimodality in their classrooms to teach common learning outcomes, even if they have anxiety about using the digital tools often associated with multimodality. For instance, our comics-creation assignments ask students to use only pencil, pen, and paper so they experience the integral role of their own hand in the multimodal composition process, as each line has the capacity to convey a different meaning, and each hand draws its lines in a different way. As comics creator Lynda Barry (2014) suggests, "There is a way of making lines and shapes that is ours alone, and the more we draw, the clearer it becomes, not just to ourselves but to others: a style unique and recognizable" (5).

Furthermore, as we will show, studying and making comics can help students better understand how they can draw upon their multiliteracies to meet the priorities outlined in the WPA Outcomes for First-Year Composition (Council 2014) in the areas of rhetorical knowledge, critical thinking, reading and composing, and multimodal processes. In what follows, we each present our experiments with comics in this compositional multiverse. The chapter is structured so each experiment is theoretically framed in the relevant literature and then proceeds in the form of a first-person account. Throughout each experiment, we refer to students using pseudonyms. First, Rebecca Thorndike-Breeze describes how she used comics as an object of study to help increase her students' genre awareness as they considered the semiotics of comics. Then, Aaron Block discusses the need to push back against what he identifies as the emerging canon of "composition-class comics" and offers approaches instructors can take to experiment more with their comics reading lists to offer more global and unconventional perspectives. Finally, Kara Mae Brown presents case studies of her experiment with composing comics to promote multiliteracies and models potential ways other instructors might do the same.

USING COMICS TO RAISE GENRE AWARENESS

Genre theorists argue that when students study repeated social actions of different genres and make rhetorical choices in response to different social contexts, they learn to recognize the implicit expectations embedded in a wide variety of rhetorical situations (Devitt 1993; Miller 1984). With this complex understanding of genre as social action, students become more empowered to take an active role in the world around them. Teaching with comics illuminates these processes and opens opportunities for both teachers and students to experiment because comics dramatize what we talk about when we talk about genre as social action. Though any precise definition of comics is hotly debated (Harvey 2001; Eisner 2008; Groensteen, Beaty, and Nguyen 2007; McCloud 1993), there is a general consensus about how image, text, creator, and reader interact to give comics meaning. In particular, Scott McCloud's (1993) *Understanding Comics* offers a compelling narrative, in comics form, of how comics audiences, creators, genres, and forms have changed within and in response to cultural changes over time. The work dramatizes how these elements are mutually constituted in culture, and beyond that, it demonstrates how studying comics form and development can open opportunities to underscore what John Trimbur (2011) calls "the historicity of the genres, the subject positions they make available, [and] the way they circulate in literate culture" (187). By working with McCloud and other comics, students can link their background and previous education—their "incomes" (Guerra 2008)— to these genre concepts. Here, Rebecca Thorndike-Breeze presents her pedagogical experiment using comics to teach genre as social action and thus help students meet WPA outcomes for rhetorical knowledge in first-year writing.

Rebecca Thorndike-Breeze

My goals for this experiment were to help students develop their understanding of genre and enhance their confidence in the power of what they create to contribute to the world around them. But my path toward these goals was not straight; I fell into analytical pitfalls that were accompanied by many small victories in the form of student insight and understanding of genre as social action. I, like many other writing instructors, am a trained textual interpreter, and despite my best intentions, I tend to privilege textual analysis over creation. Steve Westbrook (2006) notes in "Visual Rhetoric in a Culture of Fear," "to 'do' visual rhetoric in composition too often means not to work with students on authoring multimedia visual texts that combine words and images but, rather, to work on critically reading visual artifacts and demonstrating this critical reading through the evidence of a print essay" (460). In my effort to teach students how to engage with multimodal texts through McCloud's (1993) critical framework, my class fell into this reader-centric pitfall. Though valuable, developing analytical vocabulary and critical lenses through study of texts like McCloud's does not always promote *thorough* multimodal learning. Such theoretical approaches privilege reading multimodal texts over creating them, as Westbrook warns. However, there was still value in inviting my students to approach comics as an object of study; even if they were not composing their own comics, they made significant strides in understanding how image and text make meaning across genres and modes through the collaboration of comics creators and readers.

My first-year writing class studied chapter 2 of McCloud's *Understanding Comics*, "The Vocabulary of Comics," which, as the title declares, offers a critical vocabulary of the form. As described above, this text dramatizes what we talk about when we talk about genre as social action. This chapter, in particular, presents McCloud's theory of the history and development of collaborations among writers, artists, and readers toward making meaning across a spectrum of representation, from realist to abstract. Integral to McCloud's broader theory of how comics make meaning is his concept of "masking," which my first-year students seized upon.

For McCloud (1993), "masking" explains how comics creators combine images and text to make meaning in collaboration with the reader by drawing the reader *in*to the comic. To articulate this concept, he draws upon a combination of semiotics and Marshall McLuhan's concept of nonvisual awareness—our compilation of our sense of self through all five senses. McCloud (1993) explains that, in nonvisual awareness, as we use various objects, "our identities and awareness are invested" in them, over and over, every day (38). He goes on to argue that this process is inherent in the meaning making of comics, that readers identify their abstract senses of self with the abstraction of cartoons: "The cartoon is a vacuum into which our identity and awareness are pulled . . . an empty shell that we inhabit which enables us to travel in another realm. We don't just observe the cartoon, we become it!" (36; suspension points in original).

As a class, we also read Alan Moore and David Lloyd's comic *V for Vendetta* and watched the Wachowskis' film adaptation; the connection between McCloud's masking and the Guy Fawkes mask in the *V for Vendetta* texts became a focal point of class discussion, and several students took up the topic in their analytical essays. Given that the mask was adopted by Anonymous and the Occupy movement, the class-wide interest (my own included) in its significance is understandable, and students demonstrated a strong understanding of the cultural power of semiotics in their essays. For example, Jenna analyzed the how V's mask functions in the graphic novel, in the film, and in the real world through its adoption by Anonymous and the Occupy movement. Like most of the students in the class who wrote about the mask, she began her discussion with reference to Guy Fawkes himself, but her paper impressively traces the mask through culture. Jenna writes,

> The virus or meme currently spreading through culture is a reality as the protesters in the public protests in Thailand, the Arab Spring Movement in the Middle East, Turkish Airlines workers, Occupy Wall Street, and members of Anonymous all take to the streets in smiling Guy Fawkes masks. . . . The power in the face of Fawkes lies in the ability to go against the higher power that people feel are oppressing them without having to be exposed. . . . Over time, it has become clear that the original image of Fawkes has taken a turn for the best, as people now identify him as a hero and not a terrorist. It is the combination of the works of Moore and Lloyd and the manipulations of McTeigue and the Wachowski[s] . . . that have shaped the versatile symbol of the face of Fawkes into an outlet for true freedom, ready for use in our surveillance-saturated twenty-first century.

Jenna's analysis shows how creators, citizens, readers, and viewers all work together, not only to give texts meaning but also to revise and alter meaning throughout culture and history. She demonstrates understanding not only of how semiotics works in culture but also how it can be harnessed to make change in society.

My emphasis upon McCloud's theoretical framework pulled us into a reader-centric, analytical pitfall, but for instructors like me who are first beginning to experiment with multimodality, using comics as an object of study can be a steppingstone to teaching students to compose multimodally. Indeed, my students' close readings of comics helped them better understand how creators of a range of texts make choices to construct meaning and how those meanings are culturally mediated. In an end-of-semester reflection, Jenna wrote, "I have come to realize that genres are not there to limit you, but just to provide some loosely bound structure. It is an identity framework that encourages you to play with it and self-define it." Jenna demonstrates that she recognizes genres as rhetorical frameworks in which she has freedom to "play" with rhetorical choices and her writerly identity. In this reflection I see the potential for comics in the writing classroom to cultivate genre awareness through multimodal analysis, as well as student confidence in the power of their choices to contribute to culture.

QUESTIONING THE COMICS CANON—COMICS AS MEDIUM

Since comics have come into vogue in mainstream culture and the college composition classroom, the conversation about their pedagogical value has shifted from should we teach using comics? to how should we teach comics? In an era of multimodality and multiliteracies, introducing comics as a possible text or classroom medium is no longer shocking or surprising, but with wider acceptance seems to have come a degree of ossification. Geoffrey Sirc (1997) argues that the field ignored the excitement and volatility of punk in the 70s and 80s, and it seems we may be doing something similar now by treating comics as a category of literature rather than the broad and rhetorically rich medium it is.

Scholars define comics variously as "sequential art" (Eisner 2008), "a sequence of discrete, juxtaposed pictures that comprise a narrative, either in their own right or when combined with text" (Hayman and Pratt 2005), "juxtaposed pictorial and other images in deliberate sequence, intended to convey information and/or produce an aesthetic response in the viewer" (McCloud 1993), and "[a medium] that [uses] a combination of sequential art and text in order to create narrative meaning for the audience" (Jacobs 2007a). None of those definitions is entirely satisfying on its own, but when taken all together a somewhat blurry but coherent picture of what constitutes the medium emerges. In the following section, Aaron Block challenges the emerging "composition-class" consensus about comics, and offers his own experiment as a boundary-pushing model of instruction.

Aaron Block

What if the definition of comics depends as much on where you ask that question as whom you ask it of? In comic-book specialty shops, traditional bookstores, magazine racks, libraries, and especially online, the scope of the medium is almost impossibly vast: mainstream US superhero comics sit side by side with European albums and sci-fi collections like *Heavy Metal* and *2000 A.D.*; Chris Ware's structuralist masterpiece *Building Stories*; bizarre humor comics like Sam Humphries's and Caitlin Rose Boyle's *Jonesy* and Jake Lawrence's *Teen Dog*; Xeroxed minicomics about local scenes and heart break; webcomics as varied as Ryan North's *Dinosaur Comics*, Mike Norton's *Battle Pug*, even Scott McCloud's own sci-fi romance series *Zot!*; and still more, to the extent that I could fill this entire book with different examples. The point is that comics and graphic literature are too diverse and multifaceted a medium to restrict our classroom explorations to a single genre or style of expression.

But in the classroom, comics are treated like Serious Literature. Erika Lindemann (1993) and Gary Tate (1993), among others, have already discussed the role of literature in the composition classroom, and even advocates for teaching with novels tend to eschew canonical texts. We acknowledge that the purpose is not to teach students to appreciate "great writing" but rather to use essays and novels as tools for constructing arguments, or even as examples of composing in different genres. But we seem to be less confident in that approach when it comes to comics. The literature about comics in the composition classroom, and the textbooks that identify comics as a medium or a subject of study, tend to emphasize a handful of graphic novels—Marjane Satrappi's *Persepolis*, Allison Bechdel's *Fun Home*, and Art Spiegelman's *Maus* among them—as well as Scott McCloud's *Understanding Comics*. These are all justly celebrated, award-winning texts, but their prominence in the field seems to be based heavily on that reputation. *Maus* is an easy sell to both administrators and students because it won the Pulitzer Prize and is a sober, serious work. As a consequence, it has become part of the canon, with all the attendant implications for both teachers and students. Once, when I asked one of my first-year writing classes about their prior experiences with comics, a student offered that *Maus* was the only comic she had ever read. When I asked how she liked it, she said, "It was good, but I *had* to read it, you know?" That's a dispiriting, but expected, reaction to a seminal work of literature of any sort, particularly comics. But if we only focus on the legitimacy of *Maus*'s narrative and its elevated cultural status, we ignore the value of teaching comics as a medium and fail to introduce students to the complex and challenging composing practices and opportunities therein. Even if we only want students to produce nonfiction narratives and memoirs, relying on those examples still restricts their choices when composing. If comics are a medium, we should teach them that way.

Application

To address this definition and scope problem, I developed an assignment for my first-year writing course that would expose students to comics in two different ways and ask them to make composing choices after each exposure. I based the structure of this assignment on the assumption that students, who are generally unfamiliar with comics as either literature or a medium for writing, would base their composing choices on whatever models I presented to them. They'd written short literacy narratives for a previous assignment, so I used those texts as the basis for the comics assignment and asked them to repurpose their narrative, or at least a selected scene from it, into a short comic—four to five pages or so.

After introducing the idea of comics and translation, and asking them about their prior experience with or interest in comics, I asked them to read excerpts from Will Eisner's (2008) book *Comics & Sequential Art.* Scott McCloud's (1993) *Understanding Comics* is the more traditional option, but I find Eisner's text to be more practical, whereas McCloud's is more theoretical. Both are valuable, but for this assignment I wanted my students to have a handful of techniques or tools to draw from, a basic working knowledge of the creation of graphic storytelling they could then apply to their own narratives. (An added benefit of using *Comics & Sequential Art* is that examples are all drawn from Eisner's own work, which is among the most enduring and engaging in the field.)

Following classroom discussion and homework that used Eisner to provide a framework for comics as a medium, I next gave my students excerpts from Howard Cruse's *Stuck Rubber Baby* to read as an example of a professional, critically lauded comic. Like *Persepolis, Maus,* and *Fun Home, Stuck Rubber Baby* is a black-and-white pseudomemoir that confronts bigotry in multiple forms and employs an idiosyncratic cartooning style that uses largely traditional page and panel layouts but is still experimental, particularly its imagery. Rather than asking them to read the entire graphic novel, I offered a few selected passages, and we discussed them in class using terminology derived from the Eisner readings to examine and explain the choices Cruse made in crafting

Picture 1

  Sitting at the table, I was doing my writing homework, feeling tired and bored. (4–5years old)

Picture 2

  Parents and grandparents were emphasizing writing was important and forced me to read and write. (They held books, papers and pen in hand, standing beside the desk)

Picture 3

  I was sitting in the middle of the classroom, teacher told us to write according to a picuture with two swallows. (Show a picture with swallows on the blackboard)

Picture 4

  I went home and asked my mother how to write the story, holding the picture in hand.

Figure 9.1. A student's comic script demonstrates the way students adopted the style of the comics they had read.

his narrative. This discussion then prepared students to make their own choices, and the next stage of the assignment was producing scripts and rough thumbnail sketches for their comics.

As I'd expected, the drafts were generally pretty conventional and followed the grid that characterizes Cruse's work (fig. 9.1). That observation should not suggest, however, that they weren't still interesting or that the students were not engaged in the work of translating their literacy narratives into the language of comics. My goal with this assignment was not to set my students up to fail and then succeed but rather to juxtapose one type of comics craft with several others in an attempt to broaden their thinking about composing practices.

To that end, the next stage of the assignment returned to examples and sample readings, but this time we considered different sources. First was a webcomic, *GUTS: A Young Adult Television Fiasco* by Sean Michael Robinson, which details the author's experiences as a contestant on the Nickelodeon game show. While still a monochromatic memoir, Robinson's short comic employs some challenging and unique layouts. As with Cruse, we discussed the comic using terms from Eisner but did not dwell on those choices. Instead, I gathered together a tall stack of comics and graphic novels from my bookshelves, as well as a few interesting webcomics—what I dubbed my "Cornucopia of Comics"— and offered them to my students as examples. I tried to find as much variety as possible, which meant I brought in single issues of superhero comics, a few literary graphic novels, some experimental art and underground comics, and a few that cannot be so easily classified. I suggested they look through them—if not closely reading, then just idly flipping through the pages—and trade and circulate them as they saw fit. I asked them to look for anything that interested them—a page layout, a certain image or figure, a panel shape, a sound effect, a color choice, an inking move, or anything else—and when they found it, to write a short paragraph explaining what it was and why they liked it. Then I asked them to look back at the thumbnails they had already generated and use the detail they had found in some way by revising a layout or wedging in an extra panel or making some coloring notes, anything to indicate how that new element might be integrated into the script and thumbnails of the working draft.

When it came time to revise those thumbnails and scripts, several students ended up incorporating those changes into their final drafts (fig. 9.2). Of those, a few opted to drastically restructure their comics with different panel designs, imagery choices, even the tone of the captions, all in response to what they'd discovered in the stack of comics I'd given them.

Outcomes

What this activity seems to mean for comics in the classroom, then, is critical distance from canonical texts, and with it an emphasis on technique and convention. For teachers, this distance might require developing a deeper library of sample texts to draw on or even asking students to bring in comics on their own to build a reading list for the assignment. It also means accepting texts into the classroom that are not critically vetted or awarded and which fall outside the umbrella of literary comics. If we allow that comics of all varieties, whether prestigious, avant-garde, pulpy, or mainstream employ the conventions of graphic literature in equally interesting ways that are also applicable to the tasks we set before our students, we can avoid essentializing the medium.

By exposing my students to a variety of comics, and most important by allowing them to follow their own interests rather than introducing

Figure 9.2. A student's comic final draft incorporated a new panel layout that helped them tell their story in a more dynamic way.

one example as Important or Valuable, my goal was to introduce students to the comics medium as I would any other. If we avoid narrowing the scope of those media by diversifying the sources, examples, and techniques we introduce in the classroom, we multiply the composing choices available to our students considerably. Some students may opt to closely ape the approach of a favored sample text, others might mix and match with varying degrees of consistency and coherence, and still others might transform existing techniques or devices to create something new and unfamiliar. The specific results seem less important than the fact that our students have a say in the matter.

DEVELOPING MULTILITERACIES: USING
COMICS AS LITERACY NARRATIVES

Literacy narratives have long been a popular genre in writing class-rooms, and they are particularly useful for eliciting student learning incomes. The Digital Archive of Literacy Narratives, housed at The Ohio State University, defines literacy narratives as "stories about how—and in what circumstances—[individuals] read, write, and compose meaning and how they learned to do so (or helped others learn)." By asking students to tell their own such stories, writing instructors hope to accomplish several goals. First, literacy narratives help students put literacy in the context of their own personal experiences and understand the significance literacy plays in their intellectual, personal, and civic development. Also, asking students to think through their own experience with literacy can help them better understand multiliteracies, a term coined by the New London Group (1996) to encompass the "cultural and linguistic diversity" that arises from our increasingly globalized world, where culture and technology have moved us beyond the "mere" literacy of text towards literacies that include reading and writing multimedia.

Comics have been similarly poised as tools to help students come to terms with multiliteracies because of the way they combine text, image, and design in the familiar form of narrative. According to Dale Jacobs (2007b), whose work has provided a foundation for thinking about comics in the writing classroom, "by teaching students to become conscious and critical of the ways in which they make meaning from multimodal texts such as comics, we can also teach students to become more literate with a wide range of multimodal texts" (24). Indeed, in this way, comics can be thought of as what Deborah Brandt (2001) calls "literacy sponsors." She notes, "Sponsors . . . are any agents, local or distant, concrete or abstract, who enable, support, teach, model, as well as recruit, regulate, suppress, or withhold literacy" (4). Jacobs (2007a) himself draws this parallel in his article/literacy-narrative hybrid "Marveling at 'The Man Called Nova': Comics as Sponsors of Multimodal Literacy." In the narrative component of that article, Jacobs describes how an early encounter with comics sponsored a lifelong interest in multimodal texts. However, it is worth noting that Jacobs's work focuses mostly on students *reading* comics rather than writing them and thus falls into the reader-centric pitfall Westbrook (2006) has identified in much multimodal instruction. Jacobs's work helped Kara Mae Brown think critically about her own use of literacy narratives and comics in her first-year writing course and to devise the following experiment.

Kara Mae Brown

I wondered what would happen if students wrote literacy narratives in the form of comics. While I appreciated the reflection on literacy experiences literacy narratives encouraged, I found students' narratives often focused solely on traditional, textual literacies. Also, I found the genre did not offer my students much of a writing challenge since many of my students had written narratives extensively in high school. On the other hand, while comics helped my students better understand how text, image, and design could work together to create meaning, I worried that the content of their comics too often deviated too far from my otherwise writing-about-writing-themed course. After all, the other projects in the course more explicitly asked students to engage with and analyze concepts from the field of writing studies, such as genre and rhetorical analysis and fieldwork into discourse communities.

I wanted to experiment with combining the explicit thinking about writing encouraged in literacy narratives with the multimodal composing challenge of comics. Rather than thinking about reading comics as a potential literacy encounter, I wanted my students to render their own literacy narratives in comics form. Would writing literacy narratives in multimodal form help students access their own multiliteracies? I examine three case studies of student work from a project for which students composed their own literacy narratives as comics.

The Project

For the last project of the semester before the final portfolio, I asked students to create a literacy-narrative comic through a series of steps. First, similar to Aaron Block, I asked students to compose traditional literacy narratives. But, anticipating the way comics decompress narrative time (small moments can actually take up a lot of space on the page), I asked them to write literacy *moments*, particular scenes in their literacy development. Next, students translated those literacy moments into a comic script, in which they had to start considering layout, paneling, dialogue, and what images might accompany their narratives. Each of these components was peer reviewed before students drew their narratives as comics. Finally, students reflected on the project as they curated their work in their ePortfolios.

Case Study 1: Visual Metaphors for Literacy Sponsors

Clara wrote her initial narrative about her literacy education at Catholic school. It was clear from her initial narrative that Clara's work was meant as a critique of what she perceived as censorship in her education. A brief excerpt from Clara's literacy narrative reads,

> My third grade Language Arts teacher Ms. A glared down at me with frustration from her perch as I angrily scooted my chair back into my desk.
>
> "And quit making so much noise, some people are trying to get homework done."
>
> I sighed and looked down at my assignment. Memorizing the prepositions to a Yankee Doodle song. What a waste of time. But that was exactly what going to a private Catholic school in Rhode Island was: a waste of time—and money for that matter.
>
> "Aboard, about, above, across, after . . . damn it I forgot the next one."
> "CLARA WE DO NOT USE SUCH LANGUAGE!"

In the next iteration of Clara's work, the comic script, the dialogue and situation remained much the same. However, significant changes started to emerge in her descriptions of her comic's panels. For instance, "Panel 2. Dark, dismal classroom setting with Bible references covering the walls with small kitten with huge owl-like eyes (CLARA) peering down at desk as giant penguin (MS. A) swoops down from perch." Not only did Clara take a narrative that was much more plot and dialogue focused and begin to infuse it with sensory description, but she also started to think in terms of visual metaphor (fig. 9.3).

She seemed to have taken the word "perch" as a source of inspiration. While that use of the visual would have been a creative achievement on its own, Clara's choice to use animals as her main characters also contributed to the critique of Catholic schooling she began in the original. While Clara might not have been the first to use the nuns-as-penguins metaphor as a critique of nuns, she was able to use it to her advantage to comment on the harsh discipline and censorship she experienced in her literacy education (fig. 9.3). She was engaging in the kind of intertextuality James E. Porter (1986) says "presupposes certain audiences and attitudes" and "exerts its influence partly in the form of audience expectation" (38). Compared to her text-only literacy narrative, Clara's comic was more audience aware. While Clara's narrative itself still focused on Clara's traditional literacy education, rendering that experience multimodally allowed her to express her critique of that experience in a visual metaphor and increase her understanding of audience and how to appeal to their needs.

Case Study 2: Representing Imagination as an Aspect of Literacy

Hannah wrote about how the first time a teacher read to her from *Harry Potter and the Sorcerer's Stone*, she finally felt able to really focus on

Figure 9.3. Clara's literacy narrative comic. Using a multimodal form to compose her literacy narrative allowed Clara to incorporate a visual metaphor into her narrative.

a story. In her first version of the literacy narrative, Hannah described the experience like this: "*The Sorcerer's Stone*? That sounded silly. But we started to read anyway. I looked at the copy of the book in my hand as Ms. W read aloud and slowly, a world forming in my head." Much like Clara, Hannah's comic script brought out a more visual interpretation of her literacy experiences. In the script, Hannah began to give shape to the "world forming in [her] head." One panel was written as follows:

Narration Box: It was the beginning of a new era for me.
    Large panel with a drawing of the path labeled "path to obsessive fan-girling." Shows me walking down a path surrounded by magical creatures.

Figure 9.4. Hannah's literacy-narrative comic. Hannah provided images for the imaginative aspects of her literacy experience.

Maybe with heart eyes. Definitely thinking something positive. The thought bubble will have to do with the drawings. (Ex: "The dragons here have such spiky tails." If I draw a spiky tailed dragon.)

In the final comic (fig. 9.4), Hannah fulfills her promise of a "spiky tailed" hair dragon. What is remarkable about her comic, as opposed to her original literacy narrative, is that she was able to see her imagination as a vital part of her literacy development. Again, if she had not translated her work into a comic, it is unclear whether she would have given this aspect of her literacy experience the credit it deserved. In fact, the comic itself is a testament to the opening of her imagination since it demonstrates a use of that imagination.

Case Study 3: Metacognition of Literacy Development

Kyle, whose work I analyze for this third case study, misinterpreted the assignment. For his initial narrative, he did not write about an experience with literacy in any way I could interpret or he could articulate. Despite my generous interpretation of multiliteracies, I could not see a connection between literacy and the story he told of waiting in line to buy an expensive pair of sneakers. When I asked him during a conference what literacies were represented in his narrative, he could not identify them either, which made me confident this was not just a case of misreading a student's intentions but a misstep in the assignment.

Unfortunately, Kyle failed to change directions even after the first two steps of the assignment, so by the time he was ready to compose his comic, he was still working with the story about the sneakers. I conferenced with Kyle one last time to try to make sure he met the learning goal of the project: to try to better understand his own literacy experiences. In our final conversation, I asked Kyle what came to mind when he thought about the different kinds of literacy we had discussed in class and how he might connect those back to the incident with the sneakers. Finally, Kyle said that the very act of writing the comic script had been a significant literacy event. I sent him off encouraging him to think about how he might represent that in the final comic.

The last page of Kyle's final comic (fig. 9.5) shows Kyle writing the comic, rendering that act of composition as the literacy event in his narrative. The panels are superimposed on the paper with his peer review and my own comments on his script. Not only does this final comic represent an incredible turnaround for this student, but it also demonstrates Kyle's metacognition of his own writing process. What is interesting to me about this comic is not the visual component but the texture of the final product. By layering images and text, the writer seems to evoke the writing process itself while commenting on that process in the explicit content of the panels. Again, it is hard to imagine Kyle reaching this understanding, or at least being able to articulate it in such an interesting way, by writing only a traditional literacy narrative.

Results of the Multimodal Experiment

Overall, my experiment with multimodal literacy narratives was a success. Even though my students still tended to focus on traditional literacies, case study 3 shows they were able to think about their multiliteracies through the act of composing a comic. Even more significantly though, this experiment opened up new questions about how instructors might

Figure 9.5. Kyle's literacy-narrative comic. Kyle superimposed his comic panels over the feedback he received on his comic script. This metacommentary on the process showed he recognized the composition of the comic as a form of literacy.

use multimodal compositions in their classrooms. How might instructors repurpose traditional genres and assignments as opportunities for students to compose multimodally? What other writing concepts, like multiliteracies, could be explored in our classrooms through multimodal compositions?

CONCLUSION

Ultimately, our experiments with comics as multimodal texts in our classrooms expanded our own multimodal pedagogies while at the same time expanding our students' knowledge about writing. While multimodality is often associated with digital technologies, comics provided us a way to explore multimodality through technologies already familiar to us—pencil and paper—even if the composing skills, like drawing, required of the form were less familiar. These experiments helped us question fundamental tenets of our pedagogies: What are "appropriate" texts for students to read? What are "appropriate" texts or genres for students to compose? How can common assignments be remediated in multimodal forms? By pushing beyond our own boundaries, we exposed our students to a greater number of texts and more modes they might compose in a way consistent with the WPA Outcomes Statement for First-Year Composition (Council 2014) by asking them to read, compose, and think critically.

However, perhaps the most significant takeaway from this experience was the act of experimentation itself. By putting ourselves in situations in which we navigated new rhetorical situations with our students, we modeled the kind of experimentation inherent to the writing process. Rarely do writers work from a position of perfect authority. We are constantly seeking out new texts to read, encountering new genres, and experimenting with new modes. New modes are emerging at such a rapid pace that no writer and no instructor can be expected to be an authority on them all. By putting ourselves in the vulnerable position of experimenting with our students, we model for them the kind of rhetorical flexibility needed to navigate the world of texts. Knowing how, exactly, to write in any particular genre or mode is less important than the skills needed to navigate new forms: reading texts rhetorically, seeking out model texts, and using the writing process to uncover successively more successful versions of our work.

NOTES

1. Student names were changed to pseudonyms following the research protocol outlined in the IRB application.

2. These instances of semiotic synaesthesia support scholars (Gee [2008]; McCorkle [2012]; Palmeri [2012]; Welch [1999]) whose are arguments challenge orality- and literacy-divide theories by providing evidence of a symbiotic relationship between speech and writing. In this study, students remediated modalities simultaneously rather than linearly when they engaged in blending or framing one modality through perceptions of another.

3. In discussions of comics form and development, terminology is often debated among practitioners and theorists. Comics creators who both draw and write, such as Chris Ware and Ivan Brunetti, refer to what they do as "cartooning." Brunetti (2011) takes a pragmatic approach to this usage: "When we are creating comics, we

are not 'graphic novelling,' we are cartooning" (12). However, comics creator and theorist Scott McCloud (1993; 2011) prefers the phrase "making comics" because for him cartooning can include pieces of comic art that are not comics (e.g., single panels that are not juxtaposed in a sequence). McCloud's 1993 *Understanding Comics* is a seminal work of comics studies, and Thorndike-Breeze and Block both refer to his role in debates surrounding definitions of "comics." But as a whole, this chapter is concerned with the dynamic, multimodal synthesis found in both the study and the making of comics, which includes both the process of cartooning, as Ware and Brunetti describe it, and McCloud's more theoretical conception of comics.

REFERENCES

Barry, Lynda. 2014. *Syllabus: Notes from an Accidental Professor.* Montreal: Drawn & Quarterly.

Brandt, Deborah. 2001. *Literacy in American Lives.* Cambridge: Cambridge University Press.

Brunetti, Ivan. 2011. *Cartooning: Philosophy and Practice.* New Haven, CT: Yale University Press.

Council of Writing Program Administrators. 2014. "WPA Outcomes Statement for First-Year Composition (3.0)." http://wpacouncil.org/positions/outcomes.html.

Devitt, Amy J. 1993. "Generalizing about Genre: New Conceptions of an Old Concept." *College Composition and Communication* 44 (4): 573–86.

Digital Archive of Literacy Narratives. n.d. Accessed May 19. http://www.thedaln.org/#/about.

Eisner, Will. 2008. *Comics and Sequential Art: Principles and Practices from the Legendary Cartoonist.* Will Eisner Instructional Books. New York: W. W. Norton.

Finlay, Linda Shaw, and Valerie Faith. 1980. "Illiteracy and Alienation in American Colleges: Is Paulo Freire's Pedagogy Relevant?" *Radical Teacher* 16: 28–37.

Groensteen, Thierry, Bart Beaty, and Nick Nguyen. 2007. *The System of Comics.* Jackson: University Press of Mississippi.

Guerra, Juan. 2008. "Cultivating Transcultural Citizenship: A Writing across Communities Model." *Language Arts* 85 (4): 296–304.

Harvey, Robert C. 2001. "Comedy at the Juncture of Word and Image." In *The Language of Comics: Word and Image,* edited by Robin Varnum and Christina T. Gibbons, 75–96. Jackson: University Press of Mississippi.

Hayman, Greg, and Henry John Pratt. 2005 "What Are Comics?" In *A Reader in Philosophy of the Arts,* edited by David Goldblatt and Lee Brown, 410–24. London: Pearson Education.

Jacobs, Dale. 2007a. "Marveling at 'The Man Called Nova': Comics as Sponsors of Multimodal Literacy." *College Composition and Communication* 59 (2): 180–205.

Jacobs, Dale. 2007b. "More Than Words: Comics as a Means of Teaching Multiple Literacies." *English Journal* 96 (3): 19–25. doi:10.2307/30047289.

Jacobs, Dale. 2013. *Graphic Encounters: Comics and the Sponsorship of Multimodal Literacy.* http://public.eblib.com/choice/publicfullrecord.aspx?p=1334375.

Jacobs, Dale. 2015. "Comics, Multimodality, and Composition." Special issue, *Composition Studies* 43 (1): 11–12.

Kress, Gunther. 2009. *Multimodality: A Social Semiotic Approach to Contemporary Communication.* London: Routledge.

Lindemann, Erika. 1993. "Freshman Composition: No Place for Literature." *College English* 55 (3): 311–16. doi:10.2307/378743.

Losh, Elizabeth, Jonathan Alexander, Kevin Cannon, and Zander Cannon. 2013. *Understanding Rhetoric: A Graphic Guide to Writing.* London: Macmillan Higher Education.

McCloud, Scott. 1993. *Understanding Comics.* New York: HarperCollins.

McCloud, Scott. 2011. *Making Comics.* New York: HarperCollins.

Miller, Carolyn R. 1984. "Genre as Social Action." *Quarterly Journal of Speech* 70 (2): 151–67.

New London Group. 1996. "A Pedagogy of Multiliteracies: Designing Social Futures." *Harvard Educational Review* 66 (1): 60–93.

Porter, James E. 1986. "Intertextuality and the Discourse Community." *Rhetoric Review* 5 (1): 34–47. doi:10.1080/07350198609359131.

Prior, Paul. 2009. "From Speech Genres to Mediated Multimodal Genre Systems: Bakhtin, Voloshinov, and the Question of Writing." In *Genre in a Changing World*, edited by Charles Bazerman, Adair Bonini, and Débora de Carvalho Figueiredo, 17–34. Fort Collins, CO: WAC Clearinghouse.

Robinson, Sean Michael. n.d. "GUTS: A Young Adult Television Fiasco / Top Shelf 2.0." Accessed May 19, 2017. http://www.topshelfcomix.com/ts2.0/guts/.

Shipka, Jody. 2011. *Toward a Composition Made Whole*. Pittsburgh, PA: University of Pittsburgh Press.

Sirc, Geoffrey. 1997. "Never Mind the Tagmemics, Where's the Sex Pistols?" *College Composition and Communication* 48 (1): 9–29. doi:10.2307/358768.

Tate, Gary. 1993. "A Place for Literature in Freshman Composition." *College English* 55 (3): 317–21. doi:10.2307/378744.

Trimbur, John. 2011. *Solidarity or Service: Composition and the Problem of Expertise*. Portsmouth, NH: Boynton/Cook.

Westbrook, Steve. 2006. "Visual Rhetoric in a Culture of Fear: Impediments to Multimedia Production." *College English* 68 (5): 457–80. doi:10.2307/25472166.

Wysocki, Anne. 2003. "The Multiple Media of Texts: How Onscreen and Paper Texts Incorporate Words, Images, and Other Media." In *What Writing Does and How It Does It: An Introduction to Analyzing Texts and Textual Practices*, edited by Charles Bazerman and Paul Prior, 123–64. London: Routledge.

10

DIGITAL STORYTELLING IN THE L2 GRADUATE WRITING CLASSROOM
Expanding the Possibilities of Personal Expression and Textual Borrowing

Joel Bloch

INTRODUCTION

This chapter will explore the implementation of digital storytelling in a graduate L2 academic writing course. A digital story is a multimodal literacy that remixes the author's narration of a personal story with supporting texts, usually images or music either borrowed from the Internet or created by the storyteller (Lambert 2013). Christopher A. Hafner, Alice Chik, and Rodney H. Jones (2015) have identified remixing as one of the key elements of multimodality that can be introduced to students. Multimodality has been extensively discussed in academic writing (e.g., Kress 2003; 2005) and in composition courses in particular (Palmeri 2012; Selber 2004) and writing-across-the-discipline (WAC) courses (Reid, Snead, and Simoneaux 2016). Digital storytelling has its roots outside the classroom, often being used for political and social issues (Lambert 2013a) or for after-school activities (e.g., Hull and Katz 2006) as an alternative form of literacy to those that dominate traditional classroom assignments. There has been a growing interest in using digital stories in undergraduate L2 writing courses (e.g., Bloch 2015; Hafner 2015; Hafner, Chik, and Jones 2015; Nelson 2006) to meet a variety of goals for personal expression and academic discourse. There has also been interest in using digital storytelling as an alternative approach to immersing students in the potential of multimodality on the World Wide Web, as in the online course DST 106 (Burtis, cited in Levine, 2014), which attempts to give students greater control over their learning.

Regardless of the approach, digital storytelling foregrounds the voices of the students. Glynda Hull and Mira-Louise Katz (2006) argue that telling their narratives helps storytellers position themselves in

DOI: 10.7330/9781607327974.c010

relationship to their audience, thus providing the storyteller with an agentive self, much like the author of an academic text has. They build on Jerome Bruner's (1994) research on narrative to argue that these personal moments in the narrative that digital storytelling builds on provide the storyteller an opportunity to develop their perceptions of their lives as a whole. It is this agentive self coupled with the use of textual borrowing that makes digital storytelling a potentially useful form of multimodality for the academic writing course, one that can be integrated with traditional print forms of academic writing. It was both the centrality of voice in an academic paper (e.g., Ivanič 1998) and the rhetorical importance of textual borrowing (e.g., Bazerman 1988; 2013; Latour 1987) in our academic writing courses that made digital storytelling seem to be a potentially important component of the graduate L2 course.

Textual borrowing refers to collecting, remixing, and transforming previously published texts—print, digital, and aural—to create new texts, which can then be borrowed again to create even more new texts. The goals for textual borrowing in the graduate writing courses evolved with more experience teaching. Visual images could be used to express ideas from new and different perspectives. However, over time, I began to explore the more rhetorical potential of the images in developing the students' narratives.

While print texts are still the most highly valued form of literacy in most academic writing courses, research has shown large increases in the amount of multimodal composing in writing classes (Reid, Snead, and Simoneaux 2016). However, there is concern among teachers about whether the increased time requirements, as well as the increased need for technical skills, can justify its implementation (Reid, Snead, and Simoneaux 2016). Teaching multimodal literacy can require additional classroom time, which may be problematic for an approach that may not be accepted among international students. There have been questions about moving digital storytelling inside the classroom. Mark Nelson (2006) found that contextualizing digital storytelling inside the L2 classroom created a "hindrance" towards authorship, which limited its authenticity. Nevertheless, the growing popularity of digital storytelling in the classroom has developed in conjunction with the growing importance in academic writing of constructing a discoursal voice and identity inside the text (e.g., Ivanič 1998). In the remainder of this chapter, I explore the relevance of this approach in graduate-level L2 writing courses.

TEACHING DIGITAL STORYTELLING IN A
GRADUATE-LEVEL L2 WRITING COURSE

Digital storytelling was implemented in a number of graduate and undergraduate writing courses by myself and a group of graduate teaching assistants. Initially, our implementation of digital storytelling in graduate classes was similar to its implementation in undergraduate courses since the goals in both classes were similar (Bloch 2012; 2015; Bloch and Wilkinson 2013). However, our goal for implementing digital storytelling in these graduate classes evolved to remediate problems with traditional writing assignments as well as to introduce alternate forms of literacy that would encourage students to view certain rhetorical issues from a different perspective than found in their print texts. In the digital story assignment, the students were asked to mix an explanation of their major with a story about their experiences in the field. The storytelling aspect has long been a metaphor for writing an academic research paper (e.g., Medawar 1984). John Swales and Christine Feak (2011) use the metaphor in the title of their guide to writing literature reviews: *Telling a Research Story: Writing a Literature Review.*

However, this sense of authorship found in storytelling has been more problematic in forms of literacy that require extensive amounts of textual borrowing (e.g., Bazerman 2013), with a concern that traditional, print assignments may constrain the expressions and the voices of these students in ways that may be detrimental to their overall literacy development. The introduction of multimodal literacy is also constrained by assumptions about the goals and literacy backgrounds of the students.

Underlying the growing popularity of digital storytelling has been the assumption that everybody has a story to tell, and that by sharing these stories, creators can gain a degree of ownership over their stories, which, in turn, could help them claim ownership over all aspects of the academic writing process. The research on digital storytelling outside the classroom has illustrated the potential of alternative forms of literacy for promoting what Hull and Katz (2006) called an "agentive self" (44). With this perspective on agency, students can free themselves of the constraints textual borrowing can place on expressing their own claims (Bazerman 2013). Digital storytelling, therefore, may be seen as an integral part of teaching students to negotiate the constraints (e.g., Bazerman 1988) traditionally found in academic writing.

Hull and Katz (2006) show creators can appropriate a variety of texts to contextualize their own narratives in terms of their own goals and the constraints of the context. Citing Mikhail Bakhtin, Nelson (2006) argues that digital storytelling allows for a rethinking of authorship by allowing students to "populate" the ideas of others with their own "intentions" (57). Since graduate students would be expected to later publish their research (e.g., Lillis and Curry 2014), the ease with which digital stories could be shared with audiences both inside and outside the classroom fulfills a long-term goal of giving students the opportunity to create for a larger audience than only the instructor.

The research into alternative forms of multimodality literacies (e.g., Knobel and Lanksher 2007; Kress 2003; New London Group 1996) has paved the way for considering how multimodal literacies can be implemented as an alternative form of literacy in a composition course. The New London Group's argument that these new forms of literacy should "count" as much as traditional forms of literacy do can support teachers in implementing alternate forms of literacy, and this argument can be applied to any form of digital literacy.

Researchers have identified various problems students often experience with textual borrowing (e.g., Bazerman 1988; 2013; Blum 2010; Howard 1999; Pecorari 2015; Shi 2008). There has been extensive research on the connection between agency and textual borrowing in academic genres (e.g., Bazerman 1988; 2013; Latour 1987), and for many years, researchers have attempted to categorize the rhetorical purposes for textual borrowing (e.g., Geisler 2016). Andreas Karotsolis (2016) argues for four categories for classifying textual borrowing: reference citations that point to the text; evaluative citations that contain some reference to the creator's opinion; elaborative citations that are used to develop claims; and citations that comment on the creator's project. Bruno Latour (1987) introduced a more rhetorical framework for using citations in which textual borrowing can be used to support the claims of the author, show weaknesses or differences in those citations that seem to contradict the author's claims, and establish the credibility or ethos of the author.

However, this role textual borrowing can play may have detrimental effects on student writing. These problems could result from deference to the texts published by scholars in prestigious journals, which can repress the natural, evaluative power of their own voices. Charles Bazerman (2013) has pointed out that the danger of textual borrowing can be found in how the texts overpower the voice of the writer so writers can be "written" by the texts they borrow. In considering undergraduates' use of academic texts, discussions of plagiarism have often focused on the difficulties students have with textual borrowing. Susan Debra Blum (2009) found that students may not understand why they are borrowing the texts. Mike Rose (1989) similarly found students may not understand the meaning of the text, which, in his examples, could lead inexperienced students to plagiarize to complete an assignment. Although the students in the graduate courses often had much more background knowledge in their disciplines than did undergraduate students, they often had used the same copying strategies in their written texts, which could lead to charges of academic misconduct.

While textual borrowing in a digital story differs from that in an academic paper, its importance in the digital story can increase student awareness of the purposes for this textual borrowing (Nelson 2006) and its role in developing the author's voice. Therefore, combining digital storytelling with traditional academic writing can give students multiple perspectives on text creation. It was hoped that textual borrowing in this multimodal literacy could help with textual borrowing in print texts, although finding evidence for this transfer has been difficult.[1]

Implementing digital storytelling in the L2 graduate course required a greater focus on connecting multimodality with the other aspects of our academic writing curriculum, partially because there was more resistance from the graduate students to this kind of assignment. Since the work of John Swales on genre (1991), academic writing at the graduate level has been considered different from writing at the undergraduate level. Graduate students often expect to do more academically focused writing, such as research papers, than do undergraduate students. Anecdotally, a few graduate students occasionally resisted the implementation of digital storytelling, often because of the extra expenditure of time and the lack of apparent relevance to other forms of writing.

Certain aspects of digital storytelling, such as narratives, have long been metaphors fused in academic writing for reporting on research or writing a literature review (e.g., Medawar 1984), as have images and photos (e.g., Kress 2003; 2005). In this chapter, I first discuss the role of digital storytelling as a form of literacy in an academic writing class. I then examine three digital stories created by international graduate students to explore how these students responded to the digital-story assignment. The analysis of the stories presented here was influenced by the goal of implementing digital storytelling, which was to help students better understand this connection between textual borrowing and developing their own voices, so that will be the primary basis for the questions to be addressed here:

> For what purposes do students choose texts in their digital stories?
>
> How do students mix their own voices with the voices from the borrowed texts?
>
> How do the stories compare to the other print assignments given in the class?

DIGITAL STORYTELLING AS A FORM OF ACADEMIC LITERACY

In previous courses, the L2 graduate students had sometimes chosen to write about the relationship between their major and their personal life, and they sometimes struggled with integrating their own voices. For example, a Korean graduate student wrote a first draft on studying ichthyology that lacked any personal content, even though the particular assignment asked students to define a topic related to their major. In his revision, he added a section on how he had worked in his family's fish market and had spent his free time fishing, which had led him to graduate school to study ichthyology.

The main change for the graduate writing classes was in adding the digital-story assignment and then attempting to frame it as part of the academic writing curriculum. Initially, students could choose any story they wanted to tell as long as the story had a pivotal moment to focus on. Second, in order to reduce the time required to search for texts, students were encouraged to use their own photos. The digital-story assignment replaced a definition paper assignment found in John M. Swales and Christine B. Feak's textbook on academic writing (2004). In that assignment, the students often "copied" information from the Internet, perhaps because the students seemed to feel they could not add anything to what was in *Wikipedia*. Therefore, digital storytelling about the students' experiences in their disciplinary communities could add an agentive dimension to the assignment that could not be copied from the Internet, while the rhetorical goals surrounding textual borrowing could be introduced as they were with the print assignments.

DISCUSSION OF THREE DIGITAL STORIES

In this section, three stories chosen from the academic writing class for L2 graduate students is discussed to discuss how these students negotiated the constraints of the assignment.

In "Special Education," a Korean graduate student discusses his field of special education, the students he worked with, and how he met his future wife. Students often begin their stories with a series of reference citations that establish who they are and the field in which they are studying. He begins with a segment depicting his background in special education in Korea, discussing his work, its importance, and the problems he faced. Many of the key concepts reflect what was also focused on in the academic print texts. He uses images of his students to introduce his topic of the variety of students he teachers (table 10.2: images 1–4), which is mixed with the narration of his story. He uses the

Table 10.1. Digital stories discussed in paper

Country of Origin	Major Field	Topic(s)	Title
Korea	Special Education	kinds of children; reasons for coming to the United States; finding a wife	"Special Education" (http://go.osu.edu/speced)
Taiwan	Industrial Design	children's dreams; choosing a major; frustrations along the way	"The Road towards My Dreams" (http://go.osu.edu/road)
Colombia	Entomology	background; research; overcoming fear of insects; advisor; marriage	"José's Digital Story" (http://go.osu.edu/arcology)

textual borrowing of images to support his claim that these students have the potential to accomplish many things. These images both establish the identity of the student as a teacher of special education and an insight into the kinds of children he teaches. He then explores his decision to come to the United States, adding a short coda about how he met his wife, who is also a special-education teacher. This coda adds a very personal conclusion to the importance of his decision to continue his studies.

While his digital story works in explaining his major and his personal relationship to it, it includes additional aspects of a formal research paper. Each sequence of text and images seems to answer critical, rhetorical questions also asked in print texts (e.g., Swales 1991): Why is this problem important? What is the significance of the results of the study? Even the coda about his marriage adds a personal evaluation of the significance of the work, as might be found in the conclusion of an academic paper. This approach illustrates an interesting way in which, through this remixing process, the author can repurpose the remixed texts for different rhetorical purposes.

The format of the digital story also closely resembles an academic paper. This narrative begins with a problem statement about disabled children, adds a solution to the problem, and then adds a discussion of the importance of his work. The digital story, however, goes beyond the problem with evaluation often found in a print assignment by including personal experiences that serve to evaluate the significance of the author's field.

Much of what the students did with these texts raised important points about originality and transformation they often struggled with in their print texts. By placing the borrowed texts in conjunction with the author's claim, the resulting remixing can transform both texts into a new and, what Latour (1988) found to be, stronger claim. The

Table 10.2. "Special Education" (https://vimeo.com/86073327)

Image	Text
1.	How do they think of disability or people with disabilities?
2.	They are not living in other societies; they are living with us in our society.
3.	There merely have some to their tasks.
4.	So if someone would provide a little better method in order to overcome their limits, they should be better.

relationships in table 10.2 between text and image illustrate what Kress (2003) found even in more static relationships on the printed page: that an image does not just "express a thousand words" or even the same information differently, but by remixing images and texts, the content is transformed to express new meanings, in this case in more personal ways.

Many of the author's images support his claims about the potential of his students, some of which could not have been understood if he had used one mode alone. In one image, for example, the smiling face of a boy with a thumbs-up illustrates the successes the narrator expresses. The video showing the different abilities of the children supports the narrator's claim that these children have a variety of athletic abilities. While these uses of images exemplify the various rhetorical purposes for textual borrowing, the images are remixed with his own narrative, thus giving the viewers an insight into the narrative that could not be achieved with only print texts. Remixing transforms his print text into a more deeply personal statement than students' print texts usually do.

The relationships between his texts and images also illustrate how the assignment could deal with some of the students' problems with textual borrowing. Here, the student was not being be "written" by the texts as is often feared or may occur in the literature reviews of academic papers, where texts appear to have been "regurgitated" to demonstrate they have been read (e.g., Blum 2010). His own voice, boosted by the images he chose to remix with the narrative, presents a powerful story about special-education teachers while immersing the student in the same processes he would use in his academic writing.

Another course goal was to study the possible relationships between text and image in order for the students to explore how authors can control these images for their own rhetorical purposes. Using such textual borrowing for rhetorical purposes was an important focus in the course, but here again digital storytelling provided an alternative perspective. With print texts, using reporting verbs was discussed to show the difference between the students' ideas and those of the authors of the texts (e.g., Bloch 2010). The purpose of the images could not be controlled in that way but relied more on the viewer's interpretation to connect the text and the images.

In "The Road to My Dreams," a Taiwanese student narrates her decision to study industrial design and come to the United States through her mixing of text, image, and music. As I show below, the interpretation of these connections was often left to the viewer. However, the organization of her digital story retains the more traditional linear pattern of an academic paper. She begins at childhood, remixing a series of images of children role-playing to stand for the different goals the children may have. The images were borrowed from the Internet, but through her narrative, she appropriates these images to represent how she saw herself as being different from other children. The viewer can connect the images to the possible dreams of other children in order to interpret the ambiguity of her decision-making process

She explores the ability to control the texts in how she mixes the same image with different texts: she twice uses an image of a mother and daughter with different narrations showing different relationships with her mother depending on her choice of discipline to study. In terms of her roles as a student and as a daughter, she first describes herself as a rebellious daughter but later as a dutiful daughter who chooses a field of study her mother would approve.

In another sequence on possible career choices, she uses the juxtaposition of images to evaluate the possible implications of her career decisions. She uses one image of a little boy in a suit looking at a computer to represent the "practical" life she does not want to have. Operating under the constraints of the texts and her goals for using them forces the student to "turn," using Latour's (1987) argument, the image to meet her rhetorical purpose. Again, the viewer must connect the narrative and the visual texts. Here, the narration can better control that

Table 10.3. "The Road to My Dreams" (https://www.youtube.com/watch?v=eyL2SqP5L00&index=22&list=UUqFZU2ZlofNcg0BxQ9-zVSg)

Image	Text
5.	Now I am at OSU taking some design courses waiting to
6.	take the entrance exam to get into the industrial design major.
7.	I know it is not going to be easy, only eighteen students are going to be enrolled every year
8.	I am not sure how my road towards my dream will be like.

interpretation by using different discoursal forms than those found in a print text but with a similar rhetorical goal.

Another problem our instructors struggled with in the course was having the students express their identities within the constraints of an academic paper (e.g., Bazerman 1988; 2013). Contemporary research on academic writing has shown the expression of identity is a key aspect of academic writing although the students often struggled including their identities in their research. Digital storytelling provided an alternative perspective on such expression, in part because of the different processes used in remixing image and text and in part because of the greater array of semiotic materials available to use.

The students remixed these materials in various ways to express their authorial identity. One way this student remixed materials was through her choice of various images of herself: with friends and her mother, studying in a coffee shop, working at a computer, feeling frustrated, and showing her university ID to represent her final decision. In another example, the student's rhetorical goal seems to differentiate the creation of products with their design in order to explain her major. In images 5–8 in table 10.3, she explores her current situation at the university and the difficulty of her decision to choose her major. The images both depict who she is now and her future life in the design classroom, assuming she overcomes the difficulties expressed in her narration.

Her use of these images for various rhetorical purposes illustrates what A. Suresh Canagarajah (2016) calls "co-construction" to describe how English-language learners appropriate the resources of one language to create their own meanings in another language. The various semiotic materials are not languages as Canagarajah describes them but have to do more generally with how these different modes of literacy can interact. Digital storytelling allows students freedom to coconstruct meaning through textual borrowing. For instance, the student wants to represent her struggle in college by choosing a cluttered desk to represent her dilemma. She does not seem to simply represent information in a different way but through the remixing process, creating a more transformative meaning that goes beyond the original meaning.

Her ability, to expand on Canagarajah's (2016, 12) words, to "shuttle" among different modes of texts, allows her not only to create different perspectives on her life but to also give different meanings to the texts themselves. Digital storytelling allows for "shuttling" between different modes of expression (written, oral, and image) but through different forms of textuality, both academic and nonacademic, thus retaining its outside-the-classroom roots while incorporating many of the characteristics of the context in which it has been implemented. The student uses remixing throughout her movie as a means to fulfilling the goals of the assignment—to remix the personal and the professional aspects of her lives. As she narrates her goals for her future, she shows a number of images related to design and her studying at the university. Here again, the two texts represent different kinds of information, which are then remixed together to give a potentially new, transformative meaning to both texts.

The third mode of identity expression is through voice. Joe Lambert (2013) argues that it is crucial for digital-story creators to voice their own narratives. Lambert writes, "This is why my first person voice—the way I talk to myself about my own experience—is never far from the perspectives I am sharing. I realize that the story of ideas I am telling comes out of my own journey. They could not possibly fit any other human's story perfectly in alignment" (11). For our goals, voicing was seen as part of the process of creating a voice in the text. Multimodal assignments have revived the interest in integrating aurality with other modes of expression (Selfe 2009). Besides the voice of the narrator, a further use of aurality is the use of music. Choosing music is somewhat more problematic, both in legal terms and in technical terms, than choosing images since it can interfere with the narrative. In some personal stories, the music was the central feature as the students explored their own

Table 10.4. A sequence of text and image from "José's Digital Story" (https://vimeo.com /86073325)

Image	Text
9.	The United States University is one of the largest research centers in mites and ticks around the world.
10.	When a friend of my school who studied biology asked me to join her on a field trip.
11.	How can you be in danger with so many soldiers around you?
12.	The best part is that I am not dreaming alone.

relationships with the music they loved. Often it was used as an additional mode of expression for adding a level of meaning. In the digital story, the student adds a soundtrack with the refrain "nobody knows me at all," which, somewhat ironically, encapsulates the purpose of creating and sharing digital stories.

As Latour (1987) has argued, the actor in an academic paper must construct an identity in their paper. Constructing such identifies has been a major difficulty in our writing classes, but the presence of stories allows the creators to foreground their identities in ways that had been difficult in their academic papers. "José's Digital Story" tells the story of a student from Columbia coming to the university to study insects. It begins with the use of reference citations to introduce the student through an image, a map of Colombia, and a brief introduction to his research in mites and ticks (acology) at the university (table 10.4, image 9). He also uses another series of reference citations to show his movement between the university and Colombia.

The goal of his story seems to explore the tension between his goal to study insects and his early fear of them. As with the previous story, the problem to be analyzed was a personal one. His problem analysis and possible solution are first discussed in his account of how a trip to the jungle in Columbia helped him overcome his fear. His digital story follows the structure of the definition paper beginning with the problem statement outlining the contradiction between his current area of study and his initial fear of these insects he was studying, which may explain why this story is important to him.

The personal nature of his problem and the serious goals of his study were both expressed through his choices of academic and comic images of the insects. One advantage of the abundance of semiotic materials available for them to use (e.g., Hull and Katz 2006; Nelson 2006) is that they allow the student to choose both scientific and comic representations of the insects he is studying, which he seems to use to provide his audience different representations of these audiences. Unlike the kinds of photos one might expect in a scientific paper, which he does use, many of his images are of large, cartoonish bugs that seem to invoke a sense of fear, reflecting the personal theme in his digital story.

Throughout José's digital story, his texts are frequently drawn from various popular cultures. In some cases, appropriating cultural materials can lead to what is sometimes called *linguistic imperialism*, in which the meanings of the materials reflect the culture rather than the experiences of the creator. However, as was often the case, he controls these materials to explore his identity in the movie. For example, he juxtaposes the narration of his desire to be an explorer with a poster of Harrison Ford in *Indiana Jones* and an image of himself climbing a mountain.

There are critical uses of textual borrowing as well. His narration contrasts images of his research with images of his childhood fear of insects and later of his overcoming this fear on a trip to the Colombian jungle (table 10.4, image 10). As was mentioned earlier, this juxtaposition between the images and the text can create a space for the viewer's interpretation that may not be present in the conventional academic paper. By retelling his story of overcoming his fear of insects, José constructs an identity within the narrative by playfully reflecting on his limitations. He appropriates often grotesque images of insects along with his images exploring his narrative of his trip to the jungle in contrast to the more scientific images he uses later in his digital story.

As with the digital story on special education, the personal nature of the text is supported by the mixing of images with the narrative. These modes are mixed together to elaborate on both his fear and his ability to overcome this fear. Through this remixing process, the narrative is transformed into a new format, incorporating both the narrative of the academic paper and his narrative. His digital story follows the structure of the definition paper beginning with the problem statement outlining the contradiction between his current area of study and his initial fear of these insects he was studying, which explains why the story is important to him. Unlike the images taken from the Internet in his previous discussion of mites and ticks, he relies primarily on his own collection of photos for describing his life.

Differences in digital story content can necessitate inclusion of different types of images, as indicated by his often-playful use of images that demystify the insects he is studying. His use of images is more realistic when he depicts his academic community and his research. Once he has described overcoming his fear of insects, José shifts to narrating his involvement in his research on mites and his motivations for coming to the United States. He mostly uses his own images of himself doing research or of his advisor in the United States. Even the more formal images, however, retain a sense of whimsy by featuring large captions like "Mites Suck." Hampered by a lack of funding, José's journey to graduate school was not smooth, which he illustrates with separate images of maps first showing his trip to the United States and then his return to Colombia. However, the story does not end there, as his would-be advisor later contacted him and asked him to return to the jungle to search for a rare mite. This eventually led him back to the United States to find, as is also seen in the Korean digital story discussed above, not only a research topic for a PhD (table 10.4, image 12) but also a spouse. The story concludes with a mixing of the academic and personal lives of the storyteller.

The three stories discussed here illustrate another important course goal for instruction in textual borrowing: responding to the needs of the audience. Throughout his story, José uses textual borrowing to address concerns of the audience. For example, Colombia is often identified in the media as a haven for drug lords, so José feels he must counter that stereotype (table 10.4, image 11). Similarly, the insects he is studying have a negative reputation, which he feels he also needs to address. This segment (images 9–12) begins with a scientific explanation comparing his field to the study of other insects.

While the rhetorical constraints on an academic paper differ from those on a digital story, digital storytelling allowed students to explore these moves in ways that seemed to free them from the conventions of the academic paper. Students, for example, often had a problem with making evaluations, perhaps reflecting a tradition in which the data should be allowed to speak for itself. From a rhetorical perspective, José's conclusion on the importance of his research, not only to his career but also to his in life, illustrates an important rhetorical move that the graduate students often struggled with in their formal academic papers but that were more easily expressed in their digital stories.

DISCUSSION AND CONCLUSION

It is not the contention here that digital storytelling could replace academic writing assignments in a graduate-level writing class, particularly for students who will spend most of their academic careers writing print-based research papers. However, this approach is consistent with Hafner, Chik, and Jones's (2015) argument on the importance of multimodality for creating more personalized learning environments for L2 students.

There were also issues that could be dealt with in more depth than they had been previously included in the courses. Clearly, one was the issue of visual representation (e.g., Kress 2003). Another was the question of the use of visual intellectual property. Hafner (2015) argues that the principles, or what one might call the *affordances of remixing*, can be leveraged into new discussions of the approaches to textual borrowing found in different forms of literacy. Hafner sees the value of having the students address the issues of copyright textual borrowing from the Internet entails (e.g., Aufderheide and Jaszi 2012). Introducing intellectual property law was an important goal of the course since it impacts the use of textual borrowing in conventional print texts as well as multimodal ones.

Perhaps more interesting is how the students were able to go beyond our initial plans for digital storytelling. As Hafner (2015) found, L2 students do not always position themselves as authors in the ways teachers expect, nor do they use textual borrowing as is expected, particularly in their choice of images. Their recording of their narratives, as well as their need to interact during the production of the videos and their sharing their stories both inside class and online, brought a new dimension of aurality to a composition course that often lacked this mode of expression (e.g., Selfe 2009).

Our goals for achieving this personalization necessitated its being adapted to meet the needs and interests of our graduate students as well as to meet the goals of our course. Despite the connections between digital storytelling and academic writing, our course pedagogy had its own unique goals that needed to be accommodated by the introduction of multimodality, which could remediate some of the problems students had with the goals of original assignments. At the same time, the ability of the students to explore their assignment from different perspectives and for different purposes created a balance between our goals and theirs, which again was not often found in this course.

The reasons for their enthusiasm for the digital-story process were not necessarily the same as our reasons for implementing them. The aurality of the digital story, for example, helped students connect this assignment with oral-presentation skills that could be useful in their own teaching and academic careers. However, despite our revisions to the assignment, there was still some resistance to the amount of time involved in digital storytelling. As one student put it in her blog on her digital story, "I understand that the process of making a video is a good opportunity to study how to using soft of making video, but the same presentation could use PowerPoint or electronic book. That will save our time to do something else." This "something else" was of great importance to both the students and teachers, but many of the interesting findings presented here were not made clear to the students. I attempted to respond to this resistance by having them rely more on using their personal photographs than on downloading images from the Internet, which could reduce the time spent searching for images online, although as shown here, the students did not always follow this advice.

Student resistance also led us to emphasize more the potential for transfer of skills across the assignments, hoping the students would better see the importance of these alternative literacies for their print writing. There has been a growing interest in what is called "teaching to transfer," (e.g., Anson and Moore 2017; Yancey, Robertson, and Taczak 2014), which focuses on how explicit teaching can help students connect assignments. In our course, digital storytelling was taught in parallel to the print assignments over the fourteen-week semester. Although there was no pedagogical intention for this approach, the parallel design could further facilitate skill transfer across the two domains, providing that the students could see the connections between these different literacies (e.g., Perkins and Salomon 1988).

To support the transfer process, several activities were modified to promote more reflection. Students had to create a storyboard in which they matched pieces of their narratives with the images they used. They inserted a thumbnail of the image into one column of a table and the piece of text into the second column, as the figures show. To promote more reflection, the students discussed their choices of images as a way for them to think about their use of images as texts. Sometimes, previous exercises were modified for these goals. The students were then asked to reflect on why they matched an image to a piece of text.

I have struggled with this issue in various ways (Bloch 2015), and the issue of transfer is not resolved here. Gita DasBender (2016) used reflective essays to study transfer; the blogging assignments DasBender studied provided a space for reflection on the relationship between multimodal and print texts. Our students could reflect on their experiences, although they did not always focus on the rhetorical issues we were interested in but often focused on their experiences in graduate school. As this Chinese student blogged,

> First, this assignment actually give me a chance to look back and see what I did, why did I ends up studying computer science and how did I get here. These are things that I don't give much thoughts before. And it is important because sometimes we just too busy with what we are doing but forget why we are doing it at the first place. Doing the digital story give me the chance to refresh the memory. Also I learned how to use movie maker to make a small movie. That is something really useful. I can use it to create a story about my life here at the end of my time here. I believe that will be so interesting and so meaningful. And it will be much more interesting than me showing a bunch of pictures to my friends.

Many of the students blogged on the value of examining their experiences and decisions that led them to graduate school. The blogs indicated how the students could construct themselves as agents through their reflections about their experiences in graduate school. From these reflections, the instructors learned more about what the graduate students considered both important and, in some cases, frustrating about the assignment. The requirement to screen the stories for the class and sometimes post them on YouTube was also designed to help students reflect on their choices in the stories in relationship to their potential audiences. In subsequent classes, students created rubrics for having their audiences evaluate their stories.

The issue of transfer still remains an outstanding concern. Nevertheless, this analysis, as well as the students' reflections, demonstrates the value of multimodal assignments that often went beyond our own goals. Canagarajah (2016) refers to this lack of control, or what is sometimes called "chaos," as reflective of the new postmodern classroom, in which assignments such as digital storytelling fit well. While the creation of digital stories can itself be a valuable experience for graduate students to explore some of the key concepts in academic writing, such "chaos" can also be valuable for students and teachers, as control of the assignment becomes a more shared experience.

NOTE

1. Digital storytelling was not the only method used to deal with this issue. Students had to evaluate and blog about the texts they had read before writing their papers.

REFERENCES

Anson, Chris, and Jessica Moore. 2017. *Critical Transitions: Writing and the Question of Transfer.* Fort Collins, CO: WAC Clearinghouse. https://wac.colostate.edu/books/ansonmoore.

Aufderheide, Patricia, and Peter Jaszi. 2011. *Reclaiming Fair Use: How to Put Balance Back in Copyright.* Chicago, IL: University of Chicago Press.

Bazerman, Charles. 1988. *Shaping Written Knowledge: The Genre and Activity of the Experimental Article in Science.* Madison: University of Wisconsin Press.

Bazerman, Charles. 2013. *A Rhetoric of Literate Action.* Fort Collins, CO: WAC Clearinghouse. http://wac.colostate.edu/books/literateaction/v1/.

Bloch, Joel. 2010. "A Concordance-based Study of the Use of Reporting Verbs as Rhetorical Devices in Academic Papers." *Journal of Writing Research* 2 (2): 219–44. http://www.jowr.org/articles/vol2_2/JoWR_2010_vol2_nr2_Bloch.pdf.

Bloch, Joel. 2012. *Plagiarism, Intellectual Property and the Teaching of L2 Writing.* Bristol: Multilingual Matters.

Bloch, Joel. 2015. "The Use of Digital Storytelling in an Academic Writing Course: The Story of an Immigrant." In *Teaching U.S.-Educated Multilingual Writers: Practices from and for the Classroom,* edited by Mark Roberge, Kay Loesy, and Margi Wald. Ann Arbor: University of Michigan Press.

Bloch, Joel, and Mark J. Wilkinson. 2013. *Teaching Digital Literacies.* Alexandria, VA: TESOL International.

Blum, Susan Debra. 2010. *My Word!: Plagiarism and College Culture.* Ithaca, NY: Cornell University Press.

Bruner, Jerome. 1994. "The Remembered Self." In *The Remembering Self: Construction and Agency in Self-Narrative,* edited by Ulric Neisser and Robyn Fivush, 41–54. Cambridge: Cambridge University Press.

Canagarajah, A. Suresh. 2016. "TESOL as a Professional Community: A Half-Century of Pedagogy, Research, and Theory." *TESOL Quarterly* 50 (1): 7–41.

DasBender, Gita. 2016. "Liminal Space as a Generative Site of Struggle: Writing Transfer and L2 Students." In *Critical Transitions: Writing and the Question of Transfer,* edited by Chris Anson and Jesse Moore. Fort Collins, CO: WAC Clearinghouse. http://wac.colostate.edu/books/ansonmoore/transfer.pdf.

Geisler, Cheryl. 2016. "Opening: Toward an Integrated Approach." *Journal of Writing Research* 7 (3): 417–24. http://www.jowr.org/articles/vol7_3/JoWR_2016_vol7_nr3_Geisler(1).pdf.

Hafner, Christopher A. 2015. "Remix Culture and English Language Teaching: The Expression of Learner Voice in Digital Multimodal Compositions." *TESOL Quarterly* 49 (3): 486–509.

Hafner, Christopher A., Alice Chik, and Rodney H. Jones. 2015. "Digital Literacies and Language Learning." *Language Learning and Technology* 19 (3):1–7. http://llt.msu.edu/issues/october2015/commentary.pdf.

Howard, Rebecca Moore. 1999. *Standing in the Shadow of Giants: Plagiarists, Authors, Collaborators.* Stamford, CT: Ablex.

Hull, Glynda, and Katz, Mira-Louise. 2006. "Crafting an Agentive Self: Case Studies of Digital Storytelling." *Research in the Teaching of English* 41 (1): 43–81.

Ivanič, Roz. 1998. *Writing and Identity: The Discoursal Construction of Identity in Academic Writing.* Amsterdam: John Benjamins.

Karatsolis, Andreas. 2016. "Rhetorical Patterns in Citations across Disciplines and Levels of Participation." *Journal of Writing Research* 7 (3): 425–52.

Knobel, Michele, and Colin Lankshear. 2007. *A New Literacies Sampler.* New York: Peter Lang.

Kress, Gunther. 2003. *Literacy in the New Media Age.* London: Routledge.

Kress, Gunther. 2005. "Gains and Losses: New Forms of Texts, Knowledge, and Learning." *Computers and Composition* 22 (1): 5–22.

Lambert, Joe. 2013a. Digital Storytelling: Capturing Lives, Creating Community. New York: Routledge Press.

Lambert, Joe. 2013b. Seven Stages: Story and the Human Experience. Berkeley, CA: Digital Diner.

Latour, Bruno. 1987. Science in Action: How to Follow Scientists and Engineers through Society. Cambridge, MA: Harvard University Press.

Levine, Alan. 2014. "A MOOC or Not a MOOC: ds106 Questions the Form." In *Invasion of the MOOCs: The Promises and Perils of Massive Open Online Courses*, edited by Steven D. Krause and Charles Lowe, 25–39. Anderson, SC: Parlor Press.

Lillis, Theresa, and Mary Jane Curry. 2014. Academic Writing in a Global Context: The Politics and Practice of Publishing in English. London: Routledge.

Medawar, Peter. 1984. Pluto's Republic: Incorporating the Art of the Soluble and Induction and Intuition in Scientific Thought. Cambridge: Oxford University Press.

Nelson, Mark. E. 2006. "Mode, Meaning, and Synaesthesia in Multimedia L2 Writing." Language Learning and Technology 10 (2): 56–76.

New London Group. 1996. "A Pedagogy of Multiliteracies: Designing Social Futures." Harvard Educational Review 66 (1): 60–92. http://newarcproject.pbworks.com/f/Peda gogy%2Bof%2BMultiliteracies_New%2BLondon%2BGroup.pdf.

Palmeri, Jason. 2012. *Remixing Composition: A History of Multimodal Writing Pedagogy*. Carbondale: Southern Illinois University Press.

Pecorari, Diane. 2015. *Academic Writing and Plagiarism: A Linguistic Analysis*. London: Bloomsbury.

Perkins, David, and Gavriel Salomon. 1988. "Teaching for Transfer." *Educational Leadership* 46 (1): 22–32.

Reid, Gwendolynne, Robin Snead, and Brent Simoneaux. 2016. "Multimodal Communication in the University: Surveying Faculty across Disciplines." *Across the Disciplines* 13 (1). https://wac.colostate.edu/atd/articles/reidetal2016.cfm.

Rose, Mike. 1989. *Lives on the Boundary: A Moving Account of the Struggles and Achievements of America's Educational Underclass*. New York: Penguin Books.

Selber, Stuart A. 2004. *Multiliteracies for a Digital Age*. Carbondale: Southern Illinois University Press.

Selfe, Cynthia L. 2009. "The Movement of Air, the Breath of Meaning: Aurality and Multimedia Composing." *College Composition and Communication* 60 (4): 616–63.

Swales, John. 1991. *Research Genres: Explorations and Applications*. Cambridge: Cambridge University Press.

Swales, John M., and Christine B. Feak. 2011. *Telling a Research Story: Writing a Literature Review*. Ann Arbor: University of Michigan Press.

Swales, John M., and Christine B. Feak. 2012. *Academic Writing for Graduate Students: Essential Tasks and Skills*, 3rd edition. Ann Arbor: University of Michigan Press.

Yancey, Kathleen Blake, Liane Robertson, and Kara Taczak. 2014. *Writing Across Contexts*. Logan: Utah State University Press.

11

MULTIMODALITY, TRANSFER, AND RHETORICAL AWARENESS
Analyzing the Choices of Undergraduate Writers

Stephen Ferruci and Susan DeRosa

INTRODUCTION

In this essay, we investigate how students make use of different modal affordances to respond to specific rhetorical situations. To do so, we analyze students' alphabetic texts (e.g., research essays), their multimodal texts (e.g., video PSAs), and students' self-reflective narratives as they transform their material from primarily alphabetic texts to multimodal ones. Using our students' examples, we examine how writers' rhetorical awareness and their abilities to articulate their choices for design, content, and medium are affected when they are asked to engage with different modes. We see a trend emerging from students' texts and metanarratives suggesting writers develop a facility with and awareness of writing for a particular context and audience when we ask them to use multiple modes of communication. As a result, we argue students are better prepared to address complex rhetorical situations when they make use of multiple modes and their affordances.

MULTIMODAL WRITING AND ITS SIGNIFICANCE IN WRITING STUDIES

Multimodal writing, the use of multiple modes (aural, visual, tactile, gestural, etc.) for communication, has become an important aspect of research and scholarship in the field of writing studies. But it wasn't always so. Cynthia L. Selfe (2004, 72) argued that "if our profession continues to focus solely on teaching only alphabetic composition . . . we run the risk of making composition studies . . . irrelevant to students engaging in contemporary practices of communicating." Similarly, Jody Shipka (2005, 278) urged the field to "begin asking how the purposeful uptake, transformation, incorporation, combination, juxtaposition,

DOI: 10.7330/9781607327974.c011

and even three-dimensional layering of words and visuals—as well as textures, sounds, scents, and even tastes—provide us with still other ways of imagining the work students might produce for the composition course." Both Selfe and Shipka echo NCTE's Resolution on Composing with Nonprint Media: "New Media . . . are transforming the communications experiences of young people outside of school" (National Council of Teachers of English 2003). NCTE's resolution in turn reflects assertions by the New London Group (1996, 65): "The languages needed to make meaning are radically changing in" all aspects of our lives. The many ways in which digital media and tools have come to redefine and remake our personal and public lives and what we think of as writing was articulated a decade later by Pamela Takayoshi and Selfe (2007, 3); they argued that "students need to be experienced and skilled not only in reading (consuming) texts employing multiple modalities, but also in composing in multiple modalities, if they hope to communicate successfully within the digital communication networks that characterize workplaces, schools, civic life, and span traditional cultural, national, and geopolitical borders." The call is clear: we must teach students how to use multiple modalities in their writing.

Of course, multimodal writing is more than adding a picture here or some color there. It is not just that there are photos or graphs or charts in a research report but that there is deliberate choice made by the composer about why those are included. This deliberate, conscious attention raises a number of productive questions. What do writers and their audiences gain from the inclusion of images or sound, for example? How might nonmaterial modes enable both a different conception of a rhetorical situation and the ways a composer engages that situation? How might those modes assist an audience's comprehension of the message? What possibilities for communication do multimodal texts offer that are rhetorically distinct from more traditional alphabetic texts? We think multimodal writers learn that print text is not only complemented by visual or aural modes but that those modes hold an equal place in communication. Cary Jewitt (2011, 14) reminds us that "gaze, gesture and posture for instance tend to be considered a support to speech . . . and image is often thought to be in a supportive relation to writing. Multimodal research across a range of social settings casts doubt on this assumption." Throughout the production of their multimodal projects our students ask, "So we don't have to write a paper?" One of our challenges, then, is to help writers see how other modes have rhetorical functions as much as does alphabetic text and that visuals or audio do not simply complement the written word but function in equal capacity to communicate. Multimodal writing presumes communication of any kind relies on many modes, and each, taken together or separately, "contribute[s] equally to meaning" (Jewitt 2011, 15).

Since the New London Group outlined the role new media technologies would have on our teaching and students' learning, scholars have examined the *affordances* (possibilities for communication) of different modes for creating and communicating meaning, with particular attention to how digital and Web 2.0 technologies enable different kinds of communication. Takayoshi and Selfe (2007, 5) highlight specifically the rhetorical possibilities of multimodality, noting that "audio and visual composing requires attention to rhetorical principles of communication." They go on to discuss how conventional rhetorical concerns—audience, arrangement, and so forth—are equally important in visual and audio compositions. Selfe (2009, 643) argues that "composition classrooms can provide a context not only for *talking about* different literacies, but also for *practicing* different literacies, learning to create texts that combine a range of modalities as communicative resources: exploring their affordances, the special capabilities they offer to authors; identifying what audiences expect of texts that deploy different modalities and how they respond to such texts." It's worth pointing out, though, that as a field we tend to conflate the multimodal with the digital when in fact there are many multimodal analog texts that students produce. Multimodality should therefore "not to be confused with or limited in advance to a consideration of Web-based or new media texts" (Shipka 2009, W347). We agree with this distinction. In any case, our students already make use of new media and multimodal compositions in their personal and professional lives, and we must help them do so critically and effectively. For us, this means helping them think about modes rhetorically.

However, as writing scholars have argued, we need more research into how students learn through multimodal writing. Blaine Smith (2014, 13) in her review of current research states, "There is very little research focused on student learning through multimodal projects." The shift from traditional text production (e.g., an essay) reflects a growing awareness of how our students communicate but raises questions about how multimodality helps students develop writing proficiency and rhetorical awareness. Indeed, Jonathan Alexander and Jacqueline Rhodes (2014, 19) worry that "composition's embrace of new and multimedia often makes those media serve the rhetorical ends of writing and more print-based forms of composing." Asking students to work with multiple modes, then, becomes an exercise in reinscribing linear, essayistic logics instead of exploring the inherent nonlinear, episodic, and intertextual possibilities implicit in new media. Our focus on students' critical reflection on their use of different modes to address audience seeks to respond to Alexander and Rhodes's concern by placing the focus less on the text and more on the construction and articulation of the larger rhetorical situation and students' growing awareness of how to navigate that situation.

FRAMEWORKS: INSTITUTIONAL CONTEXTS AND PEDAGOGICAL APPROACHES

Our work with multimodal writing assignments began more than a decade ago while writing a genre textbook: we wanted students to see genre as a fluid, malleable, serviceable set of concepts, not as a rigid form from which little deviation is possible. So we started asking students to transform their writing from one genre into another, teaching them to see genres as possibilities, as vehicles for reaching different and diverse audiences. Transformations—students reworking their writing for new and complex rhetorical situations—might include asking students to transform material from a research brief into an open letter and reimagine that material for a new audience and purpose. Through this process, we found our pedagogy focusing more on how these transformations affected students' rhetorical choices as they produced writing.

When we combined these concepts, transformation and multimodality, we noticed a shift in our students' attention to the rhetorical situation, particularly to audience. As a result, we began designing assignments that asked students to consider other modes as they created and transformed texts. Students composed performances (for example, Prezi presentations in which they acted deliberately as though their intended audience were present), which included sound (their voices, music, other sounds as narrative moments) and visuals. Often in the presentations, they negotiated choices for expression, body language, pace, and other delivery elements such as gestural modes. Other projects our students have produced include video PSAs, explainer videos, sound essays, infographics, and animated videos. Audience is important, but we also emphasize the students' particular role as rhetors: that is, during a presentation, for instance, we ask them to assume the role of a particular organization, group, or agency who would advocate for the cause and issue they are presenting on. Role-playing, then, something more difficult to do when working with alphabetic texts, becomes a critical means to understand and teach rhetorical strategies.

Our pedagogy has changed from alphabetic to multimodal text production, and we recognize such a structure still emphasizes traditional text production over "alternate" forms. Recently, however, we have also asked students to transform their multimodal texts into bimodal texts, such as an explainer video into an infographic, which has challenged us to think about the role of transformation and modalities differently. We were curious to discover how students make sense of those transformation processes, specifically their choices for different modalities, as those choices are informed by the rhetorical situations of those texts. We believe the reflective writing component we ask students to produce during the transformation process aids in their developing rhetorical awareness beyond the linear movement from print to digital or multimodal.

Before we examine our students' writing and the ways they invoke audience in their multimodal compositions, we want to provide some context about our university and its students. As one of four state universities in the Connecticut State University system, Eastern Connecticut State University (ECSU) is a four-year, residential university and Connecticut's only liberal arts state university. As such, Eastern has a strong commitment to serving traditionally underrepresented students; many of our students are first generation. With enrollment just over four thousand, Eastern's classes are typically small, around twenty-four. Most of our students come from Connecticut, but many come from neighboring New England and mid-Atlantic states, as well as from other countries. In short, it is in many ways a typical, small northeastern university.

In our writing program, our central concern is teaching students to identify and write into diverse, complex rhetorical situations, and as such it is in line with the WPA Outcomes Statement for First-Year Composition (3.0), which posits that "rhetorical knowledge is the basis of composing. Writers develop rhetorical knowledge by negotiating purpose, audience, context, and conventions as they compose a variety of texts for different situations" (Council of Writing Program Administrators 2014). Our program offers two first-year writing courses: Eng 100: College Writing and Eng 100P: College Writing Plus. Both are similar in focus, and both work from a faculty-generated guiding list of outcomes, which are revised often to reflect changes in the field and the needs of our students. Eng 100Plus offers students an additional two credits of "lab" time, during which they work with the instructor and two embedded writing tutors; both count for full academic credit and must be taken by students within their first thirty credits. Students are placed into Eng 100 or Eng 100P either by SAT scores or by writing short placement essays that are read by a group of writing faculty during the summer. In our experiences, students in Eng 100Plus often have less sustained writing experience and/or little confidence in their abilities. Eng 200: Reading and Writing Argument, which students can take as part of the writing minor, also focuses on helping students negotiate complex writing situations and introduces them to rhetorical concepts as they create arguments in different academic and civic genres. Students in this course range from first-year writers to upper-level undergraduates, and the course fulfills writing requirements in a number of disciplines.

We typically begin our courses with a discussion of what a rhetorical situation is, then help students understand that audience, purpose, rhetor, and context are contingent upon one another and dynamic. Thus we encourage students to see the rhetorical situation not solely as a descriptive process but as a generative one as well. We introduce larger concepts of exigency and kairos to help them understand that the conversations of others on the issue inform the rhetorical situation they are imagining and writing into. Students identify and make use of what people are already thinking or writing on the issue, helping them understand that their research and writing will be a way for them to join an ongoing conversation that will continue after they stop contributing. As students become comfortable with those concepts, we also introduce the notion of genre; ideally, we would introduce it as another choice: what genre or mixing of genres would work best for your rhetorical situation? But, in most instances, we end up assigning a genre because we have a limited amount of time and we recognize the complexity of what students are being asked to do in our classes. Although we make this approach sound like a linear discussion, when we start our discussion of genres as rhetorically situated, we introduce the idea of modes: written, visual, aural, gestural, or spatial. Each mode offers up different possibilities for communication, and we ask students to consider what they gain rhetorically through the affordances of a particular mode or combination of modes.

DATA COLLECTION

From 2013 to 2016, we systematically collected material from our students; most of our samples came from either ENG 100P or ENG 200. Our initial work primarily focused on transformations from a fairly traditional academic assignment to a visual text. For example, we designed a course in early 2014 in which we taught a research brief and then asked students to transform that into a presentation. Later, we asked them to reimagine the research brief as an animated cartoon. We have also asked students to transform research briefs into public service announcements, both print and video. More recently, we have been experimenting with other kinds of transformations: a photographic essay to a sound essay, an explainer video to an infographic, and so on. In all cases, we collected from our students their drafts (either print or digital), their final draft or version, their articulation and analysis of the rhetorical situation, and their reflections on their work.

In their early process reflections, we ask students to write about their rhetorical situation and choices they might make for research (including audio, video, photos) based on audience needs, and finally, we ask them to write about what they hope to discover from their research. After they've completed a project, they analyze how their choices about the rhetorical situation affected their finished project.

CHOICES WRITERS MAKE: MULTIMODALITY AND AUDIENCE AWARENESS

Because one of our major goals is to prepare students to write for diverse and specific audiences, we work with them to articulate who that audience is; during their composing process they reflect on how they deliberately engaged that audience through the choices they made while selecting research for example or identifying appropriate visual design elements. We have found, echoing Shipka (2009, W345), that "students who explored other rhetorical and material potentials for their work were often able to account for what they did, why, and how, and this was something that students who continued to work in highly routinized ways were unwilling or unable to do." In fact, the level of detail and clarity our students provided in their reflection on their multimodal texts was a pleasant surprise and in stark contrast to what we had seen when asking them to reflect on more traditional, alphabetic texts.

Our analysis, then, of their abilities to engage specific audiences rests on both what they have composed and, perhaps more important, what they say about how they engaged their audience in their reflections afterwards. We rely heavily on that metanarrative—their sense of their own success or failure to write to their audience—in part because "for transfer to occur, teachers need to facilitate students' development of an awareness of their own writing processes" (Ford 2004, 311). Our guiding assumption in our courses is that while students may never again be asked to write in a particular genre, they will need to understand how to negotiate rhetorical demands and make choices for how best to communicate their ideas. Ford echoes Anne Beaufort's argument for developing students' "metacognitive awareness" so they can apply what they learn to other "writing situations" and for calling their "attention to the very context-specific nature of composing" (Beaufort 1998, 196). The rhetorical reflections we ask students to produce—during and after they've completed a project—allow both a metacognitive reflection on their choices and an analysis of the rhetorical situations (context-specific transfer). Again, this focus on critical reflection is in line with current best practices, as articulated in the online WPA Outcomes Statement for First Year Composition: students should "reflect on the development of composing practices and how those practices influence their work" (Council of Writing Program Administrators 2014).

The examples we work with below, drawn from both Eng 100P and Eng 200, were chosen because of the level of detail the students provided in their rhetorical reflection writing. These students articulated clearly their intent and audience, which we believe is indicative of writers making choices based on their developing rhetorical awareness and transferability of the threshold concept that writing is rhetorically situated (Downs and Wardle 2007).

AUDIENCE AWARENESS AND ANIMATED VIDEOS

One first-year student, Kate (her name has been changed), wrote about school violence for her research brief. The assignment is a fairly typical academic assignment, one that asks students to conduct and work with formal, academic research, exploring a topic of their own choosing and synthesizing that research and their own insights to produce a report that primarily informs their chosen audience but can also provide a call to action or make proposals for change, implementation, and the like. We ask students to reflect on their work throughout their composing process and to assess the choices they have made to create their research brief.

About her decision to write her research brief about school violence, Kate notes,

> I chose to write my report with parents as my intended audience because they have the expectation to be strong in these situation. Not only may their child be scared to get on the bus every morning, but the parents never want to let go with that lingering thought in the back of their head. . . . Toward the end of my report, I added the section: what can I do as a parent? This section was designed for two reasons, reassuring the reader that we are still talking to them while maintaining their attention. Secondly, to tell them what they can do as a parents.

What is interesting about her response is both her clear understanding of what the intended audience might be feeling and might need from her—she touches on the fear every parent probably felt as they sent their kids off to school after Sandy Hook or Columbine. She has clearly thought a lot about that audience and what it needs.

In reading her research brief, however, we were struck by the limited evidence of that audience awareness. The reader implied by the way she writes and organizes her research brief seems to be the default "anyone" many students imagine. In fact, at the end of her first paragraph, she writes in a thesis-like way: "With more awareness of school violence and school shootings we can decrease the rate of occurrences." This suggests a focus on policy and, by extension, policymakers (a reasonable audience, to be sure). Later, she does write, "A student's home environment and parental involvement can vastly affect the likeliness of students committing violent acts." But framed as a policy argument, it's hard to see how this addresses the intended audience of parents. There are lots of reasons for this: students are unused to writing to an imagined audience, so even when asked to do so, they have a hard time actually doing it; the genre itself could mitigate against the audience she chose—while it is not a research report that emphasizes recitation of knowledge, it is similar enough that students might not be able see the differences. Also, Kate might have been modeling her research brief on the ones we read as samples, and those tended to include policy statements.

The final section of the paper to which she alludes in her reflection above does address parents directly, sort of. The initial paragraph of that section is still about parents—she draws on research to talk about how they respond, but she has not redirected that discussion to parents. For example, she writes, "Arias [one of her sources] spoke about the level of concern parents have, that students don't even have. She also said a parent's level of concern is often triggered by other shootings or the media. This takes them into panic mode; thinking this is happening everywhere." Here, she reports on what she read rather than really synthesizing it for her intended audience, who might want to know how violence happens or what to do about it. Similarly, she writes, "However, in the event that [a school shooting] does still happen, parents need to be able to effectively communicate to their child while remaining stable themselves." It is interesting to us that though she has all the material she needs here—a clear understanding of the issue, a clear sense of purpose and audience—her report suggests a more generic audience; she seems unable to get her writing to match her sense of the audience.

***

"Inform: explain and stay calm.

Listen: let them ask questions, they may have concerns that you were not aware of.

Normalize: go back to your routine, it can be hard for a child to go through a traumatic event directly or indirectly, so keeping the morning routine can help keep them comfortable.

Encourage ways to help, ask them if there is anything that can be done to assure them everything will be okay"

(qtd. In Varma-White)

***

Figure 11.1. A call-out box from Kate's research report

Interestingly, where she is able to develop her report in ways that address her audience is in the construction of a call-out box, a visual design element of reports that highlights important information (see figure 11.1). That material is clearly meant for her intended audience of parents and as such offers them some tools for dealing with the impact of school violence on their children.

Kate's work is reflective of what we see in a lot of our students' writing: she is able to imagine the audience, sometimes in insightful ways, as she does when she predicts how parents must feel (she is herself not a parent). Yet she struggles to find a way to make her writing responsive to that audience, perhaps because students often see research and research reports as vehicles for recitation.

Once students completed their research briefs, we asked them to transform that material into an animated video using an online application that allows users to design short animations using stock characters and actions. For this assignment, students also used Audacity to record a voice-over as well as add sound effects to their animation. Only one student had ever worked with animation software before, and most found it somewhat intimidating; as a result, a lot of class time was given over to practicing and learning the software. As part of this work, students learned about the affordances animation and sound offered them. We examined other videos, visual texts, and sound essays to better understand what one could do with those modes, as well as what writers might gain from incorporating more than one mode.

For this assignment, students were assigned an audience—whereas for their research briefs they could choose their own audience, we felt that because of the complexity of the task, it might be best to limit the rhetorical choices they had to make. Students, then, had to transform their research-brief material for an audience of middle-school students. (For some, this assignment was a real challenge—particularly for one student who had chosen to write about serial killers.) They were free to define other aspects of the rhetorical situation. Kate constructed a story about two young boys, Joe and Mike, who must deal with the idea of school violence, which they learn about as they watch television.

Again, we turn to Kate's own sense of her work to guide our analysis:

> My initial reaction to this project [to transform the research brief to animation] and reimagine it for a new audience and genre was pretty negative. I thought that trying to tell 9 year olds about these tragedies [school shootings] would be too difficult; . . . I decided that the most important aspect was to make it look kid friendly and [provide] a lot of reassurance. For example, two times I have Joe reassure Mike that yes these things do happen but they are so rare at the same time. I also mention directly after Mike expresses that he doesn't want to watch this that the way he is feeling: anxious, on-edge, and scared, is completely normal.

Here, as in her discussion of the audience for her research brief, Kate shows a good understanding of her audience's needs and expectations, and in the reflection writing she did prior to designing the animated video, she articulates critical insight into what her audience might not be able to grasp: "Some aspects [of my research] that may be beyond them and their knowledge is the shooters wanting to be celebrities . . . I will need to carefully present psychological issues [explaining why shooters commit violence] because they may not be aware of them and what they are at this age." Her awareness of audience extends to understanding that some of her research would be beyond them, particularly the notion of committing horrific acts in order to gain celebrity. And she remarked in discussions about her video that she also knew she could not show certain things—actual reports on the events, for instance, even though she discusses them in her research brief (e.g., Sandy Hook). This suggests a clear awareness of the affordances of different modes, though she is not likely to have phrased it that way; watching, she knew, was different from reading.

It is further revealing that Kate synthesizes her research and makes it applicable to the new audience—she's taken the material reproduced in figure 11.1 and reworked it as a way of understanding what her audience needs from her: reassurance. To put it another way, she has used that bit of research as a frame for constructing the entire video, as she notes in her reflection: "Because most 10 year olds are aware that school violence and shootings happen, they are scared and don't know what to expect or how to prevent it."

Of course, one of her challenges as she notes above was how to take this rather mature issue and make it understandable and not traumatizing to a younger audience. She felt she could not really write about actual school shootings because she did not want to show material that was too graphic. Instead, she used the idea of bullying, a small component of her research brief, as a frame and organizing device for the video's narrative. She introduces the idea of bullying at the start of the video to help her audience understand violence. The movement then to school violence and shootings is tied to the idea of bullying, both to help the audience understand it and to give them ways to stop it. In her video, the two boys walk home from school and talk about the day's events. Joe asks Mike if he saw A. J. threatening and bullying Blake; Mike replies that he did, acknowledging "that kid can't catch a break." As Kate has the two students in her video talk about bullying, she narrates what happened: "A. J., the known bully, threatened Blake that he will hurt him. A. J. is constantly picking on his classmates, but recently has put his energy toward making Blake as miserable as possible. Ever since Blake started getting bullied, he hasn't been acting himself." She shows this event by placing the characters A. J. and Blake in front of school lockers, with A. J. yelling and waving his arm at Blake (it's worth noting that there were severe limitations with the application that forced students to be really creative in how they represented ideas and actions).

Kate makes the case in this sequence that being bullied can often lead to people becoming bullies themselves; to illustrate this, she shows Blake next to a scrolling list of consequences of being bullied. She uses similar ideas in a later segment that depicts Joe and Mike watching a news report on school violence. She narrates the report the two kids are watching: "Bullying can dramatically affect a student's well-being, both mentally and physically. Many victims of bullying show a decline in grades, depression, and are emotionally unstable. They are also more likely to have violent outbursts while in school than non-bullied students." Kate is able to link the research on bullies—a topic most kids are familiar with—to the research on school shooters. She communicates this through a depiction and narration about two young boys who have a conversation about another young boy who is bullied, understanding that her audience will be knowledgeable about such events. She knows they will get it. She ties the idea of bullying to school violence by creating a narrative that places the events in the context of her audience's lives: walking home from school with a friend, watching television, and so on. The linkage works well because it connects the familiar (bullying) with the unfamiliar (school shootings), giving her audience the tools needed to conceptualize and understand the event (she cites the 2012 Sandy Hook Elementary School shooting as her example in the video Joe and Mike watch).

MULTIMODALITY AND AUDIENCE AWARENESS: A TRANSFORMATION FROM DISCOURSE COMMUNITY ETHNOGRAPHY TO PUBLIC SERVICE ANNOUNCEMENTS

One could argue that part of what makes Kate's video successful for its audience has something to do with the medium, with the narrative function of animation. The medium encourages the use of modes for storytelling, and Kate clearly takes advantage of that. It's an argument, we think, in favor of creating space in our classes for nonacademic, nonessayistic kinds of writing. But for this next example, the writer (a student in a ENG 200) was asked to produce a discourse community ethnography (DCE) by conducting field research on a particular group of her choice and determining first whether it was indeed a discourse community, and second, what insights or conclusions emerged from her field research on the group's literacy practices.

The writers in this course had been exploring threshold concepts in writing studies (Downs and Wardle 2007; Meyer and Land 2006) and transferability of these precepts among different contexts. Transfer includes "*drawing on* both knowledge and practice and employing it in ways almost identical to the ways they have used it in the past; . . . *reworking* such knowledge and practice as they address new tasks; and . . . *creating new knowledge and practices* for themselves when students encounter . . . a failed effort to address a new task that prompts new ways of thinking about how to write and about what writing is" (Robertson, Taczak, and Yancey 2012, 1). They call this "active transfer," as students can talk about the choices they made as rhetors. For our students, writing for a particular rhetorical situation was foregrounded for every project throughout the semester. For their DCE, students had to figure out how discourse communities (DC) use different literacy practices to mediate activity. In other words, how do the group members use texts and tools common to the community's literacy practices, conventions, lexis, and so on to accomplish their goals? Then students had to transfer that knowledge for a new rhetorical situation. Also, we emphasized in our pedagogy students' metanarratives (or reflections) on what guided their choices for the research materials they used to develop ideas about the literacy practices of the DC. In sum, students' reflections during and after the project's completion encouraged them to be cognizant of their rhetorical choices during transformation and re-creation of their text for a new rhetorical situation.

A second concept frames the pedagogy for this project. Jan H.F. Meyer and Ray Land (2006, 3) define disciplinary *threshold concepts* "as akin to a portal, opening up a new and previously inaccessible way of thinking about something;" without this "the learner cannot progress." Since what differentiates the disciplines are their ways of viewing the world, Meyer and Land argue, then moving beyond these "portals" leads to a transformation or a new understanding or new way of looking at the subject matter. To provide an example in writing studies, Linda Adler-Kassner, John Majewski, and Damian Koshnick (2012, 1) point out, "We think, for example, that *situatedness* is a threshold concept: the idea that there really is no universal rule for how to write is both a complete reversal of students' previous educational experiences, and a crucial principle for building understanding of writing beyond what those educational experiences provided." In our assignment, the transformation from a DCE into a new multimodal project, students tried to understand the new rhetorical situation, the exigency driving the communicative act, and the use of different modes for a new audience; in some cases, they did so by drawing on research they completed for the DCE, as well as their own experiences as rhetors.

An example of a student transformation was Samantha's DCE, which she transformed into a series of PSAs. A fan of the television show *Supernatural,* and a member of its online "fandom," Samantha argues in her essay that the *Supernatural* fandom she participates in is a discourse community according to the six characteristics outlined by John Swales in his essay "The Concept of a Discourse Community." Beyond simply naming it as such, Samantha examines the group's characteristics such as their lexis and shared goals; she argues that the online fandom meets its goals through sharing ideas and developing "theories" about the television series' storylines, characters' motives, and so on. Perhaps most important, Sam argues in her ethnography that these complex literacy practices of the fandom transfer to some academic literacy skills she is required to use as a college student, such as analytical thinking and writing.

In her DCE "'We Are All Nerds': A Study of the Online *Supernatural* Fandom Discourse Community," Sam argues that members of this online fandom are often stereotyped by nonmembers and reviewers of the show alike. Sam quotes other bloggers to illustrate how those outside the DC typically devalue its participants. The blogger Totallytwistedwords calls the fandom "'crazy shrieking fangirls that . . . are spiteful and mean'" while another blogger, Garrett, says "'all fans are crazy, obsessed lunatics who think they know what is best for the show and who get the show confused with reality.'" To refute these claims about the online fandom participants, Sam argues that the DC members use a complex language system that serves multiple purposes:

> Many individuals use the show as a platform to hone various skills; most notably, their writing and ability to analyze. . . . Through the use of online blogging platforms, this group has developed a complex coding and tagging system that allows both their discussions and the materials that they develop to be easily accessed and understood by fellow community members. . . . Members of the *Supernatural* community must become fluent in this highly descriptive lexis if they wish to fully engage.

Sam's redefinition of the *Supernatural* online fandom as a DC with a unique lexis and knowledge-making skills testifies to her awareness of an audience that includes participants and outsiders to the online fandom. Sam acknowledges that the "outsiders" must also be privy to the details of the show in order to critique the DC fandom members. She writes to an audience of both "believers" and "doubters"—a complex negotiation on her part as a writer.

What makes Sam's analysis and negotiation of multiple audiences possible for the audience reading her DCE—"novices" and "experts" on the *Supernatural* frontier—is, in part, her details about the fandom's lexis and coda creation tools. Sam describes the fandom's complex tagging system, lexis, and its function as it appears on several popular writing websites for the show's fans:

> On . . . *Archive of Our Own* . . . users are presented with the tagging system that writers and readers use to navigate through the site. . . . *Fanfiction.Net'*s pop-up window is used by users to filter writing based on their qualifications. Writers are able to attach these descriptions to their creations in order to boost their views. Using this menu, readers can search for pieces of a specific genre, rating, language, or scenes that involve specified characters.

Sam also explains how readers might combine tags to read the postings from fandom members about particular themes, episodes, or characters. She writes, "For highly specific users, multiple tags could be used; a user could select both the 'humor' and the 'romance' tag, for example." Thus, Sam uses visuals of the tagging system and lexis and captions these images to make her argument more persuasive to an audience of "outsiders" to the fandom and its blogs.

Further, Sam argues that fans new to the DC (another part of the multiple audiences for her ethnography) utilize the literacy tool of the archive to become "knowledgeable" and eventually create new stories themselves. She explains, "It also immerses them in the lexis of the community, allowing them to later understand what different tags mean and how they can use them on their own. As these examples demonstrate, *Supernatural* fans have created their own language within their discourse community, which they have coupled with their own written texts meant to support the genre that they are working with."

What is interesting about Sam's DCE then in terms of multimodality and audience awareness is this: she discusses the online fandom of *Supernatural* and their use of a specialized lexis to define it as a DC, yet she takes her analysis of the audience's needs and goals *a step further* by visualizing the ways the members and audiences perform through the complex tagging system. (She says later in her ethnography, "The market for fan writings is detailed; those that enter it are looking for highly specific pieces, and rely on a similarly specialized language in order to quickly find what they are looking for.") By including visuals of the group's lexis (images, captions) for her DCE's audience, Sam's argument disrupts the narratives that stereotype this particular fandom and supports her claim that the fandom uses complex social-epistemic literacy practices.

Finally, Sam argues that through the fandom and its literacy technologies, fans (and audiences) are able "to provide their own personal contributions [to the show's narratives] via the writing of 'fanfiction.'" Metawriters, she claims, contribute new story lines about the show: "One specific subsection of the community, operating under the name of spn_heavymeta, is particularly known . . . for [providing] meta-analysis for every episode of *Supernatural*, with the overall purpose of determining how current story arcs impact overall character development." Other fandom writers are part of an "alternative universe of writing, commonly referred to as AU," in which they write outside the story lines or from a character who did not appear in that episode. "Within the community," Sam explains, "these creations are known as 'coda.' These stories follow the show, although they are not accepted as 'canon' (in this context, canon refers to only those events that have happened on the show. Traditionally, any outside writings are not seen as 'canon')."

Sam's conclusions that fandom members negotiate complex literacy practices to communicate, and that they engage in knowledge-making practices, reveal her keen sense of multiple-audience awareness. Through her interpretations of the fandom's visual tools (e.g., tabs, Archive of Our Own), she reveals her understanding of the rhetorical operations of this DC that help it accomplish its goals. Sam makes choices that serve her rhetorical situation and her audience's expectations, too, in particular the audience for her DCE and those novice or expert fans in the DC. Her rhetorical awareness is apparent in her use of visuals of the tagging systems and captions in order to analyze them, which illustrates the complexity of the DC's literacy practices.

TRANSFORMATION: FROM DCE TO PSAS: A DEEPER FORAY INTO AUDIENCE AWARENESS

While Sam's audience analysis for her DCE showed an in-depth understanding of multiple audiences, during her transformation from ethnography to a public service-announcement campaign, she chose a new rhetorical situation to guide the production of her multimodal project.

Students were asked to transform their DCE into a new multimodal genre of their choice appropriate to a particular rhetorical situation they would define. They could choose an issue addressed by the DC, or produce a multimodal text relevant to the work of the DC, and analyze the new rhetorical situation to determine which modes might make sense to work with. Students needed to rethink who they were as the rhetors, their audience, and the exigency of the situation guiding the production of their new "text." They could recycle some of the research or ideas used in their DCEs but only if it made sense given the new rhetorical situation.

Sam's PSA campaign, Love Yourself, Your Way, targets an audience of tweens, teens, and young adults who face discrimination and bullying because of their differences: physical characteristics, belief systems, and so on. Through her research, and common knowledge, Sam determines that this issue is fresh in the minds of her audience and that one way to get them to listen to her message is through popular-culture references. Sam chooses to use images, fonts, and themes from a popular television series, *American Horror Story* (AHS)—ones that will resonate with them. Based on her research from sites such as jasonfoundation.com and

Stopbullying.gov, she argues her intended audience for the PSAs are those most heavily affected by bullying, discrimination, and its consequences. In her reflective writing, Sam posits that a young *AHS* audience, many of whom are "empowered by their abnormalities," will relate to the images of these characters in her PSAs. Sam claims that the show itself "teaches people to embrace the physical and nonphysical differences" of people, so her intention is for the PSA campaign to "appeal to stop bullying and suicides . . . promote a message to love one's self, and embrace the things that make each of us individuals."

While Sam's PSA campaign targets an age demographic similar to the one for her DCE, a different fan base emerges (*AHS* viewers) for her audience. Also, the rhetorical situation changes further when the issues that emerge from the *AHS* series itself, according to Sam's research, are ones faced by this new audience regularly: being different and being bullied for it. For each PSA below, Sam analyzes her choices (e.g., rhetorical appeals, design choices) in her reflection writing, revealing her complex audience-analysis abilities. Knowing her intended audience for the PSAs, she writes, "Youth today are often exposed to a myriad of visual stimulus, so I believe it is important that my appeal be brief—I wanted something they could glance at, understand the message, and remember." Her choices for her PSAs' messages are based on the audience's prior knowledge of specific episodes and characters' quotes and how they resonate with viewers' own real-life experiences with these issues. For example, in her reflection on two of her PSAs using the images of *AHS* characters Fiona Goode and Jimmy Darling, she explains, "The redone Fiona Goode quote that tells everyone they are 'supreme'" and . . . "Jimmy Darling saying that though many people view different people as freaks, in reality they are 'perfect'" illustrates the show's message of "acceptance of differences."

In the PSA "They Want to Call Us Monsters," Sam focuses on character Jimmy Darling (and his physical differences, such as extrodatyly), whose fingers are partially fused together. Sam writes, "Though Jimmy initially hates his physical disability, by the end of the show, he loses his hands and commissions a man to make exact wooden replicas." She argues that his quote in the show "suggested equality and that he was accepting of who he was." Sam's message on her PSA "They Want to Call Us Monsters" is effective based on her audience's familiarity with Darling's storyline and his quotation from the show. Her message is relatable to young *AHS* fans because of the PSA campaign issue: prevention of bullying and discrimination, which sometimes lead to suicides, among this demographic. The audience, Sam suggests, knows this issue is prominent in public conversations (perhaps their schools have even promoted antibullying campaigns). In her reflection, she writes, "These youth often face bullying, as is evident by the research presented [in the PSAs] so I wanted to create a campaign that demonstrates the importance of positive self image and of treating people equally." Further, she discusses how using alphabetic text and visuals (character images) work together to effectively convey the message to her intended young *AHS* viewing audience: "[My PSAs] contain familiar images of the characters as well as reimagined popular lines from the show, both of which are couple together to form a complete messages that would be understood by any member of the AHS community."

Sam's choice for using different black-and-white images in each PSA also reveals her complex audience-analysis abilities. She writes she must "cater the appeals" to different audiences who are discriminated against or bullied for "physical disabilities, religious choice, or gender identification." Thus, her research on and experience with the *multiple audiences within the* AHS *fan community* leads her to select visuals that represent the type of discrimination faced by these characters and by the audience "reading" the PSAs.

About her choice to use the character Fiona Goode to address the members of the PSA audience who may face discrimination because of their religious practices, Sam writes, "As a witch, Fiona faces a stigma against her choice of religion—a prejudice that she pays no mind to, declaring herself 'supreme' and openly practicing. Fiona represents those of religious minorities." For the third example in her PSA campaign, Sam chooses a visual and text with care to target a very particular audience who may be persecuted because of what Sam calls "gender identities:"

> Lana [Winters] was imprisoned [in a mental asylum] because she identified as a lesbian and lived with her girlfriend, and she was forced to undergo damaging "treatment" methods in order to "cure" her. Her caregivers, primarily nuns, are demonstrated [in the PSA] by the other character Sister Mary Eunice possessed by a dark spirit, leading her to commit horrible acts.

She further discusses her choice to "contrast these two figures" (Lara and Sister Mary Eunice) in a split-screen image by posing the question to PSA readers that seems obvious to an audience familiar with this plotline: "Who was the real Monster here?"

The slogan Love Yourself. Your Way in all three PSAs admonishes the audiences to be proactive in embracing their differences despite what others may say or do and supports Sam's choice of the sponsoring organization for the PSAs, or "the rhetor," Lady Gaga's Born This Way Foundation, whose mission she analyzes in her reflection: "This foundation was perfect for . . . multiple reasons, the primary being that its founder, Lady Gaga. Lady Gaga has already been cast for season 5 of *AHS*, so her foundation could reasonably use the show as a mechanism for conveying this message. . . . It caters to young adults who have been bullied and sought to create 'safe spaces' for them. Based on this knowledge, I decided the foundation would be suitable representative for the messages [of the PSA campaign] and would convey the ethos needed."

Thus, the Born This Way logo that appears at the bottom right of all three PSAs suggests Sam's keen awareness of her choice of "rhetor," especially given her audience and its identification with Lady Gaga's work both as both a public figure and artist (and her foundation) and as an *AHS* character.

Finally, her design choices such as font style and color are incorporated with a clearly defined vision of her audience in mind. Sam explains in her reflection writing that using the bold red color and "the font similar to the one used on the *AHS* title card for some key words—such as 'Supreme' and 'Monsters' . . . remind viewers of the connection the PSAs have to their discourse community." (The bold red letters stand out and appear to drip like blood.) And about the design and arrangement, Sam indicates how she expects her different readers to navigate the PSA. She says those who look closely will notice the "facts and statistics in small white font against the gray background." Some viewers, she acknowledges, will only see "the bold red wording superimposed over the image," which she argues "is enough to get the point across." Knowing that not all audience members will look closely, Sam claims the careful readers "will come away with the statistical evidence that serves as partially a logos appeal and partially a pathos appeal." Thus, Sam's conceptualization of a new audience for her PSA campaign is further complicated through her use of distinctive visual modes: colors, design, logos, and arrangement on the page that function as rhetorical appeals, as her reflection suggests. Clearly, her choices indicate a deliberate concentration on audience and the rhetorical situation guiding her text.

MULTIMODALITY, AUDIENCE AWARENESS, AND TRANSFER: SOME CONCLUSIONS

What has struck us throughout our work with multimodality in the classroom over the last four years is the extent to which our students can both articulate and address complex audiences in ways that surpass their ability to do so when asked to write more traditional, alphabetic texts. We have seen this tendency no matter what kind of text students write—whether it is a research brief, as in the example above, or a letter to the editor, or a profile, or any of the other kinds of writing students are traditionally asked to write in first-year composition. It is interesting to us, as well, that when students incorporate different modes into their alphabetic texts, it is in those spaces that extend beyond print where they are able to connect most strongly with their audience, or, at least, gesture in complex ways towards that audience. Shipka (2009, W345) suggests some reasons for this when she writes, "Students who explored other potentials for representing their work often reported being highly engaged with that work and spent considerably more time on their texts than those who continued to produce, in decidedly less reflective ways, the highly formulaic texts that one student said had 'gotten him by' in his high school courses." Our brief examples here, and others we've gathered in our study, suggest that students' awareness of these other elements affects how they negotiate the rhetorical situations for their writing and make choices, it seems, with a keener eye towards who would care, why they'd care, and how they might be moved by the text and its message. Audience becomes a complex concept (instead of writers writing to the teacher or to "everyone" or "anyone") they must wrangle with—one that requires writers' use of rhetorical knowledge and critical-analysis skills that enable them to make conscious choices and be able to articulate why they made them for a particular audience. Both their metanarratives and the texts they produce—ones that use multiple modes—offer clear indications that students compose with significant rhetorical awareness, especially toward audiences, when they visually or audibly represent their ideas and arguments. And, as students' reflections and multimodal compositions suggest, crafting complex arguments through "storying" their texts using narratives and multiple modes resists the trope of "everyone as audience," one they seem to rely on in more formulaic genres.

Students' reflections and multimodal compositions provide evidence of their deepening awareness of their audiences and the larger rhetorical situations surrounding their compositions. Such awareness, made clear in students' choices in their compositions, seems like the kind of "transferability" of a threshold concept—the situatedness of writing—current research on transfer (Adler-Kassner, Majewski, and Koshnick 2012) argues is crucial to writers' development. Students' understanding of a particular genre or of disciplinary conventions is important. But more critical for undergraduate writers is their ability to read a situation critically and rhetorically and enter into it effectively—consciously and purposefully.

REFERENCES

Adler-Kassner, Linda, John Majewski, and Damian Koshnick. 2012. "The Value of Troublesome Knowledge: Transfer and Threshold Concepts in Writing and History." *Composition Forum* 26.

Alexander, Jonathan, and Jaqueline Rhodes. 2014. *On Multimodality: New Media in Composition Studies*. Urbana, IL: NCTE.

Beaufort, Anne. 1998. "Transferring Writing Knowledge to the Workplace: Are We on Track?" In *Expanding Literacies: English Teaching and the New Workplace*, edited by Mary Sue Garay and Stephen A. Bernhardt, 179–99. Albany: SUNY Press.

Council of Writing Program Administrators. 2014. "WPA Outcomes Statement for First-Year Composition (3.0)." http://wpacouncil.org/positions/outcomes.html.

Downs, Douglas, and Elizabeth Wardle. 2007. "Teaching about Writing, Righting Misconceptions: (Re)Envisioning 'First Year Composition' as 'Introduction to Writing Studies.'" *College Composition and Communication* 58 (4): 552–84.

Ford, Julie Dyke. 2004. "Knowledge Transfer Across Disciplines: Tracking Rhetorical Strategies from a Technical Communication Classroom to an Engineering Classroom." *IEEE Transactions on Professional Communication* 47 (4): 301–15.

Jewitt, Carey. 2011. "An Introduction to Multimodality." In *The Routledge Handbook of Multimodal Analysis*, edited by Carey Jewitt, 14–27. London: Routledge.

Meyer, Jan H.F., and Ray Land. 2006. "Threshold Concepts and Troublesome Knowledge: An Introduction." In *Overcoming Barriers to Student Understanding*, edited by Jan H.F. Meyer and Ray Land, 3–18. London: Routledge.

New London Group. 1996. "A Pedagogy of Multiliteracies: Designing Social Futures." *Harvard Educational Review* 66 (1): 60–92.

National Council of Teachers of English. 2003. "Resolution on Composing with Nonprint Media." http://www.ncte.org/positions/statements/composewithnonprint.

Robertson, Liane, Kara Taczak, and Kathleen Blake Yancey. 2012. "Notes toward A Theory of Prior Knowledge and Its Role in College Composers' Transfer of Knowledge and Practice." *Composition Forum* 26.

Selfe, Cynthia L. 2004. "Toward New Media Texts: Taking up the Challenges of Visual Literacy." In *Writing New Media: Theory and Applications for Expanding the Teaching Of Composition*, edited by Anne Francis Wysocki, Johndan Johnson-Eilola, Cynthia L. Selfe, and Geoffrey Sirc, 67–110. Logan: Utah State University Press.

Selfe, Cynthia L. 2009. "The Movement of Air, the Breath of Meaning: Aurality and Multimodal Composing." *College Composition and Communication* 60 (4): 616–63.

Shipka, Jody. 2005. "A Multimodal Task-Based Framework for Composing." *College Composition and Communication* 57 (2): 277–306.

Shipka, Jody. 2009. "Negotiating Rhetorical, Material, Methodological, and Technological Difference: Evaluating Multimodal Designs." *College Composition and Communication* 61 (1): W343–W366. http://www.ncte.org/library/NCTEFiles/Resources/Journals/CCC/0611-sep09/CCC0611Negotiating.pdf.

Smith, Blaine E. 2014. "Beyond Words: A Review of Research on Adolescents and Multimodal Composition." In *Exploring Multimodal Composition and Digital Writing*, edited by Richard E. Ferdig and Kristine E. Pytash, 1–19. Hershey, PA: Information Science Reference.

Takayoshi, Pamela, and Cynthia L. Selfe. 2007. "Thinking about Multimodality." In *Multimodal Composition: Resources for Teachers*, edited by Cynthia L. Selfe, 1–12. New York: Hampton.

SECTION IV

12

DISTRIBUTED ASSESSMENT FROM THE RUNWAY TO THE CLASSROOM
A Model for Multimodal Writing Assessment

Areti Sakellaris

INTRODUCTION

This chapter interrupts our field's print-based formulations about writing assessment and argues that we should look to the fashion industry for a model of writing assessment. The fashion industry is one rooted in a multimodal and materially sensitive environment with various participants doing different things with a text as it undergoes continuous and distributed evaluation and assessment. By evaluation, I mean making a value judgment, and by assessment, I mean collecting information to make decisions. Although I will focus on multimodal writing assessment, the model need not be constrained to multimodal writing, and it may be readily adopted for writing assessment in general. This model's value is in repositioning writing-assessment formulations in a multimodal environment and extrapolating the advantages and disadvantages of this directionality rather than our previous tendency to work from a print tradition towards the multimodal. I argue that the fashion process maps onto the writing assessment process, and I provide an example of how distributed, multimodal writing assessment occurs in a classroom setting.

Our students compose in a networked, distributed environment, and we should assess in a networked, distributed environment. Therefore, this chapter also suggests we expand our idea of authorship from a single author to a system of distributed authorship. The model of multimodal writing assessment based on distributed authorship and distributed assessment is promising because it demands rhetorical reliability and honors the differences amongst assessors; we can use reliability not primarily to score or grade individuals and their texts but as a way to create a more inclusive and generative writing-assessment process. The model of writing assessment I propose requires we redefine how we think about writing assessment, expertise, and knowledge making;

DOI: 10.7330/9781607327974.c012

we can draw inspiration from the fashion industry to redefine writing assessment as a recursive cycle through which a text is shaped by a composer who operates from a particular context informed by material and social conditions. This text circulates through a cycle of production to various participants with the expectation it will receive evaluation and assessment.

How a text is produced in the fashion industry matters just as much as the text itself because the text cannot circulate and be assessed without traces of *what it means* and *what it means having been (re)made by someone, sometime, somewhere.* What's at stake for the text, its composer, and its assessors is intimately tied to representations of ability and projected identities as composers and assessors (also composers as assessors, assessors as composers); how it was produced and how it delivers its message also matters to the audience, as it conveys information about itself, its maker, and the contexts of its production. The people best suited to assess this text are those familiar with the context(s) in which it is (re)produced and (re)circulated. That is what happens in the fashion industry, and it should happen in our composition classrooms.

PRODUCTION, CIRCULATION, AND EVALUATION IN THE FASHION INDUSTRY

The composition classroom and the fashion industry are sites where meaning making through textual production, circulation, and evaluation occur in a seemingly chaotic interplay of individuals, materials, labor, and criteria. Yet, the composition classroom tends to focus on student texts *after* the linear process of composition is completed, whereas the fashion industry tends to focus on designer texts before, during, and after composition in a multimodal environment sensitive to material, social, and labor contexts. The model of writing assessment I propose requires we reconsider the writing-assessment process as nonlinear and laced with assessment and evaluation throughout the cycle and intricately tied to the text's materiality and production. Like the ongoing debates about writing constructs and their assessment tools, the fashion industry and its educational programs struggle with what they mean by creativity and how to assess it (Freeman, Son, and McRoberts 2015, 122). However, the fashion industry relies on a combination of expert raters and those involved with the contexts of production for evaluation and assessment, from classroom assignments and design consultations to industry awards (124). Charles Freeman, Jihyeong Son, and Lisa Barona McRoberts's research (2015) suggests that a consensual assessment technique (CAT) could be a direct assessment applied throughout the industry because it evaluates "products within the group and context of which products were created, thereby minimising external ideals affecting creativity judgements" (124). Their findings that "the domain-specific knowledge of the rater was not as important as the number of raters" (127) and that raters exhibited "a level of consistency between expert and novice" (128) could transfer to the writing classroom through a model like the one I propose.

Like most writing, a fashion design typically begins in the realm of ideas. Whatever the exigency for setting out to design a collection or to compose a written text, a designer begins by gathering inspiration. A designer and their team may create an inspiration board; this board, also known as a mood board, represents argumentative claims based on evaluations of trend and color forecasts, sales information, and historical and cultural influences. These value judgments steer the creative process, acting as appeals to withstand more extensive and pressing assessment from a gamut of stakeholders tied to financial implications, as well as performing the meaning-making potential and discursive nature of fashion texts and their reproductions as images, video, and derivative (sometimes knocked-off) designs. This moment of creative and evaluative labor mirrors the brainstorming or freewriting a writer may perform in order to identify potential responses to a rhetorical situation.

The designer refers to the mood board to focus their designs; for the sake of this example, let us imagine they sketch a dress. The designer and their team may work together to source a fabric for the qualities most befitting the designer's goals for this particular dress; evaluative judgments must be made about these goals. Questions guiding the evaluation may include: Do we, as a fashion company, want this design to be a fluid silk dress that will move and conform to the body because we know our customer likes to wear her clothing from work to happy hour? Do we want this design to be a silk taffeta dress that will be more rigid in order to hold its unusual shape and rustle when our customer makes her grand entrance at a gala? This moment of critical and evaluative labor mirrors the research and critical thinking writers engage in as they consider what and how they will give shape to their compositions during prewriting and outlining.

The next stage in the fashion industry, patternmaking, is akin to drafting in the composition classroom. The designer transforms their sketch into a dress sample either by draping fabric to a padded mannequin meeting specific size measurements or by passing the responsibility to their patternmaker. Patternmaking creates a paper template or sample garment to guide production of a more finished piece or a better sample (Keiser and Garner 2008, 292). Like a written draft with its title, headings, citations, and claims tentatively arranged, a pattern contains information about the size and type of sleeve, where buttons will meet buttonholes, where a seam will join fabric pieces, and so forth and instructs the production team how to cut and assemble the sample based on the measurements and specifications of the pattern's accompanying technical pack. The technical pack is a document like an author's footnote in that it advises the production team on how to read the pattern for cutting and sewing. This moment of creative and critical evaluative labor must happen, otherwise no material transformation takes place and the process effectively halts. Composition instructors and those familiar with assessing student writing may recognize this as the moment students transform ideas and outlines to drafts.

Like a draft, the dress sample is evaluated. The dress sample is placed either on a form or on a fit model, and everyone from the designer to production assistants, patternmakers, the fit model, business partners, retailer representatives, and editors may be present at this time. A designer and their assistants may evaluate whether the design is good and coheres to the collection's theme and whether the fit or fabric is right; a retail buyer may judge whether their customers will like the dress enough to purchase it at full price; and an editor may judge whether the designer is pushing conceptual boundaries. The different concerns different participants stress parallel the different concerns a student's draft may evoke from their instructor, peer-review partner, or writing center tutor. This evaluative moment for the designer and writer suggests the ways in which both must negotiate their goals with the evaluations they receive. These evaluations need not be assessments *per se*, but we could imagine situations in which indeed the fitting stage curtails, delays, or supports further development just as moving from a written draft to final draft can be challenging for students. Circulation of the dress and written text may already extend beyond only one other individual, as I've described, so the revisions a writer makes before resubmitting the text for circulation and evaluation are similar to the redesigning and fittings a designer does before resubmitting the design.

Among those intervening to review the dress sample may be a technical designer. The technical designer is responsible for "review/development of techpacks [technical packs], fit assessment, supervising construction, and fabric issues which occur between buyers and suppliers in manufacturing" (Lee and Steen quoted in Lee and Park 2016, 59). The technical designer's attention to process, parties, materials, and products may remind writing instructors of their roles in managing the classroom iterations of process, parties, materials, and products and warrants our attention. Eunyoung Lee and Huiju Park (2016) studied how technical designers assessed the fit of virtual and actual garments in order to suggest what kinds of intervention may make virtual 3D technology more useful and accurate for technical designers (60). Their research calls attention to a major design and financial problem: "Virtual simulation technology tends to provide ideal drapes on the body."67 The problem is that ideal drapes won't show whether the garment hikes, gaps, or puckers; the technical designers could not use the technology to look closely at common fit issues (67). The technology problem the technical designers faced reminds me of how often technology can confuse our understanding of the writing constructs we want to measure, and more fundamentally, how our shift to embrace technology and multimodality may have serious limitations for writers and assessment of their work if we do not work with writers to understand their goals.

ASSESSMENT IN THE FASHION INDUSTRY

Circulation of the dress for assessment—for assessors to make decisions about how well the designer did their work—can take a few forms that resemble circulation of a student text for assessment: the dress can be worn in a runway show, a presentation, or a photo shoot, or it can be shown during meetings with potential retail buyers. It is in those meetings that true assessment happens: editors and critics respond, supporting or decrying the designer, retailers may order the item with or without adjustments (e.g., exclusive colors or style changes), brand followers make decisions about the dress—to buy or not to buy? to hate the designer or to sing praises?—and consumers make purchasing decisions (one of the most telling criteria of assessment). This stage of circulation can be multifaceted, with the initial circulation aimed at disseminating the dress to a wider audience, usually through material transformations; in other words, a runway show can be photographed, photos can be posted on blogs and social media, advertisements can extend the designer's reach to television or streaming video, a written review can describe the dress, and physical reproductions of the dress can arrive in stores for purchase. All decisions ultimately influence the retail item, and the customer's response to the item indicates how well the designer and their team anticipated the needs of and prepurchase evaluation by their audience—in other words, how well the designer and their team modeled the customer's needs, shopping motivation, and the criteria that influence a purchase. Although price may be an important criterion, Tammy Robinson and Farrell Doss (2011) explore other criteria, including reference-group influence, prestige versus imitation status, and perceived transaction risk (282).

Meanwhile, other fashion companies are assessing the dress and may decide to knock off the designer's work at a lower price point and with a quicker turnaround time to capitalize on the design's novelty. The knock-off and the speed at and degree to which the design saturates the market are additional parameters for assessment of the knock-off but also of the original design—is it "good enough" to copy? Furthermore, the designer may assess that their design was well done, and they may reinterpret it for a secondary or diffusion line targeting an audience with needs and dispositions similar but not identical to those of the audience for their signature high-fashion line. Such self-reflection and self-assessment also demonstrate the designer's ability to receive and act on evaluations: it would be remiss for a designer, a participant in the process, or a potential consumer to misunderstand the fashion process as one in which a designer works in total isolation. Therefore, the designer keeps in mind the anticipated needs of their various audiences and assessors while attending to the needs of specific assessors with specific criteria at specific moments along the fashion cycle. After sharing for public assessment, the designer receives feedback that can inform their next collection and decisions. This moment for summative self-assessment affords an opportunity for the designer to look back at their work, and it mirrors the reflection essays and portfolios students produce in the composition classroom.

Thus, the fashion process involves a series of multifaceted and multidirectional negotiations as the designer's text undergoes material transformations. As instructors, we can speculate that the designer, like students, engages in reflection most likely throughout the process; starting from the inspiration stages to the show finale, the designer must negotiate what they intend to contribute to the fashion ecology and how to do so. We see our students facing their related set of concerns about discourse community, exigency, rhetorical appeals and constraints, audience, and criteria by which they will be assessed. The fast pace of the fashion calendar has prompted designers to design collections more quickly than ever before, and designers must take into account the reception(s) their collections garner as they design and reconsider assessments of their work. Sometimes, a designer revisits a collection to rework or recast pieces they liked or perhaps didn't get entirely right; other times, a designer uses one collection as a counterpoint to another, which demands the assessors maintain a working repertoire of the designer's work. The potential reiterations may remind instructors of students revising their writing and the compressed time within which they must compose and we must assess.

Finally, just as it is commonplace for designers to have their own aesthetics, different designers have different ideas about fit, sales, market reception, what clothing should do, and the like. In other words, different designers have different benchmarks and interpretations of industry-wide criteria; more to the point, sometimes the benchmarks for a particular designer's work change to reflect the economic and aesthetic guidance of the company, which is not necessarily owned and operated by the designer. For example, the elusive Japanese designer Rei Kawakubo is considered an icon for the daring designs she creates for her line Comme des Garçons and for the business sense she and her partner-husband Adrian Joffe wield in managing diffusion collections and supporting like-minded designers. Kawakubo is tight lipped about her work, and critics often read her designs for messages, which we can understand, but her designs seek to perpetually confuse them. Like Kawakubo, students may wish to shape their work without seeming regard—or, perhaps, with clear disregard—for standards, expectations, and criteria. We also know that sometimes students are deeply motivated even if they operate in resistance, but they do not operate in isolation. Writers and designers always already operate in a system of distributed authorship shaped by distributed assessment and circulation.

Decisions about what "counts" as a good writing or good design may not be made by assessors nearest the text and most aware of its production and exigency, but they, nonetheless, assess and expect their assessment to trickle down to programs, instructors, and students; however, this is precisely the problem with writing assessment rooted in a linear, print-based tradition. "Trickle down" of criteria does not work; instead, we need a model of writing assessment that cycles through a network of participants, and such a model must embrace distributed authorship, distributed assessment, and (re)circulation as part of the production cycle in order to teach us how to better assess our students' writing and expand the breadth of the work multimodal writing assessment entails.

Like the elusive standards of "good writing," standards of good fit in the fashion industry are contingent and changing. Diana Sindicich and Catherine Black (2011) explain that customers' "satisfaction with the perceived fit of a garment may vary from the traditional definition of 'good fit' that is based on a set amount of ease [the difference between the garment's measurements and those of the model's body] located at certain body points and on the proper hang of the fabric grain in relation to the body and ground" (448). The point to notice is that "ease is an actual measurable distance, whereas fit is a relationship," and confusion about the terms, especially for the customer (448), may echo concerns about how we assess students' writing and what key terms (including, ironically, *style*) mean.

DISTRIBUTED AUTHORSHIP EXTENDS SITE(S) OF PRODUCTION

As the analogy of the fashion industry suggests, multimodality is deeply ingrained in materiality. Jody Shipka (2009) discusses the interplay of multimodality and materiality in the composition classroom to assure students they are "not composing or acting alone, but acting *with* (and sometimes even in spite of) the requirements of the tasks, the goals they adopt, and the specific material, rhetorical, methodological, and technological choices they made in service of those goals" (357). Shipka (2011) cautions against constraining what and how students compose and conflating multimodality with digital tools and digital writing; instead, she favors encouraging "students to examine the highly distributed and fundamentally multimodal aspects of all communicative practice" (84). Yet, Shipka's (2011) framework for assessment depends on students' reflection and makes it the students' "responsibility" to identify and address the rhetorical situation (87). Although students should engage in self-reflection, Shipka's focus on students-as-producers and production downplays the roles of assessment and assessors, as well as the other individuals giving shape to the context in which the composition was produced, circulated, and assessed. Shipka seems to think students single author texts—but somehow never "alone." However, a potentially more compelling interpretation of student authorship would recognize the role of distributed authorship. If authorship is distributed, we must think about the role of assessment. Assessment can distribute the "responsibility" Shipka entrusts to students through a network of assessors with different perspectives, expertise, and purposes for when and where they encounter a student text, much like what I have explained through the fashion analogy.

In the fashion industry, distributed authorship is always already happening because designers seek words, images, fabric swatches, and music and/or art, among other things, to fuel the creative process. Sometimes the inspiration is clearly evident in a design, and the same holds for writing; we can identify a kitschy printed fabric as inspired by Andy Warhol's pop art or the lines from Walt Whitman's "Song of Myself" or other texts students read with us. Writers, like designers, communicate with others; both borrow and play, reshape, and parody other textual encounters. Like Jim Ridolfo and Dànielle Nicole DeVoss (2009), I am "specifically interested in situations where composers anticipate and strategize future third-party remixing of their compositions as part of a larger and complex rhetorical strategy" (intro). Ridolfo and DeVoss define remixing—what I call *distributed authorship*—as the "process of taking old pieces of text, images, sounds, and video and *stitching* them together to form a new product," and the concept reminds us that writers typically "draw upon multiple modes of meaning-making" when producing a text (remix; italics mine). Writers put their compositions in conversation with other works quite literally and intertextually; writers also anticipate how someone else will address their work. The bidirectionality of distributed assessment mirrors the forward and back looking of a fashion designer anticipating the response from a curmudgeonly editor, savvy retail buyers, and other assessors, as well as reconsidering their previous work and that of other designers.

Distributed authorship informs us that the speed and reception of a text are different than they were before the networked classroom; it also informs us that our ideas about authorship and assessment must change to resituate composition in its material conditions and social relations. Students situate their work by the very nature of anticipating their audience's needs, which certainly include their assessor's needs. According to Ridolfo and DeVoss (2009), "When the rhetor delivers a text into a new context," a transformation of modality occurs (remix). For these transformations to occur, students must be aware of the contexts of production, as well of as circulation and assessment; otherwise, how would a student compose a text that responds to and/or anticipates audience needs? Distributed authorship encourages students to recognize—implicitly or explicitly—the material and social conditions in which a text is produced, circulated, and assessed by emphasizing the remixed—the stitched—nature of a composition: a composition is a material object made from bits and pieces of images and phrases, audio files, and motivations. Compositions never exist "in the wild" completely free of influences, pressures, and discourses; a model of writing assessment that honors distributed authorship aligns with what we signal every time we remind our students to think about their intervention in a critical conversation or conduct a rhetorical analysis on a music video. Distributed authorship acknowledges the producers who came before and anticipates audience expectations on which a text will be assessed and from which further remixing or revising may occur.

Furthermore, distributed authorship redirects the focus in composition classrooms away from composition as a single site to seeing it as spanning across sites of composition, circulation, and assessment. John Trimbur (2000) argues that our "privileging composing as the main site of instruction" has instilled a limited understanding of composition-as-production with the effect of "largely eras[ing] the cycle that links the production, distribution, exchange, and consumption of writing" (190). Trimbur maps this cycle to Karl Marx's concept of circulation (190), and I suggest instructors explicitly acknowledge the roles authorship and assessment perform in this cycle. Circulation is crucially important to the writing process and, by extension, should be important in writing assessment; how a text is produced and circulates matters. Circulation "must be seen also as ethical and political—a democratic aspiration to devise delivery systems that circulate ideas, information, opinions, and knowledge and thereby expand the public forums" (190). The point is circulation—and what happens when a text circulates in terms of authorship and assessment—should be connected to and reflective of a text's production; circulation marks a text's transformation of modality. If circulation is a multivocal, inclusive endeavor, the means of authorship and especially assessment must also be multivocal, inclusive, and distributed throughout the network of production and circulation. Therefore, we must acknowledge the role of previous and complementary authors shaping the text's production and circulation, as well as the role of different assessors who must participate in the text's assessment to shape its cultural value.

Our fixation on multimodality strikes me as an attempt to heed Cynthia L. Selfe's (2009) call to expose students to "opportunities of developing expertise with *all available means* of persuasion and expression" (618; italics in original). Yet, we cannot talk about multimodality as an end in and of itself because we risk effacing the material and social conditions of production, circulation, and assessment—each of which carries material and social implications for the text, writer, and assessor(s). Trimbur's (200) express politicization of circulation should inspire us to frame multimodal writing and writing more generally as deeply intertwined with materiality: the text's own materiality as well as its role as a product of a writer's labor to which assessments will be attached. The impact of such framing would transform texts into vehicles for creating, sharing, and critiquing what Trimbur calls "socially useful knowledge" (191). Thus, a model of writing assessment premised on distributed authorship and distributed assessment redirects our attention to "think of democracy as necessarily a communicative process that depends on an extended delivery system" (191). If we ask our students to compose texts that perform self-defined, meaningful work, it is our responsibility to treat the texts, their producers, and their assessors in a system as "popular participation in civic life" (191). In the fashion industry, Kawakubo's designs circulate her ideas, and her assessors respond; as Kawakubo's text circulates, participants engage the opportunities for inclusivity and knowledge making afforded by their performative roles.

DISTRIBUTED ASSESSMENT CHALLENGES KNOWLEDGE MAKING

This model of writing assessment stresses that meaning making happens both before production, because of a network of distributed authorship, and after production, through circulation when distributed assessment occurs. Like the fashion industry, in which a design must undergo material transformations to reach its various audiences and assessors and thereby accrue value, this model of writing assessment honors the cycle through which "writing circulates as it takes on cultural value and worldly force" (Trimbur 2000, 194). Diminishing the space for meaning making to the site of production limits the meaning-making potential of the text and limits the participants and their roles in this civic process of textual engagement. Similar to how multimodality has broadened the types of texts we invite students to produce, this model of writing assessment extends the reach of multimodality and reunites it with materiality to claim that the cycle of production, circulation, and assessment is materially sensitive; like the fabrics and laborers available to a designer at the moment they need them, no text can be produced without participating in and reflecting on what and who was available in a situated place and time with particular social, economic, cultural, and political forces weighing on the designer.

My argument for this model of writing assessment is compelled by a need to change how we make knowledge in writing studies. The recursive nature of production, circulation, and assessment in the fashion industry inspires this model of writing assessment, which can resist the classical model of production, distribution, exchange, and consumption Marx deemed problematic because of its being "a linear one, in which the moments are autonomous and sequential" (Trimbur 2000, 205). A model of writing assessment centered on distributed authorship and distributed assessment realigns our values and practices by expelling a linear process of production to assessment via circulation in favor of a cycle with moments responding "dialectically, as mediations in mutual and coterminous relations" (206). By analogizing the fashion industry and writing, I describe a model of writing based on distributed authorship and distributed assessment that strives to "understand and, potentially, to change the way knowledge circulates" by focusing our attention on "how the means of production are distributed in the first place" (212).

A promising example of changing how knowledge is made—and what kind of knowledge counts—in the composition classroom is from Denise Newfield, David Andrew, Pippa Stein, and Robert Maungedzo (2003). Newfield et al. draw attention to the intersection of learning with "learner's interests, prior knowledge, history and identity" and wonder how assignments engaging with representational forms and identity can help students "recover their voices, their histories, multiple languages and identities" (62–63). Their South African students worked on a quilt for which they collected scrap fabric and wrote poems; they then stitched it with other objects before sending it to another group of students in China. The students generally reported great satisfaction because the project allowed them to draw on their respective culture(s) and prepare a text for an audience with which they wanted to communicate in a personally meaningful way. Students' desire for assessment reveals they were clearly engaged in reflection and self-assessment, and additional assessment from others (i.e., the teacher) would confirm the quilt project had "value" for others as well (66–67). In this situation, the close connection the students felt with the multimodal text demanded assessment, and it seems Newfield et al. support assessment when it focuses on "the potential or interest of the learner" and contributes knowledge locally to the student and classroom and to the field (70). Therefore, what students create should be considered in a "broader process of making and receiving/viewing/interacting"; assessment can be a discursive process to "engage with the makers of the objects, the students, their relationship to their contexts and histories, and with the viewers of the object and process" to avoid effacing "*relationships between and beyond*" the project and classroom (75, 77; italics in original).

Newfield et al. (2003) focus education on individual learners, ask students to take on the role of experts, and disrupt who and what create knowledge. These students engage in what Trimbur (2000) calls the "production of socially useful knowledge" and challenge notions of expertise, "not from outside but from within the process of production and the circulation" (214). In other words, we cannot critique outside the cycle in which a text is embedded; we must acknowledge our place within. Thus, distributed authorship foregrounds the roles writers past, present, and projected perform as they engage with texts and textual production. Like Trimbur, I am not arguing to supplant "one group of experts for another" but to understand and "redistribute the means of production" (216). Essentially, we should expand our conceptualization of production to include circulation and assessment as moments shaping and making meaning to expand our understanding of writing assessment into a meaning-making activity that necessarily must be part of production.

Problematizing expertise demands a model of writing assessment presupposed on distributed assessment. According to Carl Whithaus (2005), "A distributed assessment system does not insist that all readers read alike" (88). Rather, this model "include[s] multiple, and potentially different, responses to a composition" in order to substantiate its purpose of providing "an accurate evaluation of how well a student writes" (88). In the fashion analogy, participants other than the designer evaluate and assess during production and circulation: various individuals perform types of labor at different sites, from cutting and sewing in the designer's studio to writing a fashion critique in an office to posting a photo with a caption on social media from a dressing room. We can engage in more multivocal, inclusive assessment practices by allowing students to give weight to criteria they identify for their own work and that of others. Whithaus(2005) states what may seem latent, but it is worth repeating: "The value of a text, of a communicative action, is determined by its reception as well as by the structures embedded within it" (95). Reception and structures—contexts of production and reception—are sites worth probing for suggestions about where and how assessment(s) may be taking place and by whom. Distributed assessment reminds us that composition and assessment are social and should be considered in light of the "interactions of a writer and her audience" (102). Assessment happens throughout: it is already distributed. In a classroom, we might imagine asking students to write a marketing pitch for a local juice business, and we might invite a professor of marketing, a marketing executive, and representatives from the juice business to assess the students' written pitches. We may also assess the pitches, and we may invite students to assess each other and themselves (self-assessment). Prior to their pitches, students would have researched, written and revised, assessed how they were doing, and conferenced to receive evaluative feedback from their instructor and/or classmates. Distributed assessment would take all these assessments into account and give weight to the different viewpoints and reports.

We are familiar with a type of distributed assessment, even if we do not name it as such and even if we do not use it more effectively: ePortfolio assessment. Whether a single assessor or a writing program convenes for ePortfolio assessment, it is distributed assessment; however, since this type of assessment tends to happen at the end of the semester, the assessment of any student text is typically limited to assigning a final, summative value and stripped it of its meaning-making potential. If we think more deeply about ePortfolio assessment as distributed assessment, we can recognize that we as assessors can double as authors in a situated production cycle. Kathleen Blake Yancey, Stephen J. McElroy, and Elizabeth Powers (2013) provide an example of how reading ePortfolios can highlight assessments's "embodied nature" to remind us that composers are deeply connected to the material and social contexts with and through which they produce and anticipate their text will circulate and be subject to assessment (12). How students compose and we assess could take up Yancey, McElroy, and Powers's extrapolation of "viewing/reading" as "a set of continuous practices" with "*multiple* reading processes that one needs to engage in" (14; italics in original). The "*multiple* reading processes" with which an assessor may assess a text or group of texts in an individual ePortfolio or across an entire class's ePortfolios is a further variation on distributed assessment in that the multiplicity of assessments could come from the same individual. The primary advantage here is that "all the 'burden' in assessment is thus not on the composer: it's a shared responsibility between composer and viewer/reader" (14). Thus, it goes without saying that any "shared responsibility" will require "we as viewer/reader . . . to do our part [to operationalize multiple reading practices]" (14).

When I consider Yancey, McElroy, and Powers's (2013) multiple readings in addition to Shipka's (2011) reservations "with how *a narrow definition of technology fails to encourage richly nuanced, situated views of literacy*" (31; italics in original), I wonder how else we might reframe our understanding of multimodality and assessment. The context of textual production is crucially important for understanding this model because authors and assessors could be at multiple locations in the cycle of production, participating in both activities perhaps simultaneously: assessors, in shaping texts in a cycle of continuous production, could be authors. Chris W. Gallagher (2014b) suggests multimodal writing assessment "more productively engage 'context' by shifting our focus from the surround to how multimodal texts *perform* contexts" (2–3; italics in original). It is helpful for us to think about the performative nature of texts because we expect performance to be assessed by multiple audiences and audience members in multiple ways, and performance invites the kind of distributed assessment Whithaus (2005) describes. More than that, performance can include multiple performers and/or be the product of a collaborative team of authors in roles with distributed responsibilities and expectations. In the fashion industry, few designers actually work alone; rather, they have the support and talent of a design team that may not get the recognition afforded whoever's name is on the label inside the dress, but they nonetheless help author the design and shepherd it through a cycle of production with other authors shaping and, yes, assessing, the design. In our classrooms, do we not ask students to collaborate during group discussions, peer review, and as they analyze cultural and/or critical discourses?, and do we not collaborate with them as their instructors in giving feedback, conferencing about their writing, and shaping the contexts and content of the course? To posit that a multimodal text performs is to posit that a text carries traces of its production—where, how, and by whom—as it transforms and is transformed by circulation and assessment.

Gallagher suggests we think about the ePortfolio as "*interface-as-encounter*" (2014b, 11; italics in original). We should extend our definition to "production-as-encounter" to consider the multilayered material transformations texts undergo as they are positioned in certain material and social relations to their composers and assessors, and we should assess them in a production cycle that facilitates distributed assessment. Gallagher describes how one student's work anticipated "multiple *kinds* of encounters" by including visuals, "Critical Thinking," and "Construction Site" signposts, among other things (6–7, 10; italics in original). The interface allowed the student to cultivate different experiences for various audiences, and the inclusion of process-related material anticipated some audiences would be interested to "learn *how* she did this work" (9; italics in original), which highlights the ways in which a text's performativity intersects with materiality in multimodal spaces situated for distributed assessment and distributed authorship, as Gallagher's article demonstrates in his representations and interpretations.

Doing this work urges us to focus on enabling the conditions for students to facilitate different kinds of encounters and thus different kinds of authorship and assessment; perhaps then we might not be so focused on interrater reliability preconceived according to psychometrics "in which reliability is defined as consistency" (Gallagher 2014a, 74). Distributed assessment, as I am discussing it, works best if we turn to rhetorical reliability. Rhetorical reliability allows us to examine how we, individually and collectively, draw conclusions about students and their texts, as well as "the nature, status, and function of our accounts" (74). This reliability is "most consistent with the way our field understands what happens when people read and write" (78) because it recognizes the importance of the production cycle's situated contexts and emphasizes assessment as contingent upon meaning making. Furthermore, rhetorical reliability also challenges notions of an expert, centralized assessor and the power dynamics inherent in such centralization because it is sensitized to "articulate (that is, to state, but also to put in meaningful relation) a range of unassimilated, inappropriate/d perspectives" (84). As in the fashion-industry analogy, with multiple kinds of assessments occurring as the result of multiple participants, rhetorical reliability "embraces and preserves reader differences" and foregrounds how an assessor's expertise is called upon and how it is used (84, 90). The model of writing assessment I am proposing ascribes its reliability in "making productive use of credible situated reader accounts" (90) and recognizes those accounts can shape a text's meaning because its assessors participate in a system of distributed assessment, and by extension, distributed authorship.

A model for writing assessment supported by rhetorical reliability invites occasions for students to revise their texts, as well as to reflect on assessments in succeeding assignments, conferences with their instructor, or perhaps a classroom roundtable. Students can be granted opportunities to demonstrate how they negotiated their goals with the assessments and can be asked to explain how they found the assessments useful. Students, instructors, and other assessors can be made more aware of all the work being done with and through a text to revise notions of expertise and meaning making to diminish classroom hierarchies. Instructors can use assessments and reflective follow-up work to identify patterns, gaps, successes, and challenges to address in their teaching and assignments. The potential implications of rhetorical reliability and a distributed model of writing assessment are particularly important because instructors—and their students and writing programs—would have more data to make informed decisions about the kind of work students are asked to compose and the contexts that can make it meaningful. As for grading of this work, instructors could negotiate with their students how the assessments will contribute to their grades; perhaps assessments would weigh evenly, or perhaps the students would develop grading criteria with the assessors. This writing-assessment process models how assessments can be local; can be dependent on various participants, purposes, and contexts; and can provide occasions for additional revision and reflection. Instructors and writing programs can demonstrate how participating in this writing-assessment model can transfer knowledge and how inclusivity need not elide differences amongst readings, composers, and assessors.

CONCLUSION

In the assessment literature, Bob Broad (2003) maintains, "We need to conduct the best inquiry we can" to identify what we value and how we correspond those values to a written text (3). Determining what the "best inquiry" is for particular classrooms, writing programs, and departments is a challenge, but it is a challenge we must consider in light of the different kinds of knowledge making students bring to our classrooms and the work they do across and beyond the curriculum. If collaborative working conditions are a real or an imagined reality for most students, and if we believe writing is part of, and responds to, socially constructed forces ranging from audience expectations and material conditions to ideologies and economies of power, then does not adopting a distributed—and by necessity, collaborative—process of authorship and assessment warrant a try? And if we acknowledge the varied technologies students compose with and within, as well as our own stress on writing as a recursive process that includes revision and managing audience(s) expectations, do we not owe it to our students to develop a theory of assessment that matches the distributed contexts in which it occurs? Like my analogy to the fashion industry suggests, the classroom need not reinscribe an exclusionary ideology of centralized authority and expertise. This more inclusive writing-assessment process invokes John Dewey's (1968) notion that democracy is a "way of life" premised on working with others to allow "differences a chance to show themselves because of the belief that the expression of difference is not only a right of the other persons but is a *means* of enriching one's own life-experience" (223, 226; italics added). Instead of democracy as a political institution, Dewey imagines it as a framework through which all individuals can contribute meaningfully when invited into a dialogic, cooperative relationship *because* of their different perspectives. What better context than the composition classroom to disrupt and postulate concepts of knowledge making and expertise in service of "enriching" our students' and our "life-experience"? On the whole, our classrooms are already interested in exploring the production, circulation, and assessment of texts, as my analogy to the multimodal and material dimensions of authorship and assessment in the fashion industry suggests.

In this chapter, I present a model for writing assessment based on the continuous cycle of authorship and assessment in the fashion industry, and this model's strength is that it interrupts our tendencies to work from a print tradition, moving instead toward a materially conscious, multimodal writing classroom. This model of writing assessment expands our understanding of production to include circulation and assessment as moments of meaning making, and it stresses the importance of contexts in order to maintain the integrity of the composition's textual production and purpose, its writer, and its assessors. Distributed authorship and distributed assessment rely on a concept of rhetorical reliability to share participation and responsibility in the cycle of assessment and authorship; assessors can perform as authors in light of the expanded sites of meaning-making potential. Compositions are likely benefiting from a system of distributed authorship and should be assessed by various participants to resituate composition and its assessment as recursive stages that do not occur after and/or in isolation from each other.

While I can imagine productive challenges for adopting such a model at the programmatic and/or institutional level, I also want to remind readers that the fashion industry routinely performs its process of distributed authorship and distributed assessment and regularly reflects on what, how, why, and who participates.

REFERENCES

Broad, Bob. 2003. "To Tell the Truth: Beyond Rubrics." In *What We Really Value: Beyond Rubrics in Teaching and Assessing Writing*, 1–15. Logan: Utah State University Press.

Dewey, John. 1968. "Creative Democracy—The Task Before Us." In *The Philosopher of the Common Man: Essays in Honor of John Dewey to Celebrate His Eightieth Birthday*, 220–28. New York: Greenwood.

Freeman, Charles, Jihyeong Son, and Lisa Barona McRoberts. 2015. "Comparison of Novice and Expert Evaluations of Apparel Design Illustrations Using the Consensual Assessment Technique." *International Journal of Fashion Design, Technology and Education* 8 (2):122–30. doi:10.1080/17543266.2015.1018960.

Gallagher, Chris W. 2014a. "Immodest Witnesses: Reliability and Writing Assessment." *Composition Studies* 42 (2): 73–95.

Gallagher, Chris W. 2014b. "Staging Encounters: Assessing the Performance of Context in Students' Multimodal Writing." *Computers and Composition* 31: 1–12. doi:10.1016/j.compcom.2013.12.001.

Keiser, Sandra J., and Myrna B. Garner. 2008. *Beyond Design: The Synergy of Apparel Product Development*. 2nd ed. New York: Fairchild.

Lee, Eunyoung, and Huiju Park. 2016. "3D Virtual Fit Simulation Technology: Strengths and Areas of Improvement for Increased Industry Adoption." *International Journal of Fashion Design, Technology and Education* 10 (1): 59–70. doi:10.1080/17543266.2016.1194483.

Newfield, Denise, David Andrew, Pippa Stein, and Robert Maungedzo. 2003. "'No Number Can Describe How Good it Was': Assessment Issues in the Multimodal Classroom." *Assessment in Education: Principles, Policy & Practice* 10 (1): 61–81. doi:10.1080/09695940301695.

Ridolfo, Jim, and Dànielle Nicole DeVoss. 2009. "Composing for Recomposition: Rhetorical Velocity and Delivery." *Kairos* 13 (2). http://kairos.technorhetoric.net/13.2/topoi/ridolfo_devoss/index.html.

Robinson, Tammy, and Farrell Doss. 2011. "Pre-Purchase Alternative Evaluation: Prestige and Imitation Fashion Products." *Journal of Fashion Marketing and Management: An International Journal* 15 (3): 278–90. doi:10.1108/13612021111151897.

Selfe, Cynthia L. 2009. "The Movement of Air, the Breath of Meaning: Aurality and Multi-modal Composing." *College Composition and Communication* 60 (4): 616–63. http://www.jstor.org/stable/40593423.

Sindicich, Diane, and Catherine Black. 2011. "An Assessment of Fit and Sizing of Men's Business Clothing." *Journal of Fashion Marketing and Management: An International Journal* 15 (4): 446–63. doi:10.1108/13612021111169942.

Shipka, Jody. 2009. "Negotiating Rhetorical, Material, Methodological, and Technological Difference: Evaluating Multimodal Designs." *College Composition and Communication* 61 (1):343–66. http://www.jstor.org/stable/40593537.

Shipka, Jody. 2011. *Toward a Composition Made Whole*. Pittsburgh, PA: University of Pittsburgh Press.

Trimbur, John. 2000. "Composition and the Circulation of Writing." *College Composition and Communication* 52 (2): 188–219. http://www.jstor.org/stable/358493.

Whithaus, Carl. 2005. *Teaching and Evaluating Writing in the Age of Computers and High-Stakes Testing*. Mahwah, NJ: Lawrence Erlbaum.

Yancey, Kathleen Blake, Stephen J. McElroy, and Elizabeth Powers. 2013. "Composing, Networks, and Electronic Portfolios: Notes Toward a Theory of Assessing ePortfolios." In *Digital Writing Assessment & Evaluation*, edited by Heidi A. McKee and Dànielle Nicole DeVoss. Logan: Computers and Composition Digital Press/Utah State University Press. http://ccdigitalpress.org/dwae/08_yancey.html.

13

MULTIMODAL PEDAGOGY AND MULTIMODAL ASSESSMENT
Toward a Reconceptualization of Traditional Frameworks

Shane A. Wood

INTRODUCTION

Multimodal pedagogy has been viewed within composition studies as an attempt to better understand and better recognize "the complex ways that texts come to be" (Shipka 2011, 13). Though relatively young in terms of scholarship and theory, multimodal compositionists continue to rethink and reimagine ways to compose in first- and second-year composition classrooms by calling for a move towards the aural, digital, spatial, visual, and, more broadly, the holistic process of composing. Multimodal pedagogy has been known to give students agency (Shipka 2011) in the formation and process of their own texts, valuing the *process* of the composition instead of the "product," which is the impetus of our field following the turn to writing-as-process in the 1970s (Murray 1976), redefining the notions of the way(s) a text could come to be. Multimodal scholarship has challenged traditional concepts for teaching writing by arguing that traditional frameworks cannot be easily applied or overtly transferred to multimodal pedagogy (Lutkewitte 2014). Claire Lutkewitte (2014) argues assertively, "We can't overlay traditional frameworks on multimodal compositions" (4). In her discussion, Lutkewitte emphasizes the evolving nature of theory and practice that shapes our discipline. As theory and practices change, so do our classrooms as we shift away from traditional frameworks. For my purposes, traditional frameworks rely on the teaching of composition through a singular mode—specifically the alphabetic text—while ignoring the possibilities for other modes (e.g., visual, spatial) to be embraced within composing processes.

Traditional frameworks limit student agency by further cultivating cultural hegemony and marginalize already marginalized voices, catering to academic expectations through reaffirming ideologies of a linguistic

DOI: 10.7330/9781607327974.c013

standard purposed for an academic audience. Ultimately, teaching composition through traditional frameworks restricts the purposes of multimodal pedagogy. The process of shifting towards a multimodal classroom that combines semiotic modes while intentionally moving away from traditional concepts of teaching composition is summarized well by Shipka (2011): "If we are committed to expanding the technologies and representational systems that composition and rhetoric, as a discipline, work with, theorize, and explore, our frameworks must support us in making the shift" (37). Shipka challenges composition studies to reconsider how *frameworks*—the systems and ideologies that construct our classrooms—reinforce a shift toward the multimodal. This question of whether our frameworks are supporting us in making the shift calls our attention to the ways in which frameworks are being used within our writing classrooms, asking us to approach these frameworks with an evaluative mindset. Analyzing and evaluating traditional frameworks can help us understand the structures in our classrooms and the purposes of those structures, thus creating a more flexible classroom space that attempts to adapt to newer pedagogies, like multimodality.

In this chapter, I call for a reconsideration of assessment that most effectively aligns with multimodal affordances. I'm not asking for a removal of assessment; instead, I'm asking for a reconceptualization. For my purposes, the traditional framework of assessment is based on the notion that a letter grade *must be* attached to a multimodal project or a piece of writing. In this chapter, I argue that assessment can be framed through the production of student labor, and that a labor-based assessment practice pushes against traditional frameworks—something multimodal pedagogy encourages—and complements the affordances of a multimodal pedagogical approach. While we have been able to move away from some traditional frameworks (e.g., the alphabetic text) through multimodal pedagogy, we have not been able to move away from others (e.g., traditional assessment).

I believe composition is at the edge of redefining traditional assessment through multimodal pedagogy; it is just not there (yet). This movement can be seen through multimodal scholarship and academic textbooks. For example, in Lutkewitte's 2014 book *Multimodal Composition: A Critical Sourcebook*, the smallest section in the edited collection—about thirty pages—is on multimodal assignments and assessment. Multimodal scholarship as a whole is still developing and discovering its own identity, including how multimodality moves away from traditional frameworks. Even terms within multimodality, like *multimedia, new media,* and *digital media,* seem too often mixed or interchanged. Discussions about what types of assignments are given, how students respond to these assignments, what this looks like in the classroom, and how these assignments are assessed are continually ongoing. Furthermore, first- and second-year writing textbooks are just now recognizing multimodality as part of composition studies and teaching writing. In 2016, W. W. Norton's *Everyone's an Author* (Second Edition) included a chapter on multimodality entitled "Writing in Multiple Modes." Multimodality is becoming a part of the way in which the field represents itself while also showing that multimodality is becoming an integral part of the field. Regardless of newness, multimodality has stamped its name on composition studies, and its emphasis on students' composing processes is a valuable affordance for our classrooms. For this reason, we need new frameworks of assessment to support these affordances.

In order to better understand how our assessment practices can support multimodal pedagogy, first I analyze what multimodal pedagogy affords the composition classroom by focusing on a few different aspects: process, student agency, and public audiences. By understanding the affordances of multimodal pedagogy, we can, hopefully, evaluate traditional assessment's presence within multimodal teaching and scholarship. My purpose is to illuminate an alternative assessment that complements multimodal pedagogy: the grading contract. The grading contract responds to the affordances of multimodal pedagogy and can be seen as one way to expand and support our shift(s) away from traditional framework(s) because the grading contract emphasizes process through labor, supports student agency through negotiation, and encourages genre and language flexibility. Additionally, the grading contract asks students to take risks, meet or subvert genre expectations, play with style and modes, and become attuned to the decisions they make as they engage in different labor processes. Therefore, in this chapter, I encourage teachers to use the grading contract as an assessment that responds to multimodal pedagogy.

THE AFFORDABILITY OF PROCESS IN MULTIMODAL PEDAGOGY

One of the greatest affordances of multimodal pedagogy is its initiative to push process in the writing classroom and encourage students to reflect on the process of composing. Multimodal pedagogy continually emphasizes process by asking students to become aware of the rhetorical choices they make through the creation of multimodal projects. The combination of different semiotic modes magnifies these choices in multimodal pedagogy. Lutkewitte (2014) broadly defines multimodal composition as "communication using multiple modes that work purposely to create meaning . . . situated and thus shaped by context, history, audience, place, time, and other factors" (2–3). Rhetorical awareness of a genre's functions and purposes is foundational in understanding multimodal pedagogy because multimodal pedagogy attempts to bring to light the entire composing process. In *Toward a Composition Made Whole,* Jody Shipka (2011) focuses on how multimodality draws more attention to process and to decisions about design, contextualizing the nature of when and where composing happens by considering outside academic spaces as a means for creating meaning inside the classroom.

Multimodal pedagogy prompts students to think about the choices they make in a way traditional assignments cannot, possibly due to the repetitive nature of traditional texts and students' numbness to them. Students are familiar with traditional frameworks based on the process of composing an alphabetic text (e.g., essay), and they know their performance is going to be evaluated by the product. Multimodality's emphasis on process counters traditional concepts, though, because it asks students to consider multiple modes throughout the process; the process becomes multifaceted. Other pedagogies (e.g., collaborative, feminist) may work to complement process as well. But if our pedagogies emphasize *process*, yet our assessments are based on traditional frameworks that value *product*, are we being effective?

Multimodal pedagogy is developing its own niche, focusing on encouraging and challenging students to think, recreate, discover, and explore the possibilities of modes outside the realms of the traditional alphabetic text and asking students to take risks through the process. Composing in digital modes, like a website, allows students to consider and reconsider layout, design, and spatial awareness. Multimodality provides the composition classroom an opportunity to understand the relationship of space, the positioning of images or texts in a lens through process, and multimodal pedagogy allows the ability to reposition images to create new meaning and emphasize process as a means of furthering exploration. Multimodality re-envisions process. Process is not stuck to a draft, per se, nor is it tied to one assignment for the purposes of the class. Process, through multimodal pedagogy, is multilayered because multimodality lends itself to continuation: the nature of websites, blogs, and social media is ongoing, never completed unless taken down or no longer updated by the user.

In 2007, Pamela Takayoshi and Cynthia L. Selfe wrote, "In a world where communication between individuals and groups is both increasingly cross-cultural and digital, teachers of composition are beginning to sense the inadequacy of texts—and composition instruction—that employs only one primary semiotic channel (the alphabetic) to convey meaning" (2). Multimodal pedagogy creates a space where meaning is developed through the process of multiple semiotic channels. Meaning-making is constructed through the act of experiencing and experimenting with various mediums and modes. True value and learning come from the process, not the end result. Traditional assessment holds multimodal pedagogy back by reaffirming the value of product over process: how often does *communication* stop in the writing classroom between teacher and student when process becomes product because the singular performance is evaluated and graded? Nearly always. The teacher may conference with the student about the grade, or discuss the purposes for providing feedback, but eventually the class is going to move forward with another assignment.

What if assessment allowed us to revisit assignments throughout the course of a semester, continuing conversations between teacher and student, complementing the nature of multimodal pedagogy? If we reconceptualize assessment and move towards a different framework, that possibility exists. Multimodal pedagogy, like composition studies as a whole, emphasizes and values process—thinking about thinking, writing about writing, composing, revising, analyzing conventions, and critically thinking about constructions—and through process, we can challenge traditional frameworks of assessment by looking at pedagogical affordances. All pedagogies offer something unique to shape teaching styles and interests, assignments and curriculum, and classroom discussions and to connect students to different genres of composing. Regardless of our pedagogies, we ask students to perform in different genres through our assignments. Multimodal pedagogy expands knowledge on genre and provides space for flexibility because it combines multiple semiotic modes, thus allowing meaning to be created through different genres. What if we asked students to work within a different means of assessment?

THE AFFORDANCES OF STUDENT CHOICE AND STUDENT AGENCY THROUGH MULTIMODAL PEDAGOGY

Another affordance of multimodal pedagogy is its focus on providing students with choices, cultivating student agency through their process(es). Claire Lauer (2014) writes that multimodal texts are "characterized by the mixed logics brought together through the combination of modes (such as images, text, color, etc.)" (24). The formation of these texts, like all texts (even alphabetic), does not happen linearly. According to Shipka (2011), students must question their own role and what they bring to the genre and rhetorical situation in a multimodal classroom: "A composition made whole recognizes that . . . students may still be afforded the opportunities to consider how they are continually positioned in ways that require them to read, respond to, align with—in short, to negotiate—a streaming interplay of words, images, sounds, scents, and movements" (21). The nature of process leads to opportunities of agency. Multimodal pedagogy provides more opportunities for agency due to its reliance on multiple semiotic modes; students are afforded both a voice and the ability to play with logics through multimodal pedagogy.

Not only that, but multimodal pedagogy breaks constructions that continue hegemony within traditional frameworks. Multimodal pedagogy attempts to embrace all student voices: "Multimodal composition allows for many voices—even those new, marginalized, or unpopular voices—to be heard" (Lutkewitte 2014, 5). A multimodal approach resists traditional frameworks that cater to specific identities, particularly individuals who have geographical, socioeconomic, and racial advantages in the US university. In traditional frameworks for teaching writing, the alphabetic text, which can take the form of an essay or research paper, usually values the academic expectation of standard edited American English (SEAE). This type of assignment, ultimately, does not value other languages or linguistic differences. In fact, it further marginalizes students of color and students whose linguistic backgrounds differ from SEAE. Because multimodal assignments provide a space for flexibility while allowing the classroom to question academic standards and norms, multimodal assignments can provide an opportunity for marginalized voices, voices restricted by traditional frameworks, to be heard. For example, multimodality already positions itself against traditional frameworks by questioning the idea of linguistic acceptance. Aural, spatial, and visual compositions push the academic norm of traditional alphabetic texts. Additionally, a multimodal classroom can evaluate the very notion of linguistic standards imposed on students in academia; students composing via text message, or other social media outlets, counters the linguistic expectations of SEAE. At the same time, multimodality and multimodal assignments can complement other pedagogies, like translingualism, that push against linguistic hegemony. Rhetorical flexibility through multimodal pedagogy allows students the affordance of approaching projects in their own way—through their own language, their own voice, their own style, and with their own backgrounds.

Traditional frameworks often limit student agency and support classroom hierarchy while reasserting hegemony and academic ideologies. Multimodal pedagogies, which focus on deconstructing power structures, can challenge such tendencies. One academic ideology that persists through classrooms and affects students is the concept of *failure*. In this ideology, failure is a plague, it is nonnegotiable, and it symbolizes ignorance. Allison Carr (2013) writes, "The effeminacy and shamefulness associated with failure . . . pervades those handbooks that represent and forward dominant ways of thinking about good writing, handbooks which, for better or worse, we trust." Even classroom resources, like handbooks, signal an idea of failure in direct relationship to student writing. But failure should not be associated with overwhelming negativity. In fact, failure can be reconceived: failure is normal; failure can be accepted; failure creates success. Through multimodal pedagogy, teachers and students work to better understand the combination of semiotic modes. Unlike traditional classrooms where students are shamed for experiencing failure, a multimodal classroom says failure is necessary. Multimodal assignments inherently value risk taking. Colleen A. Reilly and Anthony T. Atkins (2013) describe the reality of failure through multimodality: "Creating digital texts often requires that students learn new skills, which simultaneously requires that they take risks and experience failure." Multimodal assignments allow students to enjoy failure, to participate in new genres without the fear of being penalized by their choices. In the traditional framework, teachers can still value failure and risk taking, but they are ultimately tied to a standard expectation: producing and delivering a letter grade. Multimodal pedagogy expects failure, whereas traditional pedagogy expects something finished. The expectation is different, shaping the ideologies within the classroom. Ultimately, assessment helps construct these ideologies and expectations.

But assessment must mirror the nature of these assignments in order for the pedagogy to truly embrace failure. The assignment cannot lend itself to failure while the assessment punishes students for their choices. Multimodal pedagogy must reimagine assessment in order to complement its values. More specifically, a reimagined assessment that encourages linguistic flexibility, the ability to play with languages and dialects, can help us with that shift. For example, an assessment system that moves away from the ideal hegemonic SEAE and moves towards a more translingual approach can transform the classroom. Or an assessment system that moves away from the status quo of an alphabetic text and moves towards an embrace of multiple modes and risk taking can transform the classroom. Risk taking is an affordance of multimodal pedagogy and multimodal assignments, often asking students to call on everyday literacies and expanded audiences.

THE AFFORDANCES OF STUDENT LITERACIES AND PUBLIC AUDIENCES IN MULTIMODAL PEDAGOGY

Multimodal pedagogy provides students the opportunity to think outside academia to a broader, extended audience. Traditional frameworks can position students to think about an extended audience through the assignment prompt, but students know who the audience is—the teacher—and they know that, under traditional frameworks of assessment, the teacher is going to assess their work. Traditional frameworks and pedagogies may err towards a more academic audience, preparing students for more academic tasks. The multimodal classroom, on the other hand, challenges the singular academic audience. The binary of private versus public is complicated through multimodal pedagogy: "Multimodal essays allow us to see how the audience students often envision in print modes can be extended to include people beyond the classroom" (Powell, Alexander, and Borton 2011). Students also have ownership of their audiences through multimodal pedagogy (Powell, Alexander, and Borton 2011). Through digital compositions, students must negotiate audiences and spaces that are far more public than print texts inside the classroom; they already navigate such spaces in their lives outside the classroom. For example, there is plenty of agency through Twitter: an individual can decide whom to follow, reply to, or retweet; they can decide to make an account private or public, either limiting or opening their audience; and, for the most part, they can post whatever they want.

Most students already compose online, and social media has influenced daily compositions of our culture; more than likely, it is *how* students read and write on a day-to-day basis. Multimodal pedagogy asserts that other modes can provide practice in the same skills traditional approaches afford: analysis, synthesis, and research. Twitter, Facebook, Instagram, Snapchat, and blogs can illuminate rhetorical awareness as well, while also challenging the inside versus outside binary. Multimodal compositions, in particular, are everywhere, not just inside academia and not just in the Western context. Multimodal pedagogy provides a bridge: it values social media compositions; it opens the possibility for students to see how much they read and write daily; it provides new means for discussing the composing and thinking process; it invites another purpose, audience, and situation to be explored in the writing classroom; it fosters new means of critical thinking and textual analysis; and it affords a study of cross-cultural contexts.

The multimodal classroom can complicate students' perceptions of social media audiences through analytical discussions of how purpose and meaning change depending on the audiences interpreting their posts. Students practice reading and writing more through these mediums than anything else because they have personal experiences with them. By opening such spaces inside our classrooms, we might come across different ideas and concepts and language use and purposes we are not familiar with . . . and that is okay. Paying attention to other spaces as opportunities to create meaning is important to our field's relevancy, especially as multimodal communication and literacy increase (Kress 2003; 2009). But we must consider what our assessments are doing and whether they support us in our pedagogy. Reconceptualizing assessment to value flexibility by emphasizing student agency can benefit our multimodal classroom and requires a shift away from the traditional framework of assessment.

At the heart of multimodal pedagogy is the ability to challenge traditional frameworks, which I applaud, but I question whether it has done enough (yet) to resist traditional frameworks of assessment. Assessment is tricky regardless of our pedagogical approach because it *must be done*. Multimodal scholarship has provided different ways to assess multimodal assignments, illuminating what assessment looks like and how it functions in a multimodal classroom, and there is something to be learned from these types of assessments. But I believe we can do more: are our assessments really pushing the traditional paradigm as much as possible?

CURRENT ASSESSMENT PRACTICES AND THEORY IN MULTIMODAL PEDAGOGY

Chanon Adsanatham (2012) echoes the thoughts of many compositionists and multimodal scholars when it comes to the process of creating assessment: "We must engage students to become active creators/ contributors of knowledge in our teaching and evaluation" (155). The communal aspect of creating assessment through collaboration aligns with what many assessment scholars note as a best practice (Danielewicz and Elbow 2009; Inoue 2004; Reilly and Atkins 2013). Adsanatham (2012) incorporates participation by asking students to create their own grading criteria, pushing students to take agency over their own assessment. Encouraging student agency through the process of creating criteria complements multimodal pedagogy. Therefore, I build on the good work other scholars are already doing in multimodality and assessment by proposing a holistic classroom-assessment system that supports process, student agency, translingualism, student literacies, public audiences, and a multigenre approach, aligning with the ideologies of multimodal pedagogy.

Reilly and Atkins (2103) write that pedagogy and assessment "should be directly supportive," and they urge compositionists to take more risks when assessing multimodality because multimodal pedagogy encourages risk. Reilly and Atkins focus on classroom-based assessment of digital projects, and they acknowledge that multimodal composing, specifically creating digital texts, "requires" students to "take risks and even experience failure." At the same time, they admit the difficulty of assessing digital compositions. Reilly and Atkins encourage "aspirational processes of assessment," which come in the form of creating open-ended criteria, using student reflections, and constructing criteria that complement primary-trait scoring, and they note the benefit of students having a voice in the criteria process, creating "aspiration." The students create the criteria, and the classroom spends time talking about assessment, which is important to discuss in the classroom space. Other multimodal scholars attempt to reimagine and recreate assessment that deviates from the traditional. For example, Shipka (2011) offers a "statement of goals and choices" as a way to embrace the affordances of process. This type of assessment is a "highly detailed" statement explaining the process behind composing each multimodal project. In *Toward a Composition Made Whole*, Shipka moves toward valuing process and the importance of making students aware of choices in multimodal pedagogy: "What is crucial is that students leave their courses exhibiting a more nuanced awareness of the various choices they make, or even fail to make, throughout the process of producing a text" (85). This awareness allows students to discover meaning through making *choices*, one affordance of multimodal pedagogy, which allows students the ability to experience failure by taking risks—another affordance. Shipka's assessment is similar to other constructions of reflective texts composition scholars have implemented in their own classrooms and assessments (Elbow 1997; White 2005). Shipka (2011) discusses the purpose: "to rigorously document products-in-relation-to-processes and to detail the various strategies . . . they [students] employed in order to accomplish their goals and shape their audiences' reception of their work" (120). This is noble in that it cultivates student meta-awareness of the process (and their own process) of composing a text.

More recently, Lori Beth De Hertogh (2014) reimagines assessment and pushes for a "revised assessment model" in multimodal pedagogy. De Hertogh encourages "our field to rethink what we do and do not value in our current process-based assessment methods." Thinking about what we do and do not value gives us the opportunity to question our frameworks, something that should be in a continual state of revision. Shifting towards an assessment model that counters the traditional model is not easy, but De Hertogh recommends "digital badges" and believes digital badges are an "excellent" alternative to traditional frameworks of assessment. The purpose of these badges is to validate the work and accomplishments of students, while at the same time giving students something to work for in the classroom, possibly encouraging students to be aware of their processes and the effects of their choices. The digital-badge movement has been embraced and designed by large software companies like Mozilla (Open Badges) and is used inside and outside academia. Digital badges have also been suggested by other scholars (Elkordy 2012) and implemented at universities like Purdue. Digital badges are like merit badges, and their digital nature suits multimodality well. If a student completes a specific task, then, through the online program, the student "earns" a digital badge indicating their success. While new, digital badges offer a different assessment framework that complicates ideologies of traditional assessments, challenging us to reconsider what we do and how we do it when we assess student compositions.

De Hertogh's suggestion of digital badges, though, is still attached to some defining aspects of traditional assessments. For example, the digital-badge system is primarily focused on extrinsic motivations. Traditional frameworks value extrinsic motivators and work to make students get something done in order to receive some type of "reward." Other disciplines have already argued against extrinsic motivations. Research in psychology and education shows that extrinsic motivations are not nearly as successful or effective at motivating students as is intrinsic motivation (Kohn 1999). In an extrinsically based assessment system, students become fixated more on the grade, or the reward, and less on the process of learning or acquiring knowledge. The US educational system is permeated with this type of extrinsically based assessment. For students, it starts as early as five to six years old in kindergarten classes that provide "stars" or other rewards for "good" behavior (Kohn 1999). Intrinsic motivations, on the other hand, are internally based on the individual and work to foster an individual's own interests. Multimodal pedagogy caters to intrinsic motivation by providing students an opportunity to assert their own voices and make their own choices. Through an intrinsically based classroom, students are encouraged to discover what they are interested in. Multimodal pedagogy encourages this type of flexibility within the classroom and through the composing process. Assessment should also reflect these intrinsic values.

Even with these reconsiderations of assessment through multimodality, many of the alternatives still seem inherently connected to traditional assessment. While it is unlikely for assessment to break completely away from tradition, we can begin reimagining the role of assessments in our multimodal classrooms to continue conversations that resist traditional concepts of assessment. For example, in Reilly and Atkins's model (2013), even though students are creating the scoring criteria, the project is assessed via a traditional letter grade placed on the individual assignment. I believe Shipka (2011) runs into the same type of problem, assessing the individual multimodal project and the individual reflection, in her statement of goals and outcomes. Both types of assessments, ultimately, align closely with how traditional assessment is produced, and the folly comes in the *assessment process*. If the multimodal assignment is still tied to traditional assessment, it undercuts the purpose of the pedagogy. If multimodality is about *process*, the multimodal classroom must complement that process through an assessment that aligns more closely with those values. An assessment that finalizes a product based on the distribution of a letter grade is not what works most effectively in a multimodal classroom.

While multimodal scholarship has resisted some aspects of traditional frameworks well, other aspects, such as assessment, seem to linger, hindering multimodal pedagogy with traditional elements that work against its pedagogical affordances. So, what does the grading contract look like in a multimodal classroom? I believe it looks like it does in any other composition classroom, but, more specifically, the grading contract complements the multimodal classroom by answering its invitation to move away from traditional frameworks. The grading contract is an alternative method of assessment that can be applied to first- and second-year writing courses in English, and even to graduate courses. I have seen it work effectively in both. The requirements of labor can be mapped out and negotiated between teacher and students in the first week of class, which emphasizes process and student agency through negotiation. What follows is my proposed assessment alternative, which breaks from the traditional frameworks in new ways. When I use the grading contract in my class, we form the labor expectations and requirements together: the whole class is operating under the same grading contract. This approach supports and encourages collaboration while also holding us accountable to specific standards.

A SHIFT TOWARDS THE GRADING CONTRACT IN THE MULTIMODAL CLASSROOM

The grading contract is the most effective system model for multimodal pedagogy because it pushes against traditional frameworks of assessment by confronting their nature through highlighting their flaws and instilling values more consistent with multimodal pedagogy. The grading contract is an assessment system based on student labor, or the amount of work a student chooses to put in throughout the course; it invites negotiation—between teacher and student, between student and student—and through negotiation, it has specific requirements and expectations of labor. The grading contract confronts traditional limitations in assessment while simultaneously complementing values within multimodal pedagogy: cultivating process, encouraging student agency, embracing risks and failure, emphasizing genre flexibility, embracing multilingualism, and creating rhetorical awareness. In traditional assessment, how often are students ever afforded the opportunity to see how they're positioned against assessment by the institution? And how often do we consider how we're positioned as deliverers of assessment by the institution? We might be able to resist traditional assessment that keeps us tied to specific positions of power within our classrooms if we reimagine the framework. By reimagining assessment, we can find an alternative way that complements multimodal pedagogy. Because multimodality allows multiple voices to be heard, even marginalized voices, the grading contract fits more with the objectives of multimodal pedagogy. The grading contract is counter-hegemonic. It gives students the ability to construct and produce assessment. Power is redistributed, and students are in control, or at the very least, possess a greater degree of control than the traditional frameworks. Rubrics can be co-constructed and other traditional assessment expectations, such as adhering to SEAE, can be critiqued.

Negotiation is a large part of cultivating a classroom focused on process. Jane Danielewicz and Peter Elbow (2009) assert that the grading contract emphasizes process: "Contract grading focuses wholeheartedly on processes whereas conventional grading focuses much more on products, outcomes, or result" (260). Traditional frameworks of assessment, and even some of the alternatives mentioned through multimodal scholarship, have at least one common denominator—an assessment dictated by product. Traditional assessment can overvalue product to a fault. Even classrooms that have pedagogies tailored toward process—classrooms where students produce multiple drafts—are often disconnected from process because of assessment. Teachers can design curricula filled with drafts and peer-to-peer workshops in hopes of highlighting the importance of process over product, but traditional assessment, ultimately, holds them back. Students eventually turn in a "final" draft, and then the teacher must perceive the "quality" of the product and assign a grade to it. If multimodal pedagogy truly wants to move forward, it must look at the affordances of the pedagogy and the assessment system that helps construct it.

A shift towards the grading contract seems logical, as it values process. Students think about the process in a grading-contract-based course because grades are not looming around the corner. Students are not waiting to be judged just on the project. Danielewicz and Elbow (2009) explain the nature of the grading contract: "With contracts, the writing becomes what's at stake, not so much the grade. Students are more open to radical changes and are more inventive" (255). In a multimodal class, the multimodal project becomes *what's at stake*. The grading contract does not have hidden agendas: the teacher is not forming criteria or grading papers in a dark room, deciphering between papers, comparing the "quality" of one paper to another to construct some sort of judgment in the form of a symbol. Through the grading contract, students know what needs to be done; they know the amount of "labor" they must produce in order to meet the requirements for assessment.

Asao B. Inoue (2012) has written extensively on the use and effectiveness of the grading contract in his writing courses. Inoue, like me, has issues with traditional frameworks of assessment for a number of reasons, including how letter grades create "false hierarchies" and "extrinsic rewards" (78). Inoue writes, "Grades are deceptive; not only do they replace real feedback on student writing with a one-dimensional, somewhat arbitrary symbol, but that symbol often is perceived by the student to stand in for how well he or she is doing" (78). The effect of letter grades on students runs a lot deeper than just the perception of one symbol on one particular performance. The traditional grading system, which is designed to primarily assess quality (and quality is often evaluated by notions of SEAE), positions students to think of themselves as "good" or "bad" writers based on the grade. Then, students move on to the next writing assignment with this lingering perception of them as a writer in mind. But writing is far more complex than this binary, and assessment should be equally complex in terms of what it does and how it does it. Traditional assessment can restrict student agency, discouraging students from having their own voice and taking risks, while the grading contract can encourage students to do so, thus complementing the affordance of student agency in multimodal pedagogy.

The grading contract also allows students to fully consider public audiences and explore different genres without being penalized. Students can work through an assignment based on a public audience knowing their grade is not going to be based on the singular perception of the teacher, or how the teacher views quality, or whether the teacher thinks the student meets the expectations of that imagined audience. Through the grading contract, students can take risks in various genres knowing the contract affords them the opportunity to construct in different modes. The grading contract is based on the labor exerted on the project. Therefore, the motivation is intrinsic. The student, ultimately, decides the amount of labor they desire to exert on the process, which is based on their own motivation, not an extrinsic motivator like a letter grade. There are not blurred lines in the grading contract. Students are not left guessing about their grade.

Meanwhile, teachers are not left trying to figure out a grade. Danielewicz and Elbow (2009) discuss how traditional grading can be exhausting: "Teachers tend to feel obliged, for example, to figure out their borderline between B and B minus. Contract grading eliminates this kind of agonizing" (250). Traditional grading can be intimidating due to its emphasis on product and quality, and trying to figure out a grade can be overwhelming. In a multimodality-based classroom, this agonizing feeling is magnified. What does it look like to grade a website? The role of judge through a multimodal assignment is increasingly more difficult because of the nature and complexity of the different modes at play. Questions eventually arise causing more confusion: What mode should be valued more? How can I act as the audience of this multimodal project? What if that layout choice or color scheme was purposeful and intentional by the student? All of these questions and more, through traditional assessments, make me feel positioned *against* the student.

The grading contract, while eliminating the pressure of assuming the role of judge, does not inflate grades, though Danielewicz and Elbow (2009) openly confess their classroom grading contract may provide a student a B whereas the same student might "earn" a C in another teacher's course (251). In a grading-contract-centered course, the final course letter grade is "deeply meaningless" because it accounts for absences, late assignments, peer-to-peer workshops, and quality (251). The grading contract is far more complex in nature than traditional assessments. For example, a student considered to be an "excellent" writer may receive a D in the course due to labor requirements being unfulfilled. The letter grade in a grading contract possesses different values: it points to the students' labor, or the contribution the student makes in the course. The grading contract signifies what the student produced more in terms of work ethic than anything else. The value embedded within the grading contact, then, positions students against themselves, not the teacher's perception of their writing. In a grading-contract-centered course, students must self-reflect, often facing the reality of responsibility by having to answer questions about their production of labor or lack thereof. Students analyze and critique their own participation, attendance, late assignments, and other labor requirements.

At the same time, a typically defined "weak" writer might receive a B because of their diligence and effort to engage with the material, attend class, and contribute to discussion. So, one way the grading contract combats grade inflation is that it disqualifies the student who writes "good enough" to "deserve a high grade" based solely on quality while not punishing the other student due to their "lack of success" (Danielewicz and Elbow 2009, 251). Student agency is cultivated in multimodal pedagogy, and multimodality encourages students to take risks and learn from failure. Multimodal pedagogy pushes students to compose in different modes, to create new meaning and understanding. Failure is expected as students negotiate new spaces and new compositions. Furthermore, failure is valued. The grading contract complements these characteristics of multimodality by fostering students' ability to take risks. Students know they are afforded risks in a grading-contract-centered multimodal classroom; they know they will not be punished due to a choice that leads to a lack of success. The grading contract is designed for students to meet specific terms of labor, which is much more complex than the mere perceived quality of the work that discredits students on failed choices.

Teachers and students can also create and negotiate the criteria or expectations of each assignment, thus emphasizing student agency, whether it be focused on the digital, spatial, aural, or a combination of modes. This criterion helps the teacher and student understand the expectations for the assignment. For example, if the assignment asked the student to create and upload four visual images for a professional-website assignment, and the student only created and uploaded two, the student didn't meet the expectations of labor. Their decision to include only two visual images resulted in a grade not based on the perceptions of the teacher but instead based on their own decision and choices. Those choices, in the grading contract, result in consequences: the student is penalized for not meeting the expectations formed collaboratively as a class. More important, though, this assessment practice better supports the affordances of multimodality: process, student agency, student literacies, and composing in different genres.

In order to be most effective in the classroom, we must see how traditional frameworks obstruct multimodal pedagogical goals and values. In some pedagogies, traditional frameworks of assessment may work best. In other pedagogies, the tradition may have a countereffect. Multimodal pedagogy affords a lot of opportunities to question traditional frameworks of assessment as well as the nature of the classroom structure: is traditional assessment aligning with the values of multimodal pedagogy?

TOWARDS AN ASSESSMENT MADE WHOLE THROUGH MULTIMODAL PEDAGOGY

Traditional frameworks of assessment ultimately undermine the affordances of multimodal pedagogy because of their emphasis on product singularity, not process-based labor. The grading contract exposes the failures in traditional frameworks and enlightens multimodal pedagogy to teach and value labor processes. Of course, grades are still assigned under the grading contract, but the nature of the grading contract communicates something entirely different in value compared to traditional frameworks. Through the use of the grading contract, the teacher isn't assigning something to the product because the student already knows the grade—if they produce the labor processes and work in good faith, meeting the expectations of the contract, the student receives a B letter grade. The grading contract is resisting the traditional notion that the quality of the product is all that matters. Since composition studies values the process of writing, which undoubtedly usually leads to better quality, traditional frameworks do not really afford our field much, if anything, because they are designed to emphasize product-like constructions (e.g., tests, quizzes) and knowledge (e.g., cognition).

On the other hand, the grading contract affords us a lot. The grading contract complements the affordances of multimodal pedagogy: student choice/agency; an emphasis on processes, genre, and pedagogical flexibility; and public audiences. By analyzing traditional frameworks of assessment, we can begin to see how the tradition works against some of our pedagogies and against some of our students. We must consider how to make changes to the tradition, especially traditional means of assessment, in order to create better teaching and learning. Tracy Bowen and Carl Whithaus (2013) write, "Changes to composition programs, however, only happen as individuals begin to avail themselves of the opportunities to present and create knowledge in new formats" (10). I believe multimodal pedagogy allows us the opportunity to confront traditional frameworks of assessment and move towards a new format—the grading contract—that best reflects its values. That is not to say the grading contract solves everything. But what assessment method does? Do traditional frameworks *solve all our problems*? Until we begin pushing against the traditional—something multimodal pedagogy encourages us to do—we will never be able to see what other assessment options could be more effective and could align more closely with what we value in our composition classrooms.

REFERENCES

Adsanatham, Chanon. 2012. "Integrating Assessment and Instruction: Using Student-generated Grading Criteria to Evaluate Multimodal Digital Projects." *Computers and Composition* 29 (2): 152–74.

Bowen, Tracy, and Carl Whithaus. 2013. *Multimodal Literacies and Emerging Genres*. Pittsburgh, PA: University of Pittsburgh.

Carr, Allison. 2013. "In Support of Failure." *Composition Forum* 27. http://compositionforum.com/issue/27/failure.php.

Danielewicz, Jane, and Peter Elbow. 2009. "A Unilateral Grading Contract to Improve Learning and Teaching." *College Composition and Communication* 61 (2): 244–68.

De Hertogh, Lori. 2014. "Toward a Revised Assessment Model: Rationales and Strategies for Assessing Students' Technological Authorship." *Composition Forum* 30. http://compositionforum.com/issue/30/revised-assessment-model.php.

Elbow, Peter. 1997. "High Stakes and Low Stakes in Assigning and Responding to Writing." *New Directions for Teaching and Learning* 69: 5–13.

Elkordy, Angela. 2012. "The Future Is Now: Unpacking Digital Badging and Microcredentialing for K–20 Educators." http://www.hastac.org/blogs/elkorda.

Inoue, Asao B. 2004. "Community-Based Assessment Pedagogy." *Assessing Writing* 9 (3): 208–38.

Inoue, Asao B. 2012. "Grading Contracts: Assessing Their Effectiveness on Different Racial Formations." In *Race and Writing Assessment*, edited by Asao B. Inoue and Mya Poe, 78–93. New York: Peter Lang.

Kohn, Alfie. 1999. *Punished by Rewards*. Boston, MA: Houghton Mifflin.

Kress, Gunther. 2003. *Literacy in the New Media Age*. New York: Routledge.

Kress, Gunther. 2009. *Multimodality: A Social Semiotic Approach to Contemporary Communication*. New York: Routledge.

Lauer, Claire. 2014. "Contending with Terms: 'Multimodal' and 'Multimedia' in the Academic and Public Spheres." In *Multimodal Composition: A Critical Sourcebook*, edited by Claire Lutkewitte, 22–41. Boston, MA: Bedford/St. Martins.

Lunsford, Andrea, Michal Brody, Lisa Ede, Beverly Moss, Carole Clark Papper, and Keith Walters. 2016. *Everyone's an Author, Second Edition*. New York: W.W. Norton & Company.

Lutkewitte, Claire. 2014. *Multimodal Composition: A Critical Sourcebook*. Boston, MA: Bedford/St. Martins.

Murray, Donald. 1976. "Teach Writing as Process, Not Product." In *Rhetoric and Composition*, edited by Richard L. Graves, 79–82. Rochelle Park, NJ: Hayden Books.

Powell, Beth, Kara Poe Alexander, and Sonya Borton. 2011. "Interaction of Author, Audience, and Purpose in Multimodal Texts: Students' Discovery of Their Role as Composer." *Kairos: A Journal of Rhetoric, Technology, and Pedagogy* 15 (2). http://kairos .technorhetoric.net/praxis/tiki-index.php?page=Student_Composers.

Reilly, Colleen, and Anthony T. Atkins. 2013. "Rewarding Risk: Designing Aspirational Assessment Processes for Digital Writing Projects." http://ccdigitalpress.org/dwae /04_reilly.html.

Shipka, Jody. 2011. *Toward a Composition Made Whole*. Pittsburgh, PA: University of Pittsburgh Press.

Takayoshi, Pamela, and Cynthia L. Selfe. 2007. "Thinking about Multimodality." In *Multimodal Composition: Resources for Teachers*, edited by Cynthia L. Selfe, 1–12. Cresskill, NJ: Hampton.

White, Ed. 2005. "The Scoring of Writing Portfolios: Phase 2." *College Composition and Communication* 56 (4): 581–600.

(In Lieu of an) Afterword
REWRITING THE DIFFERENCE OF MULTIMODALITY
Composing Modality and Language as Practice

Bruce Horner

Questions of modality and language in writing are inevitably questions of difference: What difference does either modality or language make to composition (as a field, as a course, as an activity, as a type of text)? What constitutes difference in modality or language? What differences does either allow, or enable, for whom, and how? And what are we, as composers ourselves and as teachers and scholars of composition, to make of such differences?

Prevailing answers to these questions of difference in modality and language in composition rest on a series of interlocking assumptions: that (1) difference is good, (2) differences are enumerable, and (3) differences—at least those worth pursuing—are new. Difference is itself pursued as novelty—at least as what is new to the composer or reader or type of composition—to the point that difference and the new are conflated: what is new (i.e., identified with the present as opposed to what is past) is what is different, unless it is consigned to the old even when encountered anew (as in the expression *same old*).

In keeping with and subsuming these assumptions is the larger assumption that difference is by definition a deviation from the norm (again, as expressed in the derogatory dismissal *same old*). What is different is thus identified with what is outside the norm, the latter of which is itself identified with what is the same—an undifferentiated, uniform, existing monolith. That postulated monolith is then conflated not simply with what is seen as statistically dominant but with what is politically dominant—hegemony.

For those accepting this interlocking set of assumptions, to seek out the different (so defined) is thus to align oneself with the dominated and against the dominating. As Claire Lutkewitte (2013) puts it, for example, "Multimodal composition allows for many voices—even those

DOI: 10.7330/9781607327974.c014

new, marginalized, or unpopular voices—to be heard" (5; cf. Anderson, Stewart, and Kachorsky 2017, 105; Hull and Nelson 2005, 253). That alignment with the different/dominated, however, comes with little hope or even expectation of success (except the success of continual resistance). For, within the accepted framework, to succeed in overthrowing the dominant would require instituting a new regime of monolithic sameness, albeit one identified with modal and linguistic forms and norms recognizably distinct from those identified with the regime that has been overthrown. The latter would then have to be continually invoked as justification for enforcement of conformity to the sameness of the new as still somehow the "different" (from the "same old").[1]

FROM DIFFERENCE AS STATUS QUO ALTERNATIVE TO DIFFERENCE AS THE NORM

As suggested by this need to invoke the same/old as foil against which to define and defend and advocate for the different/new, the identification of the different with the new and as deviation from the same aligns, paradoxically, with status quo relations—despite the protestations of advocates of the different/new, and despite the appearance of pursuit of change—insofar as it accepts what the dominant has already identified as constituting change: what we are already disposed, by the dominant, to recognize as, in fact, something different and new—as, for example, "innovative." In the case of composition, and writing studies more broadly, this is what accounts for the unwitting, unintended, and disturbing alignments that have emerged between demands that we increase the range of languages and technologies deployed in writing and flexibility in their use, on the one hand, and, on the other, fast-capitalist demands for portfolio people with broad and flexible communication skills committed to constant innovation (see Dor 2004; Flores 2013; Gee, Hull, and Lankshear 1998; Horner 2016, chap. 1; Kubota 2014; Thrift 2005). In their opposition to fordist requirements for uniformity, compositionists run headlong into an embrace of fast-capitalist values and ideals of flexibility, difference, and constant innovation as the only legitimate alternative.

This is, of course, not to argue for a return to fordism but to insist on a reconsideration of what the actual alternatives might be to what immersion in both the (still-powerful) fordist and (newly powerful) postfordist regimes lead us falsely to believe is the alternative: to refuse to accept that There Is No Alternative to the alternative being prescribed. We need to rethink both the alternative that has been prescribed and that which we have come to think of as the norm to which it is posed *as* the alternative. In other words, we need to rethink what difference in language and modality might in fact be and what it is different from.

As I've already suggested, this project requires that we rethink the relation of the norm to the different (and new). Translingual theory makes this possible by its insistence on locating language temporally as practice, with any language understood to be the always-emerging outcome(s) of such practice rather than as a timeless entity against which spatiotemporally located practices are to be measured (as inevitably flawed) (Lu and Horner 2013). Relocating language as the always-emerging outcome of language practice (in Alastair Pennycook's phrase a "local practice") renders difference not a deviation from a norm of monolithic sameness but, rather, itself the norm insofar as every utterance, every iteration, is temporally different in location and, hence, in significance (Pennycook 2010). Repetitions, for example, carry a different significance *as* repetitions from what they repeat, which themselves, by virtue of being repeated, likewise change in significance to mean that which has been repeated (cf. Pennycook 2010, 43). Reiterations, then (and every utterance is in some way a reiteration), are always simultaneously new and old, the same and different, instances of what Frédéric François (1998) calls *réprise-modification*—taking up again and thereby in the process modifying what is taken up (see Donahue 2008, 98ff.). It is in this sense that, as Pennycook (2010) insists, sameness, rather than difference, must be accounted for as a phenomenological effect of the practice of iteration (50). Difference, in contrast, is the unavoidable norm rather than a deviant outcome to be pursued as preferred alternative to the norm of the same/old.

Reifications of Language and Modality as "Countables"

Translingual theory's reintroduction of temporality to considerations of language and modality to refigure difference (and sameness) is at odds with dominant conceptions of difference in language and modality that rest on purely spatial conceptions of these as enumerable resources composers may acquire and learn to draw on and deploy (like ingredients on a shelf). By omitting the temporal dimension of language and modality (and, thereby, their dependence on composers' labor as outcomes of composers' labor practices), spatial conceptions of language and modality reify both. This removal of language and modality from history renders them and their "effects" as immune to and independent of human labor, as other than the (ongoing) products of that labor. We can see this omission of the temporal dimension of modality and its subsequent reifi-cation in Jonathan Alexander and Jacqueline Rhodes's (2014) invocation of "the power of images [apparently all by themselves] to create rhetori-cal possibilities . . . and communicate powerfully in ways that a composed [alphabetic print] text cannot" (25; cf. Hull and Nelson 2005, 229, 252). Such reification commodifies language and modality. Commodification by definition occludes the necessity of concrete labor to the effectivity of the commodified work—the specific practices by which, say, an image may or may not come to be felt as "powerful."

The enumerative character attributed to language and modality as countables—language*s*, modalit*ies*—arises from the purely spatial con-ception of these. Difference, then, is imagined to be achieved by means of addition, an effort at "expansion." Thus, it is common in arguments for versions of "multimodal" composition to insist, on the one hand, on the need to engage in forms of composition deemed new while, on the other hand, offering assurances that the "old" forms—printed verbal texts *sans* images—are not to be abandoned. Instead, those working in composition are asked to recognize that compositions are made "not *only* in words" (Yancey 2004; italics added) and to opt for what Cynthia L. Selfe (2010) terms "a more capacious choice" of "openness to mul-tiple modalities of rhetorical expression" that, reassuringly, does not "leave 'writing' out of the equation" (607; cf. Alexander and Rhodes 2014, 7; Hull and Nelson 2005, 226).

The Rhetorical Appeal of Inclusion and the Erasure of Meaningful Difference

The appeal of these arguments is the seemingly irresistible one of inclu-sion and openness: in Selfe's (2009) terms, an argument that is "not *either/or*, but *both/and*" (641). But simultaneously, as Selfe and others note, this appears to be in keeping with recognition of the difference he forces of globalization are now demanding. The invocation of the demands of those forces thus renders the additions not only necessary but also better than what is to be added to (the same old), as in the notion of a new and improved product going beyond the limitations of what has preceded it. As Selfe (2010) puts it,

> The inclusion of multiple modes of rhetorical expression represents a simple acknowledgment that a literacy education focused solely on *writing* will produce citizens with an overly narrow and exclusionary understand-ing of the world and the variety of audiences who will read and respond to their work. In the twenty-first century, we live in an increasingly global-ized world where people speak different languages, come from different

cultures, learn and make meaning in different media contexts and with different expressive modalities. In such an environment, . . . literate citizens, increasingly, need to make use of *all* semiotic channels to communicate effectively among different groups and for different purposes. (607; cf. Alexander and Rhodes 2014, 4–5, 19–20)

What once may have been adequate—"literacy education focused solely on writing"—is no longer adequate to meet the needs of current conditions of globalization. And, within the framework of enumerated languages and modalities, the only available argument against this would seem to be an argument for excluding the recognizably different in order to preserve the hegemony of a single, uniform (and narrow) set of practices identified with the dominant—English only, for example, and print literacy alone—under the guise of ascribing normative values to these as having universal and universally good effects—the ideology of autonomous literacy expanded to include language as well as technological medium.[2] In other words, to question calls for such expansion and inclusion would seem to align one not merely with Ludditism but with the interests of global Empire and the fordist regime it has upheld.

Difference, so conceived, is thus understood to be inherently good insofar as it is both inclusive and a break from the old (cf. Trimbur and Press 2015, 19–20). But further, so conceived, it is also understood as a necessity for survival in these global times, when the different can be neither ignored nor refashioned into the same (i.e., assimilated) but, instead, pursued as a commercial opportunity. It then follows that more difference, so conceived, is always better: difference through addition never stops. In keeping with fast capitalism, every niche market must be identified (or created) and accessed through exploitation of difference *qua* difference as (a) good. As the Burger King ruled long ago, each of us can, and should, "Have it your way."

Paradoxically, difference so conceived erases the possibility of conflict or confusion. Instead, differences among languages, media, and cultures, once postulated, are, in the very act of being acknowledged as legitimate, simultaneously imagined as susceptible to being readily overcome. As Philippe Blanchet and Daniel Coste (2010) caution in a critique of dominant notions of *interculturalité*,

On observe . . . d'une acception « angélique » de la notion . . . qui en réduit la portée à une simple attente de « relations humaines harmonieuses malgré les différences culturelles et linguistiques. » (9)

Difference, in this conception, may be good, but it is good only insofar as it is readily overcome in our shared "relations humaines harmonieuses."

Tensions, conflicts, incomprehension are all thereby erased through embrace of this spatial concept of differences. There is no boundary we cannot cross. Or, as Deborah Cameron (2002) argues, under a veneer of linguistic difference, the same old discourse and rhetoric of "good communication skills" prevails but now with the cachet of being also new and different by virtue of the language medium deployed.

Alexander and Rhodes, in their award-winning book *On Multimodality* (2014), appear in one sense to be arguing against such a conception of pursuit of modal difference. So, against the claims that the use of media other than alphabetic print text are also writing, just in a different medium, they argue that, in fact, "not *everything* is writing" (17). But they then defend the difference between what others claim *is* the same—*writing*—by postulating specific, enumerable, fixed differences for different media. "We would do well," they argue (citing Kress), to remind ourselves that the "'distinct logics' and 'different affordances' of various media and modes are not reducible to one another," for to ignore this keeps ourselves and our students from understanding "the richness of new and multimedia" (Alexander and Rhodes 2014, 17; cf. 19). Against the poverty of writing, they advocate pursuit of the "richness" of the latter (cf. Stein 2004, 95, on multimodal pedagogies allowing for "the expression of a much fuller range of human emotion and experience"; quoted in Hull and Nelson 2005, 228). Specifically, they argue, "New and multimedia . . . play with excess, with the dis-composed, with possibilities of communication and rhetorical affects and effects that take us far beyond the reasonable, the rational, the composed" (Alexander and Rhodes 2014, 24). But note that this conception of the "new and multimedia" accepts a dominant, if reductive, essayist notion of writing as "rational," "straightforward," and "composed," in which authors "argue points, consider counterarguments, and reach reasonable, rational conclusions," against which the "new and multimedia" is then posed as alternative. Thus, despite, and by the terms of, its pursuit of the new, their argument aligns neatly with the all-too-prevalent ideology of autonomous literacy as the same/old. The possibility is not entertained that at least some writing itself might not be rational, straightforward, and "composed" but, instead, "play[s] with excess, with the dis-composed" and pursues "rhetorical affects and effects that take us far beyond the reasonable, the rational, the composed."

Here it is also worth noting that purely spatial conceptions of difference necessarily define the different in terms of form. For example, as Pennycook (2008) argues, most accounts of linguistic difference focus purely on glossodiversity, ignoring semiodiversity to the extent that glossodiversity *per se* is valued on the assumption that (1) different languages are discrete, and (2) such linguistic diversity will provide "added value" to what is communicated: like the different colors of Benetton, more of what we are disposed to recognize as different is always better (so long as it is Benetton). Likewise, we see that prevailing notions of multimodality assume both that modes can readily be distinguished from one another and that the more modes deployed, the better, insofar as the affordances of each of the modes deployed in multimodal compositions, so conceived, will add value (as "multimodal"). It is the forms of these modes of communication, rather than what composers might attempt to communicate, that is valued. At best, specific aims are identified with the forms themselves, as when Alexander and Rhodes (2014) worry lest we lose out on the "rich rhetorical capabilities of new media" by understanding them merely in terms of "print-driven compositional aims, biases, and predispositions" (19). Concomitantly, within this enumerative model, the fewer modes a composition is thought to deploy, the more impoverished, and rhetorically weaker, it is imagined to be: less is worse.

An Ecological Model of Communicative Practice

To question the assumptions underlying such valuations of purely formal difference (in language and/or mode) should not lead us to reject either the teaching and learning of different languages or the teaching and learning of different communication technologies. To explicate, it is worth recalling that just because the discourse of fast capitalism promotes such formal features of interaction as flattened organizational structures, teamwork, and collaboration, it does not follow that we should reject flattened organizational structures, teamwork, or collaboration. To do so would be to participate, once again, in the removal of forms—here forms of organization and of work processes—from the material social realm of history and to attribute to those forms, thus reified and commodified, inherent values—positive or negative—that in fact are realized only in specific temporally and spatially located practices through concrete labor. Instead, we must always ask how any such forms—linguistic, modal, organizational, work—are taken up, under what conditions, by whom, for whom, how, and to what ends: to attend to all these in terms of, and to be found only in and through, practices.

To do this requires, too, that we acknowledge immediately that even the distinctions just invoked among linguistic, modal, organizational, and work forms, however useful they may be for some purposes of analysis, are abstractions from actual communicative practice. As Louis-Jean Calvet (2006) has observed, we must adopt what he terms an "ecological" approach to language insofar as language "is not an object that can be considered in isolation, and communication does not simply occur by means of sequences of sounds" (22). Rather, it is "a social practice within social life, one practice among others, inseparable from its environment" (22; see also 10ff.).

There is, of course, a growing tradition in composition and rhetorical studies advancing what is termed an *ecological* approach (see for example Cooper 1986; DeVoss, McKee, and Selfe 2009; Edbauer 2005; Syverson 1999). The emphasis in this work has been to bring out the dynamic, complex interactions of writers and their social and material environments (as fellow agents) as a corrective to models posing writers as isolated individuals, writing as purely cognitive, and rhetorical situations as discrete and knowable sets of elements. A summary of this work is well beyond the scope of this chapter. There is likewise a diverse tradition in sociolinguistics exploring ecologies of language (see Pennycook 2010, 88–109). Relevant to my purpose, what is added to this work by Calvet and the sociolinguistic tradition in which he participates (e.g., Haugen 1972; Milroy 2001; Mühlhäusler 1996; van Lier 2004) is the ideological critique of the extraction and separation of "language" from the full continuum of means of communication any communicative utterance entails, and, by implication, the equivalent extraction and separation of individual "modes" from such utterances, with the consequent focus on the identification and combination of languages and modes as enumerable entities. Where conventional scholarship on multimodality highlights the need to consider the range of semiotic resources involved and deployed in communicative efforts, and conventional scholarship on multilinguality highlights the need to consider the range of available linguistic resources likewise deployed, Calvet (2006) emphasizes the problematics of treating any of these resources as distinct, with specific "affordances." The seemingly endless catalogue of modes, like the likewise seemingly endless catalogue of "languages" and language "varieties," is indicative of the same failure to recognize that the treatment of *mode* as a term of analysis renders, through abstraction, what in practice cannot and does not exist or work in isolation from, nor even in mere conjunction with, other likewise distinguished modes or languages but in an ecological continuum as an undifferentiated whole of communicative practice.[3] It is in this sense, as is regularly acknowledged (and, it seems, just as quickly ignored), that all texts are always multimodal, an acknowledgement that points to the seriously flawed character of the very notion of multimodality as the deployment of an enumerated set of modes (cf. Kress 2003, 184, 187; Shipka 2011, 11–13). Thus, we need not merely an ecological approach to language(s), as Calvet argues, and not merely an analogous ecological approach to mode, but rather an ecological approach to communicative practice, and the means of that practice, drawing on terms like *mode* and *language* only for purposes of analysis and not slipping from the model of the reality of communication produced by such analysis to ascribing reality to the model (see Bourdieu 1977, 29).

Brian Street's (2009) call for an "ideological model of multimodality" (31–33) is apposite here. Instead of the prevalent ideology of an autonomous model of modality that ascribes particular affordances to particular modes (just as the autonomous model of literacy ascribes particular effects to literacy removed from material social practices of and with literacy), Street (2012) argues that we must attend to (1) practices with modality and (2) the ideologies of modality these practices arise from and contribute to the sedimentation of (cf. 27–28). "Mode," like "language," is a representation made of a practice, and such representations are inevitably selective, an exercise of power over practices and those engaging in them.[4] And just as representations of language, as practices themselves, intervene in the "ecolinguistic niche" to shape subsequent practice, as Calvet (2006) has warned, so representations of mode, as practices themselves, intervene in the broader realm of communicative practice to shape subsequent practice, here specifically with composers' understanding of and engagement with what they have learned to think of as modes.

PEDAGOGY AS SITE FOR THE MEDIATION OF DIFFERENCE IN LANGUAGE AND MODALITY

To accept this ecological model of language and modality as communicative practice returns us to pedagogy as a key site for the mediation of language and modality and the difference(s) they might produce, at the level of both practices and representations of these (as also practices). Pedagogy is ordinarily understood as the occasion for the transmission of knowledge and, for composition especially, the transmission of skills. But scholars of transfer have for some time now been exploring the problematics of knowledge transfer, problematics that emerge once we come to locate knowledge itself temporally, to be found in and dependent on practice for its continually emergent existence and therefore inevitably subject to change as it is mobilized by knowers (including learners).[5] Discussions of those problematics call into radical question transmission models of pedagogy. But those discussions have been carried out almost entirely in the realm of professional academic scholarship, with the effect of giving the impression that once we (scholars and teachers) get a workable grasp on knowledge transfer, we can then more effectively engage in transfer as teachers: the problematics, that is, risk being understood instead as mere problems susceptible to technical solution. Alternatively, we might take those problematics as the subject of inquiry at the site of pedagogy, now understood not as the occasion for (futile) attempts at transmission but, rather, as the site for as well as inevitable site of knowledge transformation.

In one sense, this might be understood as an argument for a writing-about-writing (WAW) curriculum insofar as it takes writing not as a skill (or set of skills) to be transmitted to students but as the subject of their inquiry (in collaboration with teachers): engaging students not only in the practice of mediating difference in language and modality but also, and simultaneously, in (re)representing these to one another, thereby intervening through both such practices in the ecology of communicative practice.[6] One difference I would argue for, however, would be that, first, such work is not new but rather the inevitable, constant work undertaken by composition students and teachers (though this is not how that work has been represented), and second, that it need not take the form of WAW scholarship we are disposed by our training to recognize *as* WAW scholarship. Again, in place of seeking out, or representing, some kinds of questions as different/new to composition, we can instead learn to rethink the terms in which our work and its value are represented to us (and by us).

Composition/Translation/Reiteration

Translation is one promising point of departure for engaging in, reflecting on, and (re)representing difference in language (see Horner and Tetreault 2016; Jiménez et al. 2015; Kiernan et al. 2016). For conventional translation always produces difference in meaning despite claims of what translation offers. Granted, while the lack of exact equivalence effected through conventional translation from language to language (say, French to English) is commonly recognized (versus a model of encoding/decoding), the production of difference is typically imagined to distinguish the writing of translations from ordinary writing. For example, translation is distinguished, conventionally, from paraphrase, which is treated as providing the equivalent of that which is paraphrased, albeit in perhaps distilled form. And, of course, exact repetition is ordinarily understood simply as a violation—plagiarism.

But if any repetition produces difference, then repetition itself can be understood as simply one kind of translation among others that produces both sameness and difference, with its sameness as well as its difference in need of explication. In short, all composition inevitably entails such translation in its production of difference through iteration. Likewise, while clearly any "translation" from what is designated to be one mode to another is assumed to produce difference (e.g., from printed text to video), we must also recognize the difference produced through the deployment of what is ostensibly the same mode.

This, however and again, requires shifting our attention from medium to practice. As Raymond Williams (1980) has warned, what we have are not "works" as "objects" at all but, instead, "notations" "which have then to be interpreted in an active way" (47). So, whereas conventionally difference in writing is understood to arise from changes to the forms of notations deployed, or (more recently) the medium (from printed hard-copy text to, say, YouTube video), this change in writing by a change in writing only makes sense *as* a change in writing when writing is located strictly with those forms (Horner 2013, 4–5). Crudely, for example, switching from "regular" to italicized font seems to change the writing (by doing what we understand, as a consequence of our textualist bias, to *be* changing the writing). From this conventional perspective, for students to continue throughout a course to produce unitalicized writing is to maintain a sameness in their writing unremarkable in remaining the same.

Alternatively, we can ask what practices lead us to fail to remark on the continued deployment of "regular" font in a student's writing, the difference each such (re)deployment makes, and what the student might be attempting to achieve by these means. Admittedly, this might well seem perverse, an instance of a teacher asking questions about matters that are settled and not worthy of questioning. What difference does it make that a writer continues to use regular font—the default, after all? In the same way, it would seem perverse to ask of most writers in US composition classes why they (and their teachers) continue to write English rather than something else. But we can instead take that practice as legitimately open to question: to ask what produces this sense of sameness despite the inevitability of the difference such practice makes (e.g., to "English") by virtue of its temporal location.[7]

I suspect that, increasingly, it is coming to seem less perverse to ask such a question of modality: why teachers demand that, and students agree to produce, say, hard-copy print texts versus, say, YouTube videos. But as I have already discussed, the question is usually understood not as an open question but as rhetorical. That is, except for those committed to the old fordist regime in its insistence on uniformity in form ("any color car you like, so long as it's black"), the question why are you (still) composing (only) alphabetic print text? is understood to be not a question at all but a demand that teachers require and students produce texts recognizably multimodal as a means of being different—this despite the ritual acknowledgement that all texts are always (already) multimodal.

The difficulty these questions confront is that our textualist bias—a bias arising from the ideology of the autonomous model of literacy—blinds us to the operation of the various practices of engagements with forms of notation that produce a perverted sense of some texts as multimodal and others as, well, monomodal—or more of the same. John Trimbur (1990) gets at this in his analysis of what he terms the "rhetoric of deproduction" operating in the ideology of "essayist literacy." Trimbur notes that "composition textbooks . . . often tell students that what matters in written composition are the words on the page" (74). But the self-evident character of such a view of "ordinary" writing, Trimbur notes, is in fact a product of a set of reading practices by which notations and their arrangement on pages appear to be no more and no less than "the words on the page." As Trimbur explains, "For ourselves and for our students, when we learned to read and write in school, we also learned to occupy certain subject positions as readers and writers and to orient our language practices in certain bounded ways toward written texts" (74). Specifically, we have learned to engage with texts marked as "ordinary" "essayist" texts as merely "words on the page," all evidence to the contrary notwithstanding—ignoring, for example, the significance of the selection of only black and white colors (typically not recognized *as* colors), the arrangement of the letters, the kinds of publication formats in which such formulated pages of words appeared, the size and style of font, the feel and smell, not to mention taste, of the paper, glue, and so on deployed, and of course the habitual settings in which we have expected and have learned to expect to engage with such material objects (cf. Trimbur and Press 2015, 21–22). That is to say, we have learned to engage with such texts as if they were entirely *a*modal, attributing to their modal character precisely an amodality associated with ordinary writing (and reading) despite the fact that, as Gunther Kress (2003) observes, the "multimodality of our semiotic world" is guaranteed insofar as (barring severe pathologies) "none of the senses ever operates in isolation from the others" (184). (Likewise, we engage with "English" writing as more of the same "English" as a consequence of our practice of ascribing a monolith—English—to specific texts despite differences in the English written.)

An analogy may help illustrate the role of practices in producing a sense of modalities. The equivalent in music would be to read (listen) to Western classical chamber music (e.g., string quartets) as somehow more pure in form in comparison to, say, orchestral music, a matter strictly of relations of harmony, pitch, and rhythmic patterns devoid of timbre or sociocultural significance—essentially mathematics in sound (and, for the true purists, best engaged by silent [!] reading of scores to avoid any timbral or sociocultural sullying that performance might risk introducing).[8] Such an approach ignores the ways in which the experience of such purity is an effect of listening practices according to which, for example, the timbres of string-quartet music have been learned to be thought of as *a*timbral, despite their obvious timbres, and the occasions for chamber-music performance and listening (the chamber) are likewise learned to be enjoyed/experienced as transcending, by somehow removing, time and space. (All this despite the efforts and experiences of chamber-music composers and performers and listeners.)

What is needed, then, is not so much to replace or expand the types of texts to be considered ("Let's not forget orchestral and choral music!" "Let's add a piano to that quartet!"), nor to insist upon the "possession" by these other types of texts of qualities we have learned to associate with "essayist" texts ("But videos are arguments, too! And symphonies deploy complex harmonic and rhythmic patterns and relations just as much as string quartets!").[9] Rather, we must refocus our attention toward the reading/writing practices, and ideologies, that produce the effects we have learned to attribute and ascribe instead to specific forms of composition as their affordances.

From Countable to Inevitable Difference

In what might seem like the introduction of another perversity, it appears that refocusing our attention on the practices and ideologies producing effects we've learned to attribute to specific forms of composition as their affordances may well require, as an initial point of departure, attention to difference as conventionally understood in language and modality: to have students attempt to translate across languages and across modes as these are conventionally understood. John Trimbur and Karen Press (2015) have observed that while "multimodality itself is not new, nor is it a break from the past," *multimodality* "is new as a *term*, a *conceptual terrain* that surfaced at a particular historical conjuncture, goaded by the need to understand dramatic changes in the means of communication" (20–21). In other words, those dramatic changes have brought multimodality back into awareness as a point of inquiry. Following this logic, just as we can come to better grasp one language *as* a language, and become aware of linguality by learning another language, so we can come to better grasp modality by confronting modal deployments with which we are unfamiliar—as when one learns to better grasp the Western tonal scale *as* a scale by listening to other scales based on other kinds of pitch relations.[10] Curricula that engage students in experimentations with composing in media other than, and in addition to, alphabetic print have the potential to yield this. But that potential is very likely to go unrealized unless and until students are asked subsequently, but in the same course, to "return" to conventional alphabetic print composition, not (now, any longer) as the "same old" but as itself, and in its conventional forms, multimodal. That is to say, the purpose of introducing (or "allowing") composition in what we are disposed by our training to recognize as multimodal is not to expand the range of types of texts claimed to be within the remit of composition and of composition courses and their students (an expansion not only interminable but also ultimately insufferable in its alignment with fast-capitalist demands for predetermined forms of flexibility and formal innovation). Rather, it is to rethink practices of engagement with any type of text and the ideologies served and not by such practices.

Weiguo Qu's (2014) account of teaching Chinese students to translate between Chinese and English illustrates how the introduction of a second language—here, English—can lead to such rethinking. Arguing that "translation or thinking in a language that is not native de-automatizes perception and thinking" (72), Qu observes that his students, when "confronted with different languages imbued with different cultural heritages . . . have to and are able to make decisions and choices" they previously were not aware *were* choices. As he puts it,

> Critical thinking and literacy are possible only when students have more than one way of perceiving the world. . . . From being forced to make a decision and a choice, gradually students are changed to cognize the world in line with their own decisions and with what they themselves believe in. They want their own definitions, English or Chinese. It is in this way that English as a foreign language with relevant cultural heritage participates in and contributes to the cultivation of critical literacy in an alien country like China. (73)

The point is not for students simply to expand their linguistic or cultural repertoires to include English (in addition to Mandarin). Instead, as Qu notes, even the attempt to stay with conventional, authorized Chinese meanings changes in significance and represents a choice once those meanings are placed in the context of alternative possibilities (73). In the same way, the choice to produce conventional (black-and-white, Times New Roman 12-point font, one-inch margin, paragraphed) alphabetic English-medium print texts, ordinarily understood by my students as no choice at all, carries a different significance once it is understood as a choice, with specific resonances consequent on specific practices of engagement with these notations (evident when the diversity of readers' experiences with just such textual notational practices is brought to the surface).

This means, it is worth emphasizing, that the consequence of the pedagogy I'm arguing for may well be that students decide to produce conventional textual forms (as described in the last sentence) but that, despite what the textualist bias of the ideology of autonomous literacy would lead us to believe, that decision carries a different significance as a consequence of the temporal location of its production as a practice. As Min-Zhan Lu (1994) has argued about the decision of a student to replace her unconventional locution "can able to" with "may be able to," although the "product"—that is, the notational form "may be able to"— may appear to be identical to what convention dictates,

> the activities leading to [the student's] decision, and thus its significance, are completely different. Without the [student's] negotiation, [that] choice would be resulting from an attempt to passively absorb and automatically reproduce a predetermined form. . . . If and when the student experienced some difficulty mastering a particular code, she would view it as a sign of her failure as a learner and writer.
> On the other hand, if the decision [of the author of "can able to"] to reproduce a code results from a process of negotiation, then she would have examined the conflict between the codes of Standard English and other discourses. And she would have deliberated not only on the social power of these colliding discourses but also on who she was, is, and aspires to be when making this decision. (180–81)

Yasemin Yildiz (2012) notes likewise that the use of what seems like only a single language *per se* need not signal an allegiance to monolingualism. For example, as she observes, Franz Kafka's decision to write in German (only) signaled, in fact, his rejection of monolingualism insofar as, at the time of his writing, as a Jew, he lacked authorization to write German, hence his writing of German defied monolingualist ideology (34–35). Following this, the deployment of an ostensibly monomodal set of compositional forms (e.g., alphabetic print English-medium text) does not *per se* constitute monomodality. Not only is the deployment of such forms itself inherently, necessarily, inevitably multimodal; it is the practices with those forms that produce the effect and experience of them as multimodal or not. Monomodality, in short, must be recognized for its actual multimodal—or, better, transmodal—character, just as whiteness, ordinarily passing unnoticed as the unstated norm, must be recognized for the color it is.

We need, then, to return to the same/old to learn anew to recognize in the same/old the inevitably new/different. One might, for example, ask students to reread and revise texts they had produced earlier in a semester that were conventional in notational form to consider the effects of the modality of those texts, and the effects on their experience in composing those texts of the ideologies of modality that had rendered those texts' modality invisible. What uses and limitations can they see in what they attempted, and what they imagined could be attempted in composing, that might be attributed to their understanding of and assumptions about the modality(ies) to be deployed? How and why might they revise those texts, and what in their linguistic and modal character might they reproduce, and why? Likewise, they can return to assigned readings to which they had presumably assigned "monomodal" and monolingual status (if the questions of mode and language arose at all) to consider modal and linguistic features they did not notice previously and to explore what assumptions would account for the previous invisibility of these features, the practices producing that invisibility, and the effects of that invisibility on the significance they had ascribed to those texts. Such effects can be further brought to visibility by having students consider the effects of different reproductions of what is ostensibly the same text consequent on ideological understandings of each text type: for example, the reproduction of Thomas S. Kuhn's "The Historical Structure of Scientific Revolutions" in a composition reader (e.g., Lu and Horner's *Writing Conventions* [2008]) versus the first appearance of that article in the journal *Science* (1962). Students might then attempt to account for claims to the sameness of the two versions despite their inherent differences—what leads to the erasure of such differences, and with what costs? Such strategies render all texts different even in their seeming reproduction of "the same" linguistic and modal features. While all texts participate in some way with resources of modality and language, composers' (readers' and writers') uptakes of these in practice necessarily transform them in meaning as a consequence of the spatiotemporal difference of their mobilization.

It is, of course, possible to understand multimodality simply as a phenomenon of the mixture of and interplay between different (abstracted) modalities—say, between image and word and, perhaps, sound on a webpage.[11] As Carey Jewitt, Jeff Bezemer, and Kay O'Halloran (2016) put it, "Those using the term 'multimodality' generally aim to develop a framework that accounts for the ways in which people *combine* distinctly different kinds of meaning making" (4; italics added). But this is a roundabout form of approach insofar as it entails putting together, or "integrating" into a "multimodal whole," what has been rendered distinct through analysis of enumerated "modes"—putting together what was never distinct in the first place. For insofar as all texts are multimodal, and the abstractions of each mode as discrete are at odds with the full sensorium of experience, such interplay is an inevitable presence, though some practices with matters of sight, sound, touch, and so forth seem to push to the background—to render invisible or inaudible (imperceptible)—what is nonetheless part of the full effect of the perceptible (including the perception of lack, e.g., of silence, or whitespace margins). It is those practices, rather than modes, that merit our attention. For these effects arise as an outcome of the specific listening/reading/watching practices we engage in, practices that are identified with specific genres of communicative practice but that are, of course, not determined by those genres (and in fact are far more variable than is officially recognized). And this means that one further strategy by which to explore matters of language and modality—or, to be more precise, to explore what Cynthia Selfe, Tim Lockridge, and I (Horner, Selfe, and Lockridge 2015) have come to call the *transmodal*—is to invoke, encourage, and solicit these alternative experiences and the practices they are the outcome of, as well as to consider what practices produce the experience of monomodality despite its actual impossibility.

CONCLUSION

I have argued that in place of accepting and pursuing difference in language and modality as the dominant has defined what constitutes such difference—enumerable, new, and inherently good as deviation from a hegemonic norm of sameness—we learn to recognize the inevitability of difference by relocating modality and language as the always-emergent outcomes of composing practices. Further, I've argued that pedagogy, as a key site for the mediation of difference in writing, can make possible interventions in the ecology of the means of communicative practice by its representations of modality, language, and difference. In place of attempting to transmit an expanded, enumerated set of predetermined linguistic and modal choices, each with assigned affordances, we can introduce difference in language and modality as both an inevitability and as a perpetual question and point of inquiry.

In so doing, we can subvert dominant ideologies of both language and modality, and of their relations to one another, that align with the values of fast capitalism—its incessant demands for what it defines for us as the new, different, and innovative, and for flexibility in our production and deployment of these. We can counter the isolation, commodification, and hierarchical ordering of languages and modalities by foregrounding the concrete labor and agentive role of composers in continually producing and revising these through their practices of composition. Rejecting the reification of languages and modalities, such an approach may enable us to move away from pedagogies of transmission of abstractions of language and modality and allow instead for pedagogies that problematize language and modality as the always-emerging outcomes of our material social practice.

NOTES

1. Witness the campaign attacking the "four olds" during Mao Tse-tung's Cultural Revolution while simultaneously demanding uniform, complete, and unquestioning adherence to Mao Tse-tung's dictates.

2. Examples of such ascribed autonomy for language are provided in claims for the universal and universally good effects of English (see Guardiano, Favilla, and Calaresu 2007, 33, and for comparable claims for French, see France Diplomatie 2017). Similar ascriptions of autonomy to communication technologies appear in contemporary expressions of anxiety over the ostensibly damaging effects of digital forms of communication, in contrast to the putatively cognitively enriching effects of printed forms of communication (see for example Carr 2011).

3. This is what Cynthia Selfe, Timothy Lockridge, and I aim to capture by the term *transmodal* (Horner, Selfe, and Lockridge 2015).

4. See Calvet (2006, 7) and *passim*; Susan T. Gal and Judith T. Irvine (1995); James Milroy (2001, 540–41); Peter Mühlhäusler quoted in Milroy (2001, 540–41). I draw here from Horner (2016).

5. See for example King Beach (1999); Michael-John DePalma and Jeffrey M. Ringer (2011); Rebecca Lorimer Leonard and Rebecca Nowacek (2016); Nowacek (2011); Wardle (2012). I present extended arguments on this in chapters 2 and 5 of Horner (2016).

6. On writing about writing, see Douglas Downs and Elizabeth Wardle (2007).

7. As Blanchet and Coste observe, there is a need to "intégrer toute pluralité linguistique y compris 'à l'intérieure' de ce qui est considérée comme une 'même langue,'" cautioning that "l'une des formes de l'occultation de l'altérité est *l'illusion de similarité*, fréquente lorsque l'on pense parler la même langue" (2010, 14 n. 1; emphasis in original).

8. This is the concept of "absolute" music, distinguished from music with words.

9.   This appears to be what Alexander and Rhodes (2014) are particularly concerned about avoiding (4–5, 15–17).
10.   I borrow the term "linguality" from Christiane Donahue (2016).
11.   This is part of the burden of Kathleen Blake Yancey's (2004) argument.

REFERENCES

Alexander, Jonathan, and Jacqueline Rhodes. 2014. *On Multimodality: New Media in Composition Studies.* Urbana, IL: NCTE/CCCC.

Anderson, Kate T., Olivia G. Stewart, and Dani Kachorsky. 2017. "Seeing Academically Marginalized Students' Multimodal Designs from a Position of Strength." *Written Communication* 34 (2): 104–34.

Beach, King. 1999. "Consequential Transitions: A Sociocultural Expedition Beyond Transfer in Education." *Review of Research in Education* 24 (1): 101–39.

Blanchet, Philippe, and Daniel Coste. 2010. "Sur quelque parcours de la notion d' 'interculturalité' analyses et propositions dans le cadre d'une didactique de la pluralité linguistique et culturelle." In *Regards critiques sur la notion d'interculturalité: Pour une didactique de la pluralité linguistique et culturelle,* edited by Philippe Blanchet et Daniel Coste, 7–27. Paris: L'Harmattan.

Bourdieu, Pierre. 1977. *Outline of a Theory of Practice.* Translated by Richard Nice. Cambridge: Cambridge University Press.

Calvet, Louis-Jean. 2006. *Towards an Ecology of World Language.* Translated by Andrew Brown. London: Polity.

Cameron, Deborah. 2002. "Globalization and the Teaching of 'Communication Skills.'" In *Globalization and Language Teaching,* edited by David Block and Deborah Cameron, 67–82. Milton Park: Routledge.

Carr, Nicholas. 2011. *The Shallows: What the Internet Is Doing to Our Brains.* New York: Norton.

Cooper, Marilyn M. 1986. "The Ecology of Writing." *College English* 48 (4): 364–75.

DePalma, Michael-John, and Jeffrey M. Ringer. 2011. "Toward a Theory of Adaptive Transfer: Expanding Disciplinary Discussions of 'Transfer' in Second-Language Writing and Composition Studies." *Journal of Second Language Writing* 20 (2): 134–47.

DeVoss, Dànielle Nicole, Heidi A. McKee, and Richard Selfe, eds. 2009. *Technological Ecologies and Sustainability.* Logan: Computers and Composition Digital Press/Utah State University Press.

Donahue, Christiane. 2008. "When Copying Is Not Copying: Plagiarism and French Composition Scholarship." In *Originality, Imitation, and Plagiarism: Teaching Writing in the Digital Age,* edited by Martha Vicinus and Caroline Eisner, 90–103. Ann Arbor: University of Michigan Press.

Donahue, Christiane. 2016. "Mobile Knowledge for a Mobile Era: Studying Linguistic and Rhetorical Flexibility in Composition." Working Paper, Thomas Watson Conference on Rhetoric and Composition Mobility Work in Composition Series, University of Louisville, Louisville, KY.

Dor, Daniel. 2004. "From Englishization to Imposed Multilingualism: Globalization, the Internet, and the Political Economy of the Linguistic Code." *Public Culture* 16 (1): 97–118.

Downs, Douglas, and Elizabeth Wardle. 2007. "Teaching about Writing, Righting Misconceptions: (Re)Envisioning 'First-Year Composition' as 'Introduction to English Studies.'" *College Composition and Communication* 58 (4): 552–84.

Edbauer, Jenny. 2005. "Unframing Models of Public Distribution: From Rhetorical Situation to Rhetorical Ecologies." *Rhetoric Society Quarterly* 35 (4): 5–24.

Flores, Nelson. 2013. "The Unexamined Relationship Between Neoliberalism and Plurilingualism: A Cautionary Tale." *TESOL Quarterly* 47 (3): 500–20.

France Diplomatie—French Ministry of Foreign Affairs and International Development. 2017. "10 Good Reasons for Learning French." http://www.diplomatie.gouv.fr/en/french -foreign-policy/francophony-1113/promoting-french-around-the-world-7721/article /10-good-reasons-for-learning#.

François, Frédérique. 1998. *Le discours et ses entours: Essai sur l'interprétation.* Paris: L'Harmattan.

Gal, Susan, and Judith T. Irvine. 1995. "The Boundaries of Languages and Disciplines: How Ideologies Construct Difference." *Social Research* 62 (4): 967–1001.

Gee, James Paul, Glynda Hull, and Colin Lankshear. 1998. *The New Work Order: Behind the Language of the New Capitalism.* Boulder, CO: Westview.

Guardiano, Cristina, M. Elena Favilla, and Emilia Calaresu. 2007. "Stereotypes about English as the Language of Science." *AILA Review* 20 (1): 28–52.

Haugen, Einar. 1972. *The Ecology of Language: Essays by Einar Haugen.* Stanford, CA: Stanford University Press.

Horner, Bruce. 2013. "Ideologies of Literacy, 'Academic Literacies,' and Composition Studies." *Literacy in Composition Studies* 1 (1): 1–9.

Horner, Bruce. 2016. *Rewriting Composition: Terms of Exchange.* Carbondale: Southern Illinois University Press.

Horner, Bruce, Cynthia Selfe, and Tim Lockridge. 2015. *Translinguality, Transmodality, and Difference: Exploring Dispositions and Change in Language and Learning. enculturation/ intermezzo.* http://intermezzo.enculturation.net/01/ttd-horner-selfe-lockridge/index .htm. PDF. http://intermezzo.enculturation.net/01.htm.

Horner, Bruce, and Laura Tetreault. 2016. "Translation as (Global) Writing." *Composition Studies* 44 (1): 13–30.

Hull, Glynda A., and Mark Evan Nelson. 2005. "Locating the Semiotic Power of Multimodality." *Written Communication* 22 (2): 224–61.

Jewitt, Carey, Jeff Bezemer, and Kay O'Halloran. 2016. *Introducing Multimodality.* London: Routledge.

Jiménez, Robert T., Sam David, Kennan Fagan, Victoria J. Risko, Mark Pacheco, Lisa Pray, and Mar Gonzalez. 2015. "Using Translation to Drive Conceptual Development for Students: Becoming Literate in English as an Additional Language." *Research in the Teaching of English* 49 (3): 248–71.

Kiernan, Julia, Joyce Meier, and Xiqiao Wang. 2016. "Negotiating Languages and Cultures: Enacting Translingualism through a Translation Assignment." *Composition Studies* 44(1): 89–97.

Kress, Gunther. 2003. *Literacy in the New Media Age.* London: Routledge.

Kubota, Ryuko. 2014. "The Multi/Plural Turn, Postcolonial Theory, and Neoliberal Multiculturalism: Complicities and Implications for Applied Linguistics." *Applied Linguistics* 37 (4): 474–94.

Kuhn, Thomas S. 2008. "The Historical Structure of Scientific Discovery." In *Writing Conventions, edited by* Min-Zhan Lu and Bruce Horner, 312–32. New York: Pearson Academic. Originally published in *SCIENCE* 136 (3518) (1962): 760–62.

Lorimer Leonard, Rebecca, and Rebecca Nowacek. 2016. "Transfer and Translingualism." *College English* 78 (3): 258–64.

Lu, Min-Zhan. 1994. "Professing Multiculturalism: The Politics of Style in the Contact Zone." *College Composition and Communication* 45 (4): 442–58.

Lu, Min-Zhan, and Bruce Horner. 2013. "Translingual Literacy, Language Difference, and Matters of Agency." *College English* 75 (6): 586–611.

Lutkewitte, Claire. 2013. "An Introduction to Multimodal Composition Theory and Practice." In *Multimodal Composition: A Critical Sourcebook*, edited by Claire Lutkewitte, 1–8. Boston, MA: Bedford/St. Martin's.

Milroy, James. 2001. "Language Ideologies and the Consequences of Standardization." *Journal of Sociolinguistics* 5 (4): 530–55.

Mühlhäusler, Peter. 1996. *Linguistic Ecology*. Oxford: Blackwell.

Nowacek, Rebecca S. 2011. *Agents of Integration: Understanding Transfer as a Rhetorical Act.* Carbondale: Southern Illinois University Press.

Pennycook, Alastair. 2008. "English as a Language Always in Translation." *European Journal of English Studies* 12 (1): 33–47.

Pennycook, Alastair. 2010. *Language as a Local Practice*. London: Routledge.

Qu, Weiguo. 2014. "Critical Literacy and Writing in English: Teaching English in a Cross-Cultural Context." In *Reworking English in Rhetoric and Composition: Global Interrogations, Local Interventions*, edited by Bruce Horner and Karen Kopelson, 64–74. Carbondale: Southern Illinois University Press.

Selfe, Cynthia L. 2009. "The Movement of Air, the Breath of Meaning: Aurality and Multimodal Composing." *College Composition and Communication* 60 (4): 616–63.

Selfe, Cynthia L. 2010. "Response to Doug Hesse." *College Composition and Communication* 61 (3): 606–10.

Shipka, Jody. 2011. *Toward a Composition Made Whole*. Pittsburgh, PA: University of Pittsburgh Press.

Stein, Pippa. 2004. "Representation, Rights, and Resources: Multimodal Pedagogies in the Language and Literacy Classroom." In *Critical Pedagogies and Language Learning*, edited by Bonny Norton and Kelleen Toohey, 95–115. Cambridge: Cambridge University Press.

Street, Brian. 2009. "The Future of 'Social Literacies.'" In *The Future of Literacy Studies*, edited by Mike Baynham and Mastin Prinsloo, 21–37. Basingstoke: Palgrave Macmillan.

Street, Brian. 2012. "New Literacy Studies." In *Language, Ethnography, and Education: Bridging New Literacy Studies and Bourdieu*, edited by Michael Grenfell, David Bloome, Cheryl Hardy, Kate Pahl, Jennifer Rowsell, and Brian Street, 27–49. London: Routledge.

Syverson, Margaret A. 1999. *The Wealth of Reality: An Ecology of Composition*. Carbondale: Southern Illinois University Press.

Thrift, Nigel. 2005. *Knowing Capitalism*. London: SAGE.

Trimbur, John. 1990. "Essayist Literacy and the Rhetoric of Deproduction." *Rhetoric Review* 9 (1): 72–86.

Trimbur, John, and Karen Press. 2015. "When Was Multimodality? Modality and the Rhetoric of Transparency." In *Multimodality in Writing: The State of the Art in Theory, Methodology, and Pedagogy*, edited by Arlene Archer and Esther Breuer, 17–42. Leiden: Brill.

Van Lier, Leo. 2004. *The Ecology and Semiotics of Language Learning: A Sociocultural Perspective*. Dordrecht: Kluwer Academics.

Wardle, Elizabeth, ed. 2012. "Writing and Transfer." Special issue, *Composition Forum* 26. http://compositionforum.com/issue/26/.

Williams, Raymond. 1980. *Problems in Materialism and Culture*. London: Verso.

Yancey, Kathleen Blake. 2004. "Made Not Only in Words: Composition in a New Key." *College Composition and Communication* 56 (2): 297–328.

Yildiz, Yasemin. 2012. *Beyond the Mother Tongue: The Postmonolingual Condition*. New York: Fordham University Press.

ABOUT THE AUTHORS

SARA P. ALVAREZ is a PhD candidate in rhetoric and composition at the University of Louisville and a multilingual writing fellow at Queens College, CUNY. Sara's research interests intersect the fields of critical applied linguistics, bilingualism, and education. Sara is the winner of the 2015 National Council of Teachers of English (NCTE) Early Career Educator of Color Leadership Award and the corecipient of the 2015 Conference on College Composition and Communication (CCCC) Research Initiative Award.

STEVEN ALVAREZ is an assistant professor of English at St. John's University. His research explores the languages and literacies of Latin American immigrant communities in the United States Northeast and South. He is the author of *Brokering Tareas: Mexican Immigrant Families Translanguaging Homework Literacies* (SUNY Press) and *Community Literacies en Confianza: Learning from Bilingual After-School Programs* (National Council of Teachers of English).

MICHAEL BAUMANN is a doctoral student at the University of Louisville where he researches critical-cultural rhetorical studies of identity, multimodal composing, and new media writing. Having published in *Kairos* and *Reflections*, both journals of rhetoric, theory, and writing pedagogy, he's currently researching for a monograph-scale project about queer college instructors' rhetorical acts of "coming out" or "passing" in their writing classrooms.

JOEL BLOCH has a PhD in rhetoric from Carnegie Mellon University. He has published books on technology and writing, intellectual property and plagiarism, and multimodality and articles on technology, plagiarism and intellectual property, and digital literacies. He is currently retired but teaches one course per year on publishing.

AARON BLOCK is an associate teaching professor in the English Department at Northeastern University. He teaches first-year writing and advanced writing courses, and his research interests include grading and evaluation, comics and graphic literature, and labor rights.

JESSIE C. BORGMAN is a graduate student at Texas Tech University. She has taught online since 2009 and taught face to face prior to teaching online. She has published multiple articles and book chapters and has presented at several conferences including *CCCC, C&W,* and *TYCA*. Her research interests include online writing instruction, course design, genre studies, two-year colleges and writing program administration, and the OWI Community (www.owicommunity.org), a website and social media group dedicated to collecting and sharing online writing instruction resources.

ANDREW BOURELLE is an assistant professor of English at the University of New Mexico, where he teaches classes in composition, creative writing, rhetoric, and technical communication. His scholarship has been published in *Communication Design Quarterly, Composition Forum, the Journal of Business and Technical Communication, the Journal of Teaching Writing,* and other academic journals. His research about comic books as sites of multimodal literacy has been published in the anthologies *Class, Please Open Your Comics: Essays on Teaching with Graphic Narratives* and *Teaching Graphic Novels in the English Classroom: Pedagogical Possibilities of Multimodal Literacy Engagement.*

TIFFANY BOURELLE is an assistant professor of English at the University of New Mexico, where she teaches graduate classes in online and multimodal pedagogies and directs the university's online first-year composition program, called eComp, which emphasizes multimodal literacy in online classes. Bourelle's scholarship has been published in the *Journal of Technical Writing and Communication, Kairos, Technical Communication Quarterly, WPA Journal,* and other peer-reviewed journals. For an article published in 2016 in *Computers and Composition,* Bourelle and her coauthors won the Computers and Writing Ellen Nold Award for Best Article in *Computers and Composition.*

KARA MAE BROWN is a lecturer with potential security of employment in the writing program at the University of California Santa Barbara, where she is also the program coordinator for the writing and literature major in the College of Creative Studies. She teaches courses in academic and creative writing, writing studies, and public discourse. Her research interests include writing pedagogy, assessment, online writing instruction, and writing program administration. She also publishes works of short fiction and narrative nonfiction.

JENNIFER J. BUCKNER is an associate professor of English at Gardner-Webb University in Boiling Springs, North Carolina, where she teaches courses in writing studies and new media for undergraduate and graduate students. Her research interests include soundwriting pedagogy, embodied perceptions of materiality, multimodal accessibility for temporarily abled and disabled bodies, and semiotic remediation practices.

ANGELA CLARK-OATES is an assistant professor of English at California State University, Sacramento, where she serves as the writing program administrator in addition to teaching a wide variety of English classes. She earned her PhD in curriculum and instruction from Arizona State University, where she was the administrator of the Writers' Studio, an online writing program with an emphasis on multimodal literacy. Her scholarship has been published in the journals *Communication Design Quarterly* and the *Journal of Writing Assessment,* as well as the anthologies *The Framework for Success in Postsecondary Writing: Scholarship and Applications, The Next Digital Scholar: A Fresh Approach to the Common Core State Standards in Research and Writing,* and *Working with Faculty Writers.*

MICHELLE DAY is a doctoral student in rhetoric and composition at the University of Louisville, where she is also a graduate teaching assistant, assistant director of composition, and a graduate assistant for U of L's new Cooperative Consortium for Transdisciplinary Social Justice Research. Her research interests concern the intersections among trauma, pedagogy, and community engagement, particularly when/as mediated by digital media.

SUSAN DEROSA is an associate professor of English at Eastern Connecticut State University where she teaches courses in writing studies, rhetoric, and creative nonfiction. She coauthored the textbook *Choices Writers Make: A Guide* (Pearson, 2011) with Steve Ferruci, and they have published scholarship and presented their research at conferences on multimodal writing, writing centers, and writing pedagogy. She has served as a steering-committee member of the Northeast Writing Centers Association since 2002. Currently, she is coediting with Steve a special issue of *WLN: A Journal of Writing Center Scholarship* on multimodality and the writing center for spring 2018.

DÀNIELLE NICOLE DEVOSS is a professor of professional writing and director of graduate studies at Michigan State University. Her research interests include multimodal composing, copyright and intellectual property in digital spaces, and social and cultural entrepreneurship. She is currently working on two book projects: *Type Matters: The Rhetoricity of Letterforms* (with C. S. Wyatt) and *Explanation Points: Publishing in Rhetoric and Composition* (with John Gallagher).

STEPHEN FERRUCI is an associate professor and coordinator of first-year writing at Eastern Connecticut State University, where he helped design and implement the new media studies major and teaches courses in multimodal writing and film. His work has been published in *The Writing Instructor, English Education,* and the *Journal of Teaching Writing.* With Susan DeRosa, he has presented on writing centers, writing pedagogy, and multimodal writing. They coauthored the textbook *Choices Writers Make* (Pearson, 2011), and they are currently guest editing an issue of *WLN: A Journal of Writing Center Scholarship* on multimodality and the writing center.

LAYNE M. P. GORDON is a doctoral student and assistant director of the University Writing Center at the University of Louisville. Her research interests include writing program administration, literacy studies, and political economic theory. She has also published "Beyond Generalist vs. Specialist: Making Connections between Genre Theory and Writing Center Pedagogy" in *Praxis: A Writing Center Journal.*

BRUCE HORNER is Endowed Chair in Rhetoric and Composition at the University of Louisville, where he teaches courses in composition, composition pedagogy and theory, and literacy studies. His recent publications include *Rewriting Composition: Terms of Exchange*(Southern Illinois, 2016), *Crossing Divides: Exploring Translingual Writing Pedagogies and Programs,* coedited with Laura Tetrault (Utah State, 2017), *Economies of Writing: Revaluations in Rhetoric and Composition,* coedited with Brice Nordquist and Susan Ryan (Utah State, 2017), and *Translinguality, Transmodality, and Difference: Exploring Dispositions and Change in Language and Learning,* a digital monograph coauthored with Cynthia L. Selfe and Tim Lockridge (*Enculturation/Intermezzo,* 2015).

MATTHEW IRWIN is a PhD student in American studies at the University of New Mexico. Also a widely published art critic, he is a two-time NEA arts journalism fellow and a two-time finalist for the Warhol Foundation/Creative Capital Arts Writers Grant. Irwin holds an MFA in creative writing from San Diego State University and teaches composition at the University of New Mexico.

ELIZABETH KLEINFELD is a professor of English and writing center director at Metropolitan State University of Denver. She teaches courses on rhetoric and composition theory and practice. She has coauthored a textbook on multimodal and multigenre composition and has published articles on writing center work, digital rhetoric, and student source-citation practices. Her work has appeared in *Praxis* and *Computers and Composition Online.* Her current research focuses on disability studies, inclusivity, and plagiarism.

ASHANKA KUMARI is a doctoral fellow in the rhetoric and composition program at the University of Louisville. Her research interests include graduate-student professionalization, identity studies, multimodal composing, and popular culture.

LAURA SCENIAK MATRAVERS is a fourth-year doctoral candidate in rhetoric and composition and a graduate research assistant in the School of Interdisciplinary and Graduate Studies at the University of Louisville. Her dissertation research focuses on the professional and scholarly practices of two-year college writing faculty. She is currently working on a book project about mobility work in composition (with Bruce Horner, Megan Faver Hartline, and Ashanka Kumari).

JESSICA S. B. NEWMAN is a PhD student and fellow in the University of Louisville rhetoric and composition program. Her research interests include writing center studies, community-engaged scholarship, and listening studies.

MARK PEDRETTI is assistant professor of English at Providence College and holds a PhD in rhetoric from the University of California at Berkeley. He is currently at work on a cluster of projects to bring "big data" and natural language-processing techniques to writing and writing center studies and is developing a book manuscript on the ideologies of multi-modal composition. He has previously published an article in *Composition Studies* (fall 2016) on how students understand essay projects to be "done."

ADAM PERZYNSKI is an assistant professor of medicine and sociology in the Center for Health Care Research and Policy at MetroHealth and Case Western Reserve University. His publications cross many disciplines and include journals like the *Journal of the American Medical Association*, the *Journal of Racial and Ethnic Health Disparities*, and *Sociology of Health and Illness*. As a methodologist, his research expertise ranges from focus groups and ethnography to psychometrics and structural equation modelling. Dr. Perzynski's work represents a career-long effort to infuse the study of biomedical scientific problems with the knowledge, theories, and methods of social science.

BREANNE POTTER is a writing instructor at Clarkson College and Central Washington University. She graduated with a master's in rhetoric and writing from the University of New Mexico in 2016, where she studied professional writing, first-year composition peda-gogy, online pedagogy, multimodality, and second language learning. She lives in Omaha, Nebraska, with her husband and two children.

CAITLIN E. RAY is a PhD student at the University of Louisville, where she teaches composi-tion and literature classes. She has presented and published on ableism and theatre-based teaching practices.

ARETI SAKELLARIS is a PhD candidate in rhetoric and composition at Northeastern University. She is interested in service learning, community engagement, teacher research, and decolonial theory. She completed her MA in English at Northeastern University with her thesis, "(Shadow) Literacy Sponsorship in the Archive: Woody Guthrie's Correspon dence with Alan Lomax at the Archive of American Folk Song." Areti earned her BA in English and history from Connecticut College and also holds an AA in merchandise prod-uct development from the Fashion Institute of Design & Merchandising in Los Angeles. Areti's work in fashion inspired this piece.

KHIRSTEN L. SCOTT is a doctoral candidate of English, rhetoric, and composition at the University of Louisville. She holds degrees in English language and literature from Tougaloo College (BA) and composition, rhetoric, and English studies from the University of Alabama (MA). Khirsten's research lies at the intersections of cultural rhetorics, namely African American rhetoric, historiography, and digital humanities. Specifically, her work is centered on HBCU communities and the rhetorical affordances of institutional narratives for revisionist presentations of HBCU histories.

REBECCA THORNDIKE-BREEZE is a lecturer in the Massachusetts Institute of Technology's Comparative Media-Studies/Writing division, where she teaches writing, rhetoric, and communication. She earned her PhD in literature from Northeastern University. Her teaching and research interests include rhetoric, writing studies, affect theory, comics and graphic novels, British realisms and modernisms, and animal studies. She also researches the role of emotional labor in collaborative processes and has published essays on affect in the realist and modernist novel.

JON UDELSON is a PhD fellow at the University of Louisville studying rhetoric and compo-sition. His research interests relate to style, voice, authorship, and digital writing as they pertain to issues of composition and pedagogy.

SHANE A. WOOD is a graduate teaching assistant and doctoral candidate in English rheto-ric and composition at the University of Kansas. His research interests include writing assessment, genre theory, and multimodality. He received his MA in English composition theory at California State University, Fresno, and his BA in English at Western Kentucky University.

Rick Wysocki is a doctoral student and teacher at the University of Louisville. His research interests include archival research methodologies, new materialism, the rhetorics surrounding age and aging, and maker/hackerspace research. His work has been published in *Present Tense: A Journal of Rhetoric in Society* and *Enculturation: A Journal of Rhetoric, Writing, and Culture*.

Kathleen Blake Yancey, Kellogg Hunt Professor of English and Distinguished Research Professor at Florida State University, has served as president/chair of NCTE, CCCC, and CWPA. Currently, she leads the Writing Passport Project, a multisite research project focused on writing transfer. Author/coauthor of over one hundred articles and book chapters, she has authored/edited/coedited fourteen scholarly books—most recently *Writing Across Contexts: Transfer, Composition, and Sites of Writing* (2014); *A Rhetoric of Reflection* (2016); and *Assembling Composition* (2017). She is the recipient of several awards, including two CWPA Best Book Awards; CCCC's Research Impact Award; and FSU's Graduate Teaching Award, which she has won twice.

INDEX